PRAISE FOR

CAN EVERYBODY SWIM?

A SURVIVAL STORY FROM KATRINA'S SUPERDOME

"In the sagas of Hurricane Katrina, the Superdome stands above a flooded New Orleans like a giant space saucer too packed with refugees, and refuse, to manage a launch. Bruce S. Snow has written the most thorough account I've seen of what it was like to be trapped in there, hour after hour for almost a week. With his mother, a dog and a shifting posse of allies, he watches New Orleans 'shelter of last resort' give way to thirst and hunger and then to the depravity that can come with terror and despair. He digs to the root of persistent rumors—of mass murder, rape, and wantonness—and comes up with credible explanations of what really went on. It's a dystopia right out of Dante, and yet Snow offsets misery with flashes of gallows humor and the glow of his gratitude for the men and women who bucked the herd and proved capable of tender mercies."

—Jed Horne, author of *Breach of Faith, Hurricane Katrina and the Near Death of a Great American City*

"Those of us who lived through Hurricane Katrina (inside or outside of New Orleans) remember well the horror stories (and rumors) that were reported out of the Louisiana Superdome, where some 20,000 evacuees survived in the days after the storm. Here is a genuine and authentic tale of the apocalyptic anarchy that reigned inside the 'feces-dome'—the fear and panic, the hunger and thirst, the boredom and the racial tensions that people experienced inside this Hades, this netherworld of human existence. Bruce Snow marshals his considerable writing talent to tell the real story of those who survived this surreal nightmare, presided over by the U.S. Army. Snow's is a genuine new voice of non-fiction writing reminding us of Tom Wolfe's exhilarating 'new non-fiction' of the 1960s—if the mere recording of the truth of slices of American life is stranger than fiction, you do not need to invent it."

—Günter Bischof, Marshall Plan Professor of History, University of New Orleans

"One of the best memoirs to come out of the aftermath of Hurricane Katrina, Bruce S. Snow's real-life tale of survival after his world was blown away is a testament to how quickly our lives can change and to the kind of resiliency and strength ordinary people are capable of when the chips are down."

—David Koon, *Arkansas Times*

"A masterfully written account of the human misery and ultimate survival of those who lived through the worst natural and manmade disasters in U.S. history."

—Norman Robinson, retired veteran news anchor for WDSU New Orleans Channel 6 (NBC), Media Consultant, Motivational Speaker

CAN EVERYBODY SWIM?

A SURVIVAL STORY FROM KATRINA'S SUPERDOME

BRUCE S. SNOW

et alia press

Little Rock, Arkansas
2016

Published in the United States of America by:
Et Alia Press
1819 Shadow Lane
Little Rock, AR 72207
Etaliapress.com

ISBN: 978-1-944528-98-0
Library of Congress Control Number: 2016910763

Cover Design by Amy Ashford, Ashford Design Studio,
ashford-design-studio.com
Layout Design by Kathy Oliverio
Edited by Erin Wood

Those images that do not belong to the author are printed by permission of Jim
Sterrett and are individually credited as they appear in the book's interior.
The map illustration on page XI is an original work by Allison Tucker,
commissioned especially for use in this book. Author's photo on back cover by
Lacey West.

The brief quote on page XIV of the introduction is reprinted by permission
of HarperCollins Publishers from PAPILLION by HENRI CHARRIERE.
COPYRIGHT © 1969 BY ROBERT LAFFONT. TRANSLATION FOR U.S.
EDITION COPYRIGHT © 1970 BY WILLIAM MORROW & COMPANY, INC.

DEDICATED TO
FREDERIQUE FRANÇOIS

DOLJA

1997 - DECEMBER 24, 2010
SUPERDOME SURVIVOR, DEVOTED COMPANION, FRIEND

CHANCE BROUGHT US TOGETHER.
LOVE WILL ENSURE THAT WE NEVER PART.

"As I write these thoughts I had so many years ago, thoughts that come back now to assail me with such terrible clarity, I am struck by how absolute silence and total isolation were able to lead a young man shut up in a cell into a true life of the imagination. He literally lived two lives. He took flight and wandered wherever he liked: to his home, his father, his mother, his family, his childhood, all the different stages of his life. And more important still, the castles in Spain that his fertile brain invented induced a kind of schizophrenia, and he began to believe he was living what he dreamed."

—Henri Charrière, *Papillon*, 1970

Substitute *my roof* for the word *cell* and that's pretty much the idea.

—Bruce S. Snow, 2016

INTRODUCTION

I was there.

It was the media event of the year. People across the country were watching their televisions. Comprehensive news coverage spanned the entire globe; America held its collective breath for an entire week: they were all watching me. I was there.

Due to this extensive coverage, the events of late August and early September 2005 along the Gulf Coast are forever etched into the collective American subconscious. Good or bad, these events will engage some sort of mental video recall for nearly every citizen with a television set in the English speaking world and beyond. The images, all of the sobering images, were replayed over and over and over again on the big networks and their affiliates. Images of cars and homes poking out of filthy brown water, images of people's lives and livelihoods dotting the endless surface of the brown water, images of brown water that nothing could contain. Men and women, children, babies, the elderly, and the criminals—all caught on camera and broadcasted via satellite. Some were looting stores and floating flat screen TVs on inflatable rafts through flooded streets.

The world saw seemingly countless people waving from rooftops at passing helicopters, hoping to find relief from all of that brown water. Human beings stranded atop their tiny islands of memories, all begging for help, hoping to escape the flooding and the broiling, subtropical sun. The City of New Orleans lies within the Tropic of Cancer and is therefore a subtropical City. Torrential thunderstorms pour rain onto the streets and fill the canals regularly. The pump and levee system works astonishingly well despite the City's topographical challenges. Low lying areas may collect water during an especially heavy downpour, but usually within an hour it's all gone.

A full week's worth of round-the-clock news coverage, that's what people remember from the Hurricane. Some details are remembered more clearly than others, and these details vary greatly from one individual to another. Personal opinion fills in the remaining spaces. A tragic chapter in American history taught entirely through the camera's lens.

Without fail, whenever Hurricane Katrina comes up in conversation, the first thing people ask me is, "Was it really as bad as they were showing on TV?"

The emphasis is always on really.

Whether they believe the news stories to be exaggerated or that they were part of a greater cover-up is, once again, a matter of personal opinion. But, regardless of the individual's feelings on the matter, the question never changes. "Was it really as bad as they were showing on TV?"

I've learned that the only honest way that I can answer this question is, "I don't know what they were showing on TV. I was there."

The simplest of machines failed in New Orleans. Pumping machines. Turn it on, simple. Earthen levees—not even machines—just piles of dirt and concrete, they failed, too. No nuclear bombs, just brown water and the crazy music it made in the darkness of night. And when the water finally did recede, you might have thought a hydrogen bomb had gone off in the City. Whether water or fire, when there is too much of either, man-made structures don't stand a chance.

This was a large-scale human tragedy and to retell it would be impossible if mention were not made of what I saw others doing. The people are what make the story. But all of the events will be told through me. I had the good fortune to meet and talk with people from many different backgrounds, all affected and brought together by events far out of their control—people under immense and indescribable stress. In this narrative, I recount how their paths crossed mine and how we affected each other's lives, however briefly, for good or for ill. More than a million people were directly affected by Hurricane Katrina, and each one has a story worth telling. Ten years have passed since what I like to refer to as the B.C. and A.D. moment of my life. A new existence began as soon as I left the attic of my home on Mandeville Street. The life I'd been living ended that day, and as time passes and the Earth keeps spinning, my memories of who I was and where I was seem to fade away.

My most vivid recollections of the events surrounding the Hurricane come to me in terrifying dreams. A mid-afternoon catnap is the typical time for these dreams to appear. A distant, forced-down reality pours from my subconscious and I return wholly and completely to late August and early September 2005. My mind deposits me into the thick of the turmoil. I can feel the breathless humidity on my skin, the sunshine blinds my eyes, and my nose is filled with the terrible smells of stagnant water and the inch of piss and shit that covered the bathrooms and hallways of the Louisiana Superdome. And with that is also the unmistakable smell of death. Fresh death. Human death. And it's mere feet from where I am lying in bed, hundreds of miles from 2005, in my current home in Little Rock, Arkansas. It's 1:30 in the afternoon.

I take the retelling of these moments in time with all seriousness. I am not trying to make light of any portion of the situation. The conditions inside the Superdome were repulsive; real human beings were suffering all around me. It was some depressing shit. But I can't present the truth, my thoughts, without both the serious and the asinine. It's how my brain works. I mean no disrespect to anyone whose life was wrecked by Hurricane Katrina. I'm just trying to come to terms with my share of it.

Aside from myself and my mother, the dog, and the hippo, all of the names in this tale have been changed in order to protect the individuals mentioned hereafter, especially myself.

This is my attempt to give shape and clarity and a big middle finger to my mid-afternoon nightmares. This is my attempt to confront the past and grip tightly onto something that I can consider positive, productive and, above all, sane.

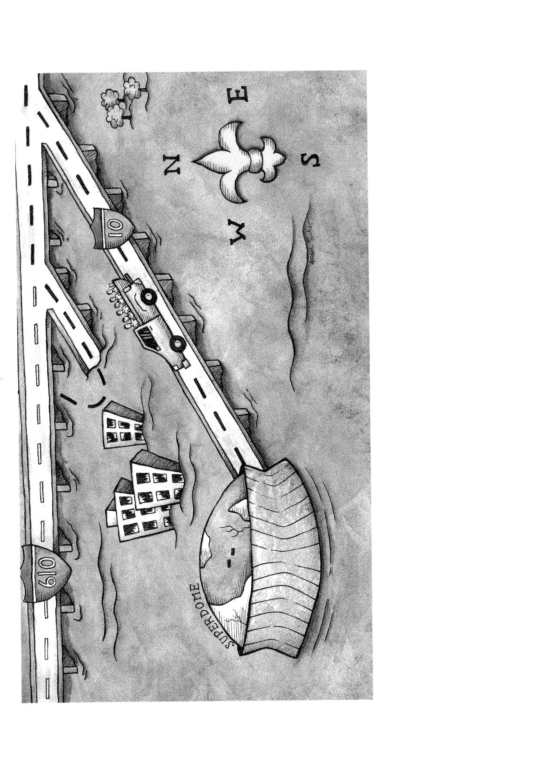

SUNDAY
AUGUST 28TH, 2005

Countdown to Landfall

Satellite images of the multicolored, vicious swirl overlying the entire Gulf of Mexico were in my peripheral vision, but I wasn't paying much attention. The sun filtering through the Venetian blinds of my grandparents' home began to fade. It would be the last sunset of my old life. Sitting still in my worn blue chair, my heart raced astride my thoughts. The room felt terribly close and warm. I lit a cigarette, and it tasted like battery acid on my tongue.

Throughout the day, friends had called as they headed out of town, evacuating to one destination or another. They asked when my family and I were leaving and where we were going. "Maybe we can meet up." When I told them my grandparents were in Florida and that we'd decided to stay, silence followed.

Some asked–others begged–me to come with them. They had extra space and weren't evacuating too far. "Just come along. Let this thing blow over, and we'll be back in a couple days." I must admit it was an attractive invitation. A couple of nights in a hotel playing drinking games, eating fast food, and swimming in a pool with friends was very tempting, but there was only room for one in each of those golden opportunities. I couldn't leave Mother, Uncle G and his wife Jimena, and my furry black companions, Dolja and Klaus. Before hanging up, my friends wished me good luck.

Eventually, the phone stopped ringing. The gravity of that silence pulled me in. Ugly thoughts flashed through my mind as I pondered potential outcomes. All of my friends had evacuated to points as far away as West Texas and Kentucky, others only as far as Baton Rouge. Regardless of where they'd gone, they were all gone.

My panic was rising, so I walked outside to get some air. Outside, I found a desolate ghost town. Nothing moved unless the wind motivated it; the leaves and branches stirred, creating a gentle whirling sound, very much like running water. The breeze blew softly, without major gusts. I neither saw nor heard anyone. Not a single automobile moved on Mirabeau Avenue, a fairly busy street, nor on Elysian Fields three blocks away, normally a major thoroughfare day and night. Stillness. My neighborhood totally devoid of life. I wandered my block in a catatonic stupor, nothing moving around me but the gentle breeze. Everyone was gone. Not just my friends, but everyone. The City had been emptied, and we were all alone. Our home, just a tiny island of light in the silent metropolis.

Wandering the neighborhood, my family's conversations replayed in my mind. This house survived Betsy and Camille without a scratch. This neighborhood is some of the highest ground on the East Bank. Everyone is wasting their time and money evacuating. This one will pass over, dump some rain, and move on, just like all the others.

But what if it didn't?

We hadn't spent the day rushing around in a state of urgency, just taking a few precautions. We ate. We filled some plastic water jugs Mother and I had been too lazy to throw away with water from the bathtub. We normally park our vehicles on the street, but we drove my little pickup and my uncle's big twelve-passenger van up onto our sloped lawn. Pulling the cars onto the lawn was standard battening-down-the-hatches while awaiting a tropical storm or hurricane. The sloped lawn allowed our engines and front ends to sit about five feet above street level, and three feet at the tailpipe. Was this enough?

Once back inside from my walk, I stared at the giant swirling red, blue, and green radar image on the television and felt unsure. Recently, the system had made a slight turn to the east, and now its path was charted directly at the City, seemingly right to my address. The winds had risen significantly, and stronger gusts shook the trees.

Was there still time to leave? Where would we go? How would we get there?

We had no lack of transportation, but each mode had its drawbacks. My uncle's big van was the obvious choice to move us all and the dog, but it didn't run very well. Uncle Gene mostly used it for short A-to-B trips. The thing would overheat or worse before we found X or Y. My little truck ran well enough and would have certainly been the more fuel-economic option, but it was a "little truck." A 1994 Nissan, it could seat four, but the rear seats were tiny and terribly uncomfortable except for the shortest of rides. In the driving force of a Category 5 hurricane, riding in the bed of the truck wasn't an option. Also at hand was my grandfather's early-80s Toyota 4Runner. With big tires and four-wheel drive, it would have been my first choice. And then there was his late-70s camper conversion van, also parked on the lawn. The camper van had beds we could fold out and a two-burner stove, microwave, toilet, and shower. Not too shabby. It had been driven cross-country many times, but that didn't matter. We didn't have keys for either one.

And how far would we get?

I might have had a quarter-tank of gas and $15 cash. Mother could overdraft her ATM card, maybe, but if not, she only had about a $40 balance, the remainder of August's Social Security deposit. Uncle Gene was out of work. Jimena had a job and worked and saved as much as she could, but she also sent money to her teenage children in Ecuador. I wasn't going to attempt to coerce her into supporting all of us on an adventure into the unknown with the storm just over twelve hours away. Not after we'd already committed ourselves to riding it out. As for the other two, we couldn't hope to squeeze any money out of a little black dog and a stuffed hippo.

The radar continually repeated the same image. A multi-colored, churning blob filled the entire television screen; it would advance an inch or two, then return to the starting point, advance an inch or two, and then go back to the starting line, over and over and over again.

The images, my thoughts, the possibilities—everything was flashing. It became apparent that I was driving myself insane. That's when I knew it was time to begin *the ritual*.

Everyone living in New Orleans has a hurricane ritual. I'd cemented mine into refined perfection, meticulous and unequalled by modern man. I'd already celebrated this rite once this season when Hurricane Cindy gave us some rain and high winds. I muted the television and turned on my stereo, a motley matching of components I'd acquired one-by-one throughout the years. I loved my stereo. I knew what I wanted and found it still in the disc tray from a previous listening. Disc two, track one of Led Zeppelin's *Physical Graffiti,* a track called "In the Light." A nine-minute piece of audio-sonic poetry. It had been my "happy place" song for about a month. I set the player to repeat. Next, I cracked open a beer and sat at my computer to play a real-time sim-based game in which you build castles, grow food, and raise troops to fight in the Crusades. To play and win a single game can take hours, and I had hours to give. The rules are simple: drink, play, win, pass out, or play until the power goes out. Either way, don't forget to drink. The hurricane ritual had begun.

After a few beers, all of the apprehension melted away, for a while.

Mother lay napping on the couch. After hearing "In the Light" two or three times, I turned off the repeat mode and allowed the player to move through the rest of the disc. Nearing the end of beer number four, I was managing a healthy castle and had repelled several waves of attacking infidels. The storm's outer bands were reaching the City, the wind came in stronger gusts, and lines of rain clouds raced over the house in quick succession. This was it. Bring it on. I'd held up my end of the deal. The ritual had been going on for close to two hours and, like the storm, was gaining momentum. Yet somehow our lights hadn't flickered once.

It was past midnight when the phones rang for the last time. I mean it. The last time from that day to this. The hand-held cordless phone was in the living room next to Mother. I had a land-line phone on the desk where I sat doing my fighting in the kitchen. I told her to go back to sleep, and answered the phone. I knew who it was. I recognized the number.

"Whoa."

"Whoa . . ."

And that was it for a moment.

Not much else needed to be said. I noticed a hauntingly unique tone in her voice that screamed, "I have no control over what is happening or what may happen next." I wondered if my voice sounded the same way.

After listening to my breath and hers for a bit, I tried to move on, "So . . . they keeping you real busy at the station, Simone?"

"Hell, yeah. I'm sitting in my car, charging my phone, listening to a CD. I don't need to be here to listen to a CD. This is fucking . . . just so fucking stupid." Simone worked as a clerk in the warrant office of the New Orleans Police Department at their headquarters building. NOPD had ordered all hands on deck for its employees. Despite this command, many seasoned officers fled the City. Scared for her job, Simone had gone to work. Now she sat in a parking garage, triple-parked with police and civilian vehicles. She couldn't leave if she wanted.

I'd met Simone about eight years prior to Katrina. She was dating one of my good friends, and over time we became very close. For several years, I considered her to be the perfect woman for me—the one I wanted to be with forever and other nonsense of the sort. Half a decade of rejection and her then-recent disappearance cooled these emotions, and I began to see her more as the one true unrequited love of my life, in a purely Woody Allen sense. So what if she didn't physically love me? It was more than worth it just to have someone around I really knew and could talk with openly, not to mention the years of inside jokes we reveled in.

As for her disappearance, until the spring of 2005, I hadn't seen her for nearly two years. She'd gotten pregnant and had a beautiful baby daughter. Now she was adjusting to life as a mother and trying to make things work with the girl's father.

Only forty-eight short hours before this last phone call, I'd taken her out to a Friday night dinner at Lorenzo's Restaurant in Metairie.

Several of my friends worked at Lorenzo's. Simone and I ate at the bar and made small talk with the bartender, another good friend named Jay. After the customers made their exits, the bar area filled with the servers and cooks, ready to enjoy their shift drinks. It wasn't long before all conversation was taken over by one of the waitresses, Sandra, and her emphatic diatribe concerning the swirling images on the big screen over the bar.

"I'm fucking leaving."

Alberto, the head chef, chimed in, "They haven't declared an evacuation yet. We're still open tomorrow and you better come to work."

"Are you crazy?! No one's going to work tomorrow. We've all got to go. If you don't leave, you're fucking retarded. It's a Category 5 and it's huge. It takes up the entire Gulf," Sandra exclaimed.

"But it shows it's going to Texas," Alberto countered.

"It doesn't matter, asshole. Look at how big it is! If that thing comes anywhere near us, we're all screwed. Look, I'm fucking leaving, and so should everyone else. You're stupid if you try and stay."

This back-and-forth went on until all the money was counted. Simone and I had stepped outside to join the night's entertainment. Four members of the crew had gone to a nearby grocery store to buy gallons of milk, step one in the gallon challenge. It's pretty easy to do. Just get a bunch of milk and start drinking. Whoever can get down the most before throwing it back up wins. We laughed and laughed as they chugged through the ice cold gallons of vitamin D, and then laughed even harder as it started to come back up. When Roger, one of the busboys, released about a quart in one stream, raised his head and, eyes watering, said, "It's still cold . . ." I knew this was not the sport for me. I've always had trouble with dairy. All that milk would turn my guts into curds for days.

No one really wins the gallon challenge, and yet we all had a good time. Before long, a huge white puddle stretched from one end of the parking lot to the other. Lorenzo himself arrived and chewed us all out for the mess we'd made. So the next hour was spent hosing all of the regurgitated milk into the street, causing still more laughter. Watching, and laughing, and hosing, the monstrous swirling storm on the television screen had been the furthest thing from my mind.

As Simone and I talked on the phone, my game on pause, all of that laughter and all of that milk seemed like ancient history.

"Simone, we're the only ones here. Everyone else in the whole City is gone."

"I know. It's so quiet. If shit gets bad, what will y'all do?"

"We've got water and food and stuff. It'll be bad for a few hours, after it passes over. If the lights don't come back on for, ya know, more than a couple days, then maybe we may do something. Or if the roof flies off, we'll figure that out, too."

"Word," she said in agreement.

Simone told me the office was abuzz with talk of the volume of people showing up at the Superdome. She'd heard there might be two or three thousand, maybe more. Historically, the Superdome is opened during major weather events to provide citizens without means to properly evacuate a safe structure in which to ride out the storm, and then go back home. The Superdome was never intended to house and feed people for a week, and certainly not 20,000 of them.

"Damn. A couple thousand people, huh?"

"Yeah, they've been letting people in since Friday afternoon. But now that it's on, it's . . . you know . . . ON."

"Word. Glad I'm out here in chilly Gentilly. I still have eighteen beers in the fridge and I still have power. I'm going to make it to the end."

"It's not supposed to be over us until like eight in the morning, jackass."

We talked for another hour or so, made plans for next weekend, stuff like that. But it would be many weeks before we'd see each other again. Simone has fair skin, celestial blue eyes, and that particularly New Orleans way of enunciating everything. Early on, I'd noticed something special about her and tried very hard to make her my friend. She's one of my favorite people. On that night in late August 2005, we were the last two people on Earth, and we were scared. More than ever before, I wanted to hold her in my arms as the wind and thunder swallowed our every heartbeat. But, she was miles away and had used up nearly all of the gas in her car idling in the garage. She might need to charge her phone again.

I said goodbye to the last person in the City I knew, outside of my own home—and a very important person at that—who was directly exposed to the conditions of days two, three, and four in post-Katrina New Orleans. There were times when I feared the worst for her. And there were many times over the coming days when just the thought of seeing her again was what kept me going. In the coming week, I wouldn't have a single moment's privacy, and yet throughout it I felt intensely alone. Like Mad Max, but in a football stadium. There would be life-changing and life-threatening events ahead. Saying goodbye to Simone cut the last tie to myself as I understood myself to be. Saying goodbye to Simone, hanging up the phone with her, enacted the ordeal, my trial by water.

It was nearly four in the morning when we ended our call. The sun would be up in less than two hours, and the worst Katrina could dish out would hit shortly after that. My eyes were leaden, back stiff. Rain, wind, and thunder came at us in waves, one band and then another would roar through just a bit louder than its predecessor. I looked around the kitchen, which doubled as my "office." Along the windowsill were a couple action figures and other knick-knacks. I took them down and gently arranged them in an empty laundry basket on the floor, fearing that they'd be damaged if flying debris took out the window. After that, I grabbed another beer and re-entered the battle. No time for sleeping while the giant approaches.

The wind had strengthened into a continuous gale. I noticed the darkness turning into gray. There was to be no true dawn that day, just a brightening of the world through a cloud-blackened sky. All at once, the band overhead would pass, the sun would throw down bright, brilliant light for a couple of seconds, and then there would be clouds and thunder again. The wind wasn't subject to this patching effect of light and dark. It kept on blowing ever stronger.

The CD player had stopped long before. That Led Zeppelin disc would become the sole prisoner in a watery grave. The room was becoming bright when the computer screen went black. I opened the fridge; the light inside was off. It had stopped running. The power had quit.

I grabbed a beer, woke up my mother and said, "Grab your shoes; it's time."

"Okay, baby. Let me brush my teeth."

"That's a good idea. The lights just went out. Let me light a candle for you."

I stepped out onto the patio and lit a cigarette. Dolja came running toward me from his nest in the garage. Also with him was Wednesday, a little gray alley cat. My grandfather would always adopt an alley cat and, interestingly enough, they all became close companions of Dolja. He'd even try to know them in the biblical sense. He's a small dog, weighing about sixteen pounds. Wednesday took a look at me, took a look at the sky, and ran directly under the house.

Uncle G opened the back door of the main house wielding a flashlight. He said, "Bruce, the power's out."

"Yeah, we're coming. She's brushing her teeth."

"Jimmy's making coffee."

"Mom'll want some. I'm good," I said, raising my beer.

And so the sun rose on our family, and we began this most ultimate of days. I ran back inside my place, the back apartment, to grab another beer and Klaus the hippo. I passed over the H. G. Wells novel I'd been reading and left it on the coffee table. Klaus makes an excellent pillow. There was naptime ahead, not reading time. How different things in my nuclear life would be if I'd grabbed the 75¢ thrift store paperback and left Klaus to drown. I walked inside my grandparents' home to join my family, to face the tempest.

MANDEVILLE STREET SOLJAS

There were four of us at 4899 Mandeville Street. Well, four and a half, really. I'll explain. This is the home my lovely grandparents purchased in 1972, nine years after arriving in the United States nearly penniless. Luckily, my grandparents were away visiting their younger daughter in Florida, my Aunt Helen. Thank God. Present for Katrina were my mother, my Uncle Gene, or G, short for Eugenio, and his wife Jimena. Like the rest of my family, Jimena is from Ecuador. They'd been in the United States for several decades, and she'd been living in this country for about two years. Her English was poor, but proficient enough to communicate. I'm the first member of my family to have had English as my first language. My Spanish is miserable; I understand much more than I can speak.

That's two out of four and a half. I make three and a half. And next comes my mother, Cecilia. Mostly, I simply call her Mother. St. Cecilia is the patron saint of music. And while Mother is anything but a saint, throughout my life she has exposed me to a wide spectrum of fantastic music. Everything from Earth, Wind and Fire to Frank Sinatra, Dean Martin, and Gladys Knight, to the whole of Motown, to Santana and Pink Floyd. Even more obscure guys like Michael Franks. She has always been one of those people who *needs* music, and she has a deep emotional attachment to certain songs. I love this about her.

Mother had been battling illness for years by the time she and Katrina crossed paths. Around 1996, she was declared legally blind and forced to give up her driving privileges. Seriously, she hasn't driven a car in nearly twenty years! In late 2004, her Social Security disability claim cleared, allowing her to receive proper medical attention via Medicaid. CAT scans and MRIs revealed tumors in her brain and in both breasts, all benign. At 45, she had a full hysterectomy. Her woman parts were a web of pre-cancerous tissue. First came the Gamma knife surgery for a brain tumor in early 2005. They placed her head into a cage and screwed it into her skull at certain points to prevent her head from moving while the lasers did their work. She came home with large bruises on either side of her forehead and little red points where the screws went in. She looked like Latina Frankenstein. Mother was the first to make the Bride of Frankenstein analogy. She can always laugh at herself, another thing I love about her. Spring 2005 was the hysterectomy. They cut her open, pulled everything out, and stitched and stapled her closed. The incision wasn't healing properly, and a couple staples actually fell out one day in the shower. We rushed her to the hospital and they closed her up again. By late August 2005, as Katrina bore down on us, she was left with a big scar and a tender belly.

The healing process and medications left her more or less couch-ridden for much of the year leading up to the hurricane. Much of it an air-conditioned, prone position, hot flash nightmare. She took a medication called Depakote every day. It helped to stave off seizures and balance her mood. That all came to a screeching halt when the flood forced her out into the City to walk for hours in the broiling Louisiana heat. Needless to say, I was deeply concerned for her health throughout the coming events.

Last, but certainly not least, comes the half to our four and a half. The glue that bound us. A seven-year-old mutt named Dolja. He was part Miniature Pinscher, mostly Rat Terrier. I took in Dolja in early 1998. A friend's sibling found him as a stray with no collar and a temperament that could be described as pitiful at best. Dolja, if I'm not mistaken, was a term first coined by New Orleans rapper Master P on one of the first albums released by No Limit Records. Or maybe it was a Cash Money Records kind of thing. I forget, but in more than one song the guy was rapping about "blowin' that dolja" in a smoky room or some such. A slang term for weed.

In February 1998, I moved into the mother-in-law's apartment attached to 4899 Mandeville Street. The address reads 4899 ½ Mandeville St. on an envelope. To my knowledge, the post office no longer allows halves. Papi, my grandfather, had this addition built onto the house for his aging mother, Helen. My aunt is her namesake. In December 1997, Grandma Helen moved to a retirement community in St. Augustine, Florida, close to her daughter, yet another Helen. Living alone was awesome at first, but before long I began to feel pretty lonely back there behind the big house, by myself.

Dolja and I met at the perfect moment, for both of us. I needed a friend and he needed anyone. It was hard at first. I'm not a textbook, fully certified "dog person." I had a dog as a kid; I wasn't a good dog person then either. Dolja didn't need a dog person. He just needed a human being. Whoever he'd run away from must have abused him. Every time I stood over him and leaned down for a pet, which was mandatory (Dolja is less than sixteen inches tall at the shoulder), he'd cower and shake and shiver. If left alone, he would whine and yelp as if I'd never return. He broke my heart. And not being the proper dog person to fix the damage done to his mental well-being, it took time to gain his trust. By Sunday, August 28th, 2005, we'd been together more than seven years, and he trusted me with his life.

So, there's the crew: four adults speaking two languages, one small dog, and a hippopotamus. Yes, a hippopotamus. The inanimate member of the 4899 gang. A fat, plush hippo the size of a leg bolster pillow, full name Klaus Aloysius Devadander Abercrombie von Heepo. His middle names are "long for mud, so I've been told," a reference to the band Primus and their hit, "My Name is Mud." The rest, the Klaus von Heepo portion, is actually a mistake on my part. I'm a total History dork, so when I found myself naming a stuffed hippo, I pulled the name "Hipper" from my mental database. I remembered that Klaus von Hipper was a German Admiral during the First World War and sounded like a good name for a hippo. Two years later, while reading another book on the First World War, I discovered my mistake. The man's name was Admiral *Franz* von Hipper. By that time, it was far too late for a name change.

I found Klaus in 2002. He's my rescue hippo. Walking through a store, I saw him in a bin with some kind of dried gunk on his face. When asked, the manager told me he would be sent back to the distribution center to be incinerated. The store didn't clean stuffed animals that got dirty. Instead, they sent them back to be destroyed, and ordered more. This was protocol. He gave me four dollars off the sticker price on the hippo. I took him home and cleaned his face. It sounds crazy, but Klaus was a very real part of my life. And Mother's, too. We hosted a small gathering for the hippo's birthday the month before the storm. Klaus added a much needed third personality to our daily routine.

Mother, Uncle G and Jimena, myself, a dog, and a hippo. That was the team on Sunday, ready to ride out the storm in our Gentilly home.

MONDAY
AUGUST 29TH, 2005

KATRINA: HER SOUND AND HER FURY

The four of us sat around the kitchen table sipping coffee and praying for a good outcome. The next couple of hours would make or break our little family. My mother, uncle, and I were calm for the most part, but Dolja and Jimena were beginning to show real signs of the strain. Normally, Dolja would run and hide at the first sound of thunder. He was lying on a couch pillow, keeping his fears to himself.

Jimena, on the other hand, had begun to show signs of a growing hysteria. She'd never experienced anything like this before. The empty streets, the howling winds, and the near-complete blackout of the sun. The candles in the center of the table gave off a macabre, shifting light that made our faces look waxen and dead. The fact that the three of us appeared so calm, I'm sure, added to her anxiety. Silent tears marched down her cheeks, and she began to chain smoke, as Mother and I were doing, subconsciously.

The scene was far too real for me. My Walkman radio could barely be heard above the furious gale. The time had come for the full strength of Katrina's might. I excused myself to run back into my apartment, ten feet from the house, for a moment so I could brush the beer and nicotine from my teeth, and grab a couple more beers for what was about to come. My declaration was met with a volley of protest from my three companions.

"No, don't go! We've got to stay together!" they said.

Finally, I negotiated three minutes to go next door while Mother waited for me, standing at the back door of the main house. I returned in the allotted time, clinking two beers in my hand. I would have never guessed that it would be the last time I'd see my apartment as it was, as I still see it in my dreams. I also wouldn't have guessed that those three minutes were to be the last time I'd use running water or flush a toilet for a solid week. Once back in the main house, I threw one beer in the freezer—though the power was off, it was still cold in there—and opened the other.

My mother held the dog; Jimena, the flashlight. Uncle G held Jimena. We were forced to shout at one another to be heard. I grabbed the radio, the hippo, and a pillow to sit on. And the four and a half of us made for the hallway that separates the dining room from the bathroom and two of the bedrooms. We made ourselves as comfortable as we could in the narrow hallway and waited for the worst to pass. The noise intensified. I tried listening to the radio, but all I could hear was garbled voices. The small headphone speakers were terribly underpowered and could only be enjoyed in a closed, quiet room; they couldn't compete with the lashing rains and powerful gusts.

Through the windows, not much was visible. The sky was darker than I'd ever seen at nine in the morning. More like a clear night with a half-moon floating above. Not pitch black, but certainly not a summer morning in late August. The wind beat the sides of our home with such terrible fury that it was able to penetrate every microscopic point of entry. This created a sound akin to the wailing of ghosts in a bad horror movie. It felt like every bad thing I'd ever done in my life had found me and was seeping through the cracks to take me away with it. These ghoulish cries drove Jimena to more tears and started Dolja to shaking. Mother stroked his head and held him close, mumbling prayers to keep the spirits at bay.

The twilight darkness created by the thick, black clouds made the hallway a gloomy, depressing place. For sake of circulation, we'd opened the doors to the adjacent rooms, and the natural light from the exterior windows allowed a dim and diffused light to enter our tiny safe room. That is, of course, excepting those heartbeat milliseconds when the entire house would illuminate like one of my Abuelita's New Year's Eve gatherings.

It's difficult to try to turn words on a page into the most brilliant flashes of lightning that may have ever hit planet Earth. Our house popped with dazzling white light, like a gigantic disco strobe with the hiccups. It's even harder to turn words into sound. Glorious and ominous, like jet planes taking off all around you. The thunder reverberated through every nail, every floor board, every vital organ and toenail. BOOM! The sound waves hit our home continuously, not like a rumble of thunder, but like a shotgun going off in every room of the house at once. Big Sonic BOOMS washed over us from all directions at once. I could *feel* the thunder hitting me in the chest.

At some point in my life, I heard that when lightning strikes, if you slowly count the seconds until you hear the thunder, you can calculate about how many miles away the lightning flash occurred, or something to that effect. The equation may not be scientifically "perfect," but light travels faster than sound, and all that jazz. This practice works just fine for an afternoon thunderstorm, sitting on a friend's porch passing a blunt, but this is Katrina. Just forget all that shit. The magnificent flashes and the nerve-shattering claps occurred simultaneously, like the muzzle flash and report of the heavens' own artillery exploding in the very hallway in which we sat. The thunder shook the house. No, seriously. Shook the house. As an earthquake must still shake a proper, modern earthquake-proof building, I imagine the ground tremors must still vibrate the structure, but it's made for this, so it won't fall apart. It's no earthquake in New Orleans, just tremendous thunder claps. And we were not in a modern earthquake-proof building. We were in a sixty-plus-year-old termite-eaten Gentilly residence, set on a stack of cinder blocks. The sound waves created by the lightning strikes all around pounded the earth beneath. The ground around us relayed this force up through the foundation pilings, the cinder blocks, and through the entire wooden frame of 4899 Mandeville Street. I could feel the shotgun crack of thunder as it passed through the very grain striations of the wooden beams overhead and underneath. BOOM. All at once. The flash and the crash. BOOM. Add to this the constant, almost sublime, rumble of all the distant thunder. The average thunderstorm count one-two-three-BOOM type thunder, the sustained 100-plus-mile-per-hour winds, the wailing fucking ghosts, and the crazy sheets—hell, blankets—of rain pounding our home. We endured the barrage at maximum intensity there in the hallway for close to three hours.

After an eternity, Uncle G dared, "It's letting up . . ."

We all strained our ears. He was right. The rain torrents had slackened to slapping sheets of a heavy downpour, much more like a thunderstorm common to sub-tropical New Orleans in the summertime. It took us some time to appreciate this change, for the wind continued to gust with unabated power. We'd been in the cramped hallway for hours when we decided that the worst must have passed and stood up on our sore legs. We wandered from window to window to survey the damage. Much to our surprise, the world was still there. A couple of downed trees and street signs, the awning over our front porch had detached and landed atop Uncle G's van, but it hadn't busted the windshield. The van had already looked beaten to death. No one would notice a few more scratches.

My little green truck parked next to the van appeared to be in perfect health. We made our way to the backyard patio for a much-needed cigarette.

The wind still came in strong gusts, and driving rain fell from above, but the intensity had diminished from a 10, like what we experienced in the hallway, to about a 5 on the terror scale. The sky had lightened and the outdoors had gained the appearance of something resembling daytime.

"G, look!" I shouted.

A section of the corrugated aluminum roof covering the garage had come loose and was flapping in the wind. Just a corner of the section over the little window, totally reachable from the ground. The garage at our house had long ago been converted from a place to store cars to a place for my grandparents to hang out. Amenities included couches, chairs, a decades-old stereo, even a wet bar. Within the prior six months, Jimena and Uncle G had bought them a flat screen television for the garage, so they could watch their novellas and baseball games on a 50-inch LCD.

The space was decorated with dozens of vintage bar lights my grandfather had collected. Some of the brands advertised on these electric signs had been out of business for well over thirty years. They were all functioning, all lit up, and some would even spin or had other moving parts inside. They were beautiful, they all worked, and they were all plugged into some kind of electrical outlet. Add to this Abuelita's sewing machines and equipment, as well as the laundry appliances, and you can appreciate why the loss of a section of this roof would have been catastrophic. Falling rain and electronic appliances simply don't mix.

"G, we've gotta do something," I said.

"No!" Jimena shouted. "Don't go out there. What if it falls on top of you?"

I stepped in and asserted control of the situation. "What if? What if we sit here and watch the roof blow off the garage, knowing we could have stopped it,

Jimmy? This is why we didn't evacuate. To protect the house. C'mon G."

G hugged his wife and calmed her. I grabbed an oily work towel from the patio and a milk crate to stand on and dashed into the rain. The slightly rusted flapping corner of the roof required more than one attempt to catch, but once I got a grip on it, I held it down with all the strength in my two hands. The wind desperately wanted it back. Uncle G had run to Papi's toolshed around the side of the garage and came speeding toward me carrying an enormous C-clamp, a kind of mobile table vise for wood cutting. We both stood on the milk crate, me holding the flap, G tightening the clamp.

"It's good," he shouted at me. And together we ran back under the cover of the patio roof, thoroughly soaked. "We did it, Bruce!"

"Hell the F yeah!" I shouted.

The wind still created ripples along that section of roofing, but the clamp was holding. We'd saved the garage. Morale soared over our accomplishment. There were hugs and high-fives all around. Time for another cup of coffee and some dry clothes. Katrina had thrown her best at us and we'd bested her. We'd saved the garage. Everything else would be fine. Everything was going to be okay. These prideful delusions would prove to be very short-lived.

Buoyed by this tactical victory, Uncle G and I decided to take a quick walk on the other side of the fence, out into the abandoned ghost town, for a reconnaissance. Why not? We were already wet. The rain had slackened into a light summer shower. The gentleness of the precipitation was disguised by darkened skies and the wind, which had lost very little of its brutal strength. We stepped out from under the protection of the patio overhang, through the six-foot privacy fence, and out into the naked light of the cloud-covered day. Things didn't appear to be so bad. The storm drains were doing their jobs, no water had collected in the streets. Several small trees were down, some in yards, some in the streets, but all the large trees in sight had stood firm. I could see that our neighbor's shed, up a block and across Mirabeau, had collapsed in on itself. Some of the wreckage had blown into the street to intermingle with the trees and other debris scattered across the neighborhood. We walked maybe halfway down our block on Mandeville to check out the homes of friends. The story was the same: some small trees down, plenty of yard debris, nothing catastrophic. Nothing that a couple rakes, maybe a saw, and some elbow grease couldn't repair. There were no signs of life out there. No other curious people snooping around, no dogs barking, and no squirrels. Just Uncle G and me in this ominous, gray-skied *I am Legend* scenario. The feeling of being in a movie of some kind or a fantastic alternate reality was never too far from my thoughts. Every bit of life had been removed from a vibrant and thriving neighborhood. That's not to say that things were quiet or still, not in the least. The gale-force winds assured there would be no true silence on the deserted streets.

We started on our way home, back the way we'd come. As we approached the corner, something stopped Uncle G where he stood.

"Look at that. That's not good."

A manhole cover in the middle of the street was releasing small gulps of water up into the street. Pumping one brown mouthful at a time up through the pry bar hole, like some kind of filthy aorta. We watched as the large, flat manhole lid filled and the water poured over the rim onto the wet street. On our walk, the rain completely stopped falling. No rain would fall on my head for the next week.

Another manhole across the street also went under. The storm drains on the curbs were steadily submerging. All of these puddles quickly united into one flat sheet of water from one curb to the other, creeping up the grass line to the sidewalk where we stood. This process couldn't have taken more than five or ten minutes.

"I wonder what's wrong with the pumps," I said.

"Yeah, that's no good. It's the drain, right Bruce? Should be sucking the water up, not pushing it out into the street."

"Word. They'll figure it out. Let's go back inside. I need a nap." The beers were really starting to weigh on me.

"Sad. Set me up with the radio, Bruce Juan."

Once inside, I grabbed Klaus the hippo, stretched out on the loveseat in the living room, closed my eyes and nodded off. The rising water had swallowed the sidewalks, and the wind continued to send the occasional ghost spinning through our home, but I was exhausted. Sleep came quickly for once.

When the Levee Breaks

We had no way of knowing that less than a mile away the London Avenue Canal had broken its levee, almost in a straight line from our front door. The levee broke just north of the point where Mirabeau Avenue crosses the London Avenue Canal, flooding neighborhoods on the east side of the waterway. Our side of the waterway. The image of a furious tidal wave may come to mind, and for the homes right against the canal walls this certainly must have been the case. Over a month later, I would see one of these houses washed from its foundation and pushed more than thirty feet into the middle of Warrington Avenue.

Less than a mile down Mirabeau from where we were, there was no tidal wave—just a severely upset water table. Everything under the streets now overflowed onto the streets, slowly rising and rising in volume. Sounds of commotion woke me from my nap. I slid my shoes on and went to see what was happening.

"No, baby, just stay inside," Uncle Gene pleaded.

Jimena shouted, "*Lo vistes. Lo veo la gata*! Wednesday!"

Sitting on the back steps having a cigarette, Jimena had spotted Wednesday, our gray and white outdoor cat. She'd heard her running across the metal garage roof and called her name. The cat stopped a moment, looked her way, and then kept going. By then, the water was inundating the patio, about a foot deep. The bottommost concrete step leading up to the door had been swallowed by the warm, brown water backing up from the drains and manholes on the streets.

"Wednesday!" Jimena continued.

Uncle G and Mother were urging Jimena to let Wednesday go. If she was on the roof, she was up high. I stressed that cats were survivors by nature. It would take more than a foot of water in the yard to do in an alley cat.

The tears rolled down her cheeks. Jimena is a good woman. She wasn't going to let it go.

Into the water she went, calf-deep. I'll admit, I was mortified. I'd seen with my own eyes this translucent, sludgy looking liquid pulsing up from underground. I have no training in city planning or civil engineering, but I know that when I flush a toilet, it goes down into the white porcelain hole, I assume through pipes beneath the bathroom floor. Now, I'm no plumber, either. Since I don't see pipes running through the yard, I also assume that the pipes go underground, the same place the current water in the yard is coming from. The oily, Earl Grey tea-colored stuff in front of me didn't smell particularly bad, but I wasn't about to take any chances.

But there she was, standing in that mess, chasing a cat that had already disappeared.

"Wednesday!"

Even if the cat did come, Wednesday would have had to swim to Jimena. Every cat I've ever known will do just about anything to prevent itself from getting wet. Jimena's pleas were desperate. All the emotion she was feeling about the storm and the wind and the rising water poured out of her as she pleaded to the cat to come to her. Wednesday had chosen to go it alone. It was the last time I'd see Wednesday that week, but not the last time ever. Six weeks later, Wednesday and I would briefly cross paths in the backyard on a sunny afternoon in October. Wednesday had nothing but a snarl for me, which I took as a big, "Fuck you, pal." Moments later, my Abuelita would catch sight of her and, overcome with emotion, begin screaming her name. And with that, the cat would dart away into history.

I was still sleepy. I left them on the back steps and headed inside to the hippo and the loveseat. I passed Dolja, stretched out on a cushion on the dining room floor. He appeared relaxed, chin resting on his paws, but from the way his eyes darted around, I could tell he was still feeling pretty stressed. The thunder and wind probably kept him awake all night. The anguish in Jimena's voice surely wasn't helping to calm him. Maybe he realized that it was his friend she was calling for out there. The gusting gales of shrieking wind still stirred up a lot of noise.

I picked him up and brought him to the couch, laid him on my stomach, and let my shoes fall to the floor. A few deep breaths and I could feel deep sleep coming to snatch me away. I'd only been out for an hour to an hour and a half, and been awake for twenty-four. Dolja loosened and started to breathe more easily. Separate, there was chaos, but together on that loveseat, a man and his dog both allowed themselves to relax.

"Aaaaah!" I heard Jimena scream.

"No, no, no!" Uncle G followed.

"I told her to let it go," added Mother.

"Shut up, Ces," said Uncle G.

"Aaaaah!" Jimena continued to scream.

Dolja leaped off of me, leaving claw marks on my belly. I could see the three of them enter from the kitchen.

"What happened?" I asked. Over Jimena's sobs, Mother told me that Jimena had slipped and fallen into the water.

Skwoosh Skwoosh

I heard the knobs turn. She was in the tub starting a shower—the last time, I think, any of us used running water. All of the pipes under the house were submerged, and I definitely wouldn't have drunk the water coming out of the faucet, but I can totally understand feeling the need to rinse off with anything available. When she was done, she seemed much calmer and said the water had remained clear for the duration.

Happily, I resumed my place on the couch and shut my eyes. The last I checked, it was around one in the afternoon.

Sweating and confused, I woke to the sound of Jimena crying and the smell of smoke and burning in the air. I slipped on my shoes and ran toward the kitchen with Klaus the hippo under my arm. The kitchen was full of smoke. What a shame it would be to lose the house to fire during a flood.

Jimena had burnt some food on the stove. I rubbed the sleep from my eyes to be sure I was seeing things correctly. It looked like she'd attempted to cook a frozen pizza in a pan on the gas stove. Mother sat in her favorite chair in the kitchen, the one right next to the phone. Dolja lay curled up in her lap. She looked anxious and angry at the same time.

"What's going on?" I asked.

"She was afraid to use the oven," Mother replied, rocking back and forth in her chair.

"Why?"

"Go look . . . "

I walked toward the back door where Uncle G stood flapping a towel, trying to fan some of the smoke out of the kitchen. Jimena stood next to him in the hallway, head in her hands, muttering prayers in Spanish.

"It's getting higher, Bruce Juan. This shit will be in our house soon."

"No it won't," Mother shouted from the other room. "There's just something wrong with the pumps."

Astonished at the water level I was seeing from the back door, I cried out, "Holy shit. How long was I asleep?"

"Less than two hours," replied Uncle G in a solemn voice. For a man born in Ecuador, Uncle G has a fairly light complexion. At that moment, he looked paler than a bed sheet. I placed my arm around his shoulder.

"Mom's right. They just need to kick the pumps on and it will suck all of this crap off the streets."

"I know, Brucey. I'm just worried for Jimmy. She ain't never seen anything like this before."

"Neither have you, motherfucker," shouted Mother from the other room.

I couldn't help but laugh. "C'mon Mother, we gotta stick together here. She's alright to be emotional."

She had more than a right to be emotional. The water had risen from less than a foot on the patio to over four. Four feet of calm, placid, opaque, brown water, through which it was impossible to see the ground beneath. Only one step below the back door remained dry. The other five steps had been consumed by the rising tide.

Across the turgid pond, I could see one dry step leading to my apartment. My front door appeared a hundred feet away instead of maybe a half dozen short steps. I stared longingly at my door from the top step of the main house. The liquid chasm that separated the two doors may as well have been the Atlantic Ocean. I wasn't going chest-deep in that muck unless I had absolutely no choice.

I always used to say that if my house were on fire, I would run back into the inferno to grab only two things: Klaus and the C.F. Martin acoustic guitar Paw-Paw, my grandfather, left me in his will when I had just turned ten. I'd never touched a guitar in my life, but he must have known something about me that I didn't yet, and wouldn't for seven or eight more years. Now, I love writing and playing songs. I love music. I love performing music and have written dozens of original songs and have played these songs with some of the best friends this life is likely to bless me with. It all started with a few power chords on Paw-Paw's guitar, and as I stood on the back step of the main house looking at my front door, I was thinking about that guitar. Thinking about the placement of our submerged patio furniture and the best route to get to the door of my apartment.

When I got there, I could grab other stuff, too. More batteries for the radio, the old Gameboy, beer, cigarettes, food, the copy of *In the Days of the Comet* by H.G. Wells I'd been reading. I don't read much sci-fi, but the book caught my eye sitting in a box of random stuff my friend's dad had set out by the trash. The paperback looked old, but clean enough, so I took it home. Though I own another copy now, I have yet to motivate myself to finish reading it. I probably never will. Katrina's flood waters have forever claimed the contents of those last few chapters.

These and other items swirled through my mind as I stood on the new shoreline of the Gulf of Mexico, my back step. I can't tell you how long I stood there contemplating, but I knew the entire time that I wasn't going in. No matter how I maneuvered in my effort to stay dry, I'd still get wet in some places, and that would be totally unacceptable. After all, the house wasn't on fire, and that was the imaginary scenario I'd created and sworn to. And besides, the pumps would start getting rid of all this water any moment now. Call me naïve, but the thought that the pumps wouldn't come on never entered my mind. This is the City of New Orleans. The only way the City can exist where it does is because of the pumps. However, the pumps can't do anything with broken levees, and there was no way of knowing that one had burst just down the street. I opened the door and went back inside to eat some of the half-burnt, half-raw frozen pizza Jimena was slicing up.

It seemed perfectly reasonable at the time. The pumps would stop all of this fluid madness from filling the backyard and slowly working its way up the steps and into our home. The pumps were going to make this all go away. The rain stopped falling hours ago; how much higher can the water possibly get without more rain falling? The water couldn't possibly get any higher. This is Gentilly Ridge, high ground. The pumps would suck all of this crap back into the storm drains, back to perdition, and away from our family's home.

I can admit now that this sounds like lunacy. It sounds naïve. It sounds stupid and delusional. In hindsight, it sounds like all of these things. In hindsight, this was the time when we should have started hauling our water upstairs to the attic, as well as our food and anything else we would need for survival. Nine gallons of bathtub water in jugs sat on the belt of the treadmill in the old TV room adjacent to the kitchen. I would be thinking about that water a lot before long.

The pumps hadn't come on. The four of us looked at our reflections staring back at us on the glass-still surface of the brown water and sank into shock.

As the water inched its way up that last step, the four of us were drowning in a paranoia, compounded by inertia. The pumps were going to fucking come on. That's all there was to it.

I heard my mother shout something from the other end of the house. She was standing in the dining room, hugging the hippo against her chest, her face flushed with despair.

"Oh, no no no," she was saying. Our attention had been fixed to the rising water level on the back patio. Some time had passed since we'd looked out front. Mandeville Street had become an ocean while we'd been fixated on the pond in our backyard.

A thin, reflective sheet of water—so thin it looked perfectly clear, not shit brown like the rest of the vast sea outside—covered the tile floor of the front porch. The front porch area of our house had been enclosed long ago and served as an ante-room to the main entrance. To enter the home through the front door required a minimum of four keys if everything was locked tight. The door to the porch only allowed entrance onto the porch. An iron security door came next, followed by the actual front door of the house. The water line was only inches from where the porch tiles crossed into the wood flooring of our living room. A mad scramble for towels, old cushions, pillows, whatever; we stuffed and smooshed these items into a water-repellent barricade.

Then we stood back and watched our barricade saturate.

We completely lost control of our lives at that moment. From then on, freedom of movement, freedom of decision, they disappeared. Katrina was at the helm and we could only hang on for the ride.

"Gene, Gene, it's Mommy and Daddy's house. Oh no no no . . ." Mother cried out, tearing at her shirt like a prophet in the Old Testament.

Uncle Gene lost it, too. "Ces . . . the house? It's in Papi's house."

Collectively, Uncle G and Mother had lived in this house for half a century. I added another fifteen years. It is in this space that our lives happened. Our Christmases, our birthdays, Thanksgiving turkeys, the most explosive arguments, and the tightest, closest hugs.

"Go Away!" Jimena shouted at the top of her lungs, as if the sheer force of her words would push the waters away. Her words proved as futile as any of our other efforts—the towel barricade, the C-clamp on the garage roof. Hell, the garage was filled almost to the rafters. The new flat screen and everything else inside was ruined. The cars on the lawn, my truck, G's van, and Papi's mobile home were all engine-deep. The water had cut us off from the rest of the world, and now it was in our house with us.

Our dismay at watching the water swallow up the front porch and advance into the front door soon turned into outright horror. The old hardwood floors we'd been walking on for decades didn't stand a chance against the rising, turgid soup. Puddles were forming in every room, soaking into rugs and pooling at the lowest points, puddles slowly and steadily growing with every passing moment. Fifteen minutes later, we all had wet feet. Each step we took splished and splashed, sending ripples across the surface in every direction.

The decision to flee came suddenly. Uncle G and Jimena each stuffed some clothes and what little cash they had into some backpacks. I grabbed a half-empty jug of fresh, not-bathtub water, Klaus the hippo, and a bag of Doritos I'd been snacking on. Mother had the dog. One at a time, we ascended the steps leading to the attic, like four astronauts climbing into the escape pod. After Jimena's fall into the brown soup, we'd all become terrified of the water. It was filthy, and though it didn't outright stink, we all believed that our home was filling with raw sewage.

Like every other bit of available space, the attic at 4899 Mandeville Street had been converted into a chill spot by my grandparents. The exposed floor beams of the attic were completely covered in plywood, turning our attic into a long, narrow A-frame room, which was ALWAYS incredibly hot. A couple of people throughout the years, including Simone, had lived up there, but only during the winter months. Sometime around 1997, Papi built a false wall across the section of the attic adjacent to the ladder, roughly the size of the second bedroom in the mother-in-law's apartment. In other words, small. A doorway draped with a long curtain separated the "room" from the rest of the attic. The little attic getaway had fallen out of use by the summer of 2005.

An old transistor radio sitting on a tiny dressing table with a mirror back, a vintage Coca-Cola wall clock, and a vintage Pepsi Cola decorative outdoor thermometer adorned the false wall. An ancient steel-frame twin bed and a cushy circular rug, several pillows and cushions, and an enormous black sea chest rounded out the furnishings. To the left of the attic stairs is a side-by-side window with no screens. This window was never locked. This window served as my and Uncle G's top secret way of breaking into the house if we were ever locked out. From the left window, it was about two feet down to the roof, which covered the flooded patio.

Getting out of the window had always required some delicate maneuvering. To exit the window, one first had to get their right leg out of the window and set their right foot on the roof. This move always scares people the first time they try it. Next, you exit ass-first, and then torso. The other foot is still stuck up in the window and requires an assist from one hand as the other holds onto the window frame for balance. To get into the window, you have to lift your left leg in, get your head in, and spring with the right foot up into the window, pulling and straining your weight through a 16-square-inch opening. My buddy Chief stands at 6'4" and he's made it through. It sounds tough, but you just have to know what you're doing.

Katrina's low pressure, high winds, and overcast skies produced an extraordinarily mild late-summer afternoon for the sultry City of New Orleans. The maelstrom outside made little impact on our attic, however. Though it must have been less than seventy-five degrees outside, the Pepsi thermometer read ninety-one. With four of us crammed in the room with a dog and a hippo, I quickly made an exit and stepped onto the roof. Once I had both feet under me, the cool wind embraced me from all sides. I felt alive as I never had before, or since.

Out there, fully exposed to the wind and the panoramic view of the flooding, was amazing, unlike anything I, or you, or very few people, have ever seen. My old familiar neighborhood looked so foreign. The reflections of the flooded homes danced on the water's surface. The gray sunlight and the sweeping wind added to the almost dreamlike quality of my surroundings. I made my way up the slope of the patio roof to the roof section of the addition to the main house. Unlike the dramatic slope over the attic or the gentler slope of the patio, the roof over this portion sits nice and flat. Wide and open, this section of rooftop represents the most open space on our property. A couple of friends and a couple twelve-packs had spent a couple of interesting evenings out on the flat roof. Under this portion of the roof was the sitting room where Klaus and I had taken a nap not too long ago, Papi and Abuelita's bedroom and master bath, and Mother's bedroom.

A clear, open expanse the size of all three rooms below became my sensory deprivation tank for the next several hours. A deep, personal change occurred in my very being, somewhere between the hours of 7 p.m. Monday, August 29th, and 6 a.m. Tuesday, August 30th, 2005. I blame this experience on a lost night of sleep and the utterly un-fucking-real shit I saw all around me. Like a shaman wandering in an unfamiliar desert, I'd embarked on an introspective journey not unlike the trip associated with any psychedelic drug.

I wandered through my mind, sifting memories, but found it difficult to hold on to any single one. The images I'd conjure would whirl and swirl around my skull like the winds whipping my body. The harder I tried, the more difficult it became to remember. I couldn't see my childhood pet Pug, couldn't see the face of my first crush, or presents under a Christmas tree. I tried to focus on Simone, but couldn't find her either. Everything was brown water. I began to worry if I'd ever see those things again.

These heavy thoughts were whisked away by the tempest. The still-frame memories I'd been trying to hold onto gave way to a frenetic moving picture show. My life, both the real and imagined moments, intertwined with the clouds racing overhead. I blinked twice, and I was free from it all. I had no identity. No end and no beginning. I was the wind. I was the storm. I was the conduit of Heaven and Earth. Then it all came crashing down, and the truth hit me like a gust of cold hurricane wind. I was nothing but a tiny speck of light in a dark, sad City.

The sun slowly being eaten to the west, across Mandeville Street from me, and the gray clouds swirling above were perfectly reflected by the surface of the water. The thin sheet we witnessed swallowing our front porch from the dining room downstairs appeared to be an ocean from up on the roof. The vehicles parked on the lawn were completely submerged, and the bed of my pickup, loaded up to an equal level with the rest of the street, appeared like a walled off monument, some sort of perverse reflecting pool stolen from the rest of the sea.

Shifting patches of orange sunlight broke through seams in the scattering gray clouds. The flat roof was being swept over by winds steadily whipping in excess of forty miles per hour and gusts probably double that. Tight ripples stretched across the shining surface when the gusts blew.

THE PARTY PEOPLE

I'd only been outside for a few minutes when I discovered that we were actually not alone in the neighborhood. I could hear hoots and shouting, like a lively party was going down a few streets away. People I'd never met, out on a roof somewhere, apparently having way more fun than me. It sounded like they were swimming and drinking and having a damn good time. I swear on my hippo's life, I even heard the garbled wash of a distant boom box. They'd brought a boom box to the end of the world. Why didn't I think of that?

They continued wailing and carrying on. My best guess is that the people I was hearing were on Western Avenue, two streets away. Despite the wind and water and beautiful sunset, the end of the world was painfully boring. Surely, given the circumstances, they'd allow me to join in their revelry. But how to get there? I was standing on my roof, looking over a vast inland sea, the entire house below me now three-to-four feet deep. I didn't want to get wet, that's for sure, but they sounded like they were having a ball, and I was totally alone up there. I wanted to have fun, too. These mystery party people, to me, were as accessible as the year 1776. I was just not meant to be there. Well, I thought, if I can't just show up, maybe I can at least make contact.

In my circle of friends, if you need to get someone's attention from far away, there is only one surefire method: the guttural, uvula-swinging exclamation we refer to as the Viking Yell. The Viking Yell starts deep in the chest, vibrates the lowest chords in your throat, and fills the air around you with a supernatural growl. If an elephant's grunt can be heard a dozen miles away, then a good Viking Yell should travel at least two blocks. Only one way to find out.

I inhaled deeply and let it rip, "Whhuuuuuuuuuuuuuuuuugh!"

To my delight, they started shouting back! What seemed impossible only an hour before was really happening. I'd found other people out there in Waterworld and I'd made contact with them! When the pumps got rid of all this funky ocean, which would start happening any moment now, I'd walk over there and introduce myself and say, "Hi, I'm the guy who was yelling at you from my roof; you yelled back. Got any beers?" Warm and enduring friendships are made under such conditions, and at that moment I felt that I needed some friendship desperately.

I heard splashing in the water nearby, but didn't see anything. A discernible voice called out, "Hey, who's up there?" Oh shit. I'd attracted attention. I didn't know if this person or people could be dangerous or what. All I knew was that I was helpless to fight off an attack. I crouched down and climbed my way to the apex of the roof in a prone position, hoping to see and not be seen. My apprehensions melted away when a saw a skinny, shirtless, hipster sort of guy wearing a backpack, a fedora, and sunglasses rowing a tiny boat with a two-by-four. I slid back down to the flat roof to present myself from a more civilized height.

"Hey, how's it going?" I called.

He sized me up, apparently decided I, too, was harmless, and said, "How's it going man, want to come for a ride?"

I must admit, I did. I wanted off that roof. I wanted a cold beer or a shot. I wanted human contact, but he was down there and I was up on the roof. The only way down that I could see was to jump onto the roof of Uncle G's van, down the front windshield, and step into his canoe from the hood. It sounded do-able, but how in the world would I get back up there? What about my mom and family? Somehow, abandoning them to go party didn't seem like the right thing to do.

"No thanks. Got other people here in the attic." He showed no visible emotion. The party people continued to shout.

The guy in the boat said something to the effect of, "You're lookin' out, that's cool man. Good luck."

And with that he started rowing away, toward the party people, my party people. Those were my party people. But looking at all that thick brown water, I knew that I was better off high and dry than in a boat with this guy with no supplies, soaking wet, and covered in shit water. High and dry, the only way to be.

As the guy in the boat rowed up Mirabeau, I saw him flip his canoe and go head-first into the drink. His skin didn't immediately start melting off. That was a good sign at least. He righted his craft, climbed back aboard, and after paddling with his hands to catch his two-by-four, he rowed away out of sight, westbound on Mirabeau. I wonder what happened to that guy over the next couple of days. His story must be at least as interesting as the tale I'm recalling now.

The wake from Gilligan's rowboat rippled into nothing and the surface of the water appeared a perfect reflection of the sunset above. The breeze swirled all around, not from one specific direction, but from every direction at once, enveloping me. This created surface ripples on the otherwise swimming pool-still surface of my brown ocean. I could see gray clouds racing across the pink light of the setting sun on the water's surface.

I could see the tree branches swaying, and I could also see me, my silhouette, reflected on the surface of the water. At that moment, I felt like the last man on Earth. I felt like a cave painting or the anonymous image on a damaged old photo. Something long forgotten, the chalk outline of a dead man.

I stepped away from the edge and toward the middle of the flat roof and let out one last full-force Viking Yell. Over the shifting wind and swooshing tree limbs, I could hear my name being called out in desperation. It was my mother's voice. I ran as quickly as I could to the attic window.

"Bruuuuce!?!"

"I'm coming."

"Are you okay? I've been yelling for you!"

"I couldn't hear you. A guy offered to take me on a boat ride."

"No!" she managed to blubber out.

The attic room had become emotional in my absence. Jimena was red-faced and wailing, Uncle Gene doing his best to console her.

"I heard you screaming. I didn't know if you were okay."

"I'm fine, Momma." I stuck my head into the window and kissed her cheek. She begged me to climb in and stay inside.

"In a minute. It'll be dark soon."

I grabbed my camera, flashlight, and a cigarette and went back to the flat roof. I snapped a few photos and, after deliberating on the sanitary ramifications of my actions, went ahead and urinated off the side of the roof and into the pool. The sun had fully set and flash pictures weren't coming out right. I climbed into the attic window and rejoined my family.

Immediately, the emotional gravity of the small attic room sank my high spirits. Life was far too real in there. Tears and sighing all around. Air stagnant and hot. I longed for the whipping cool breeze out there on the flat roof. I felt like maybe I would have been in a better place rowing with the guy in the boat, saying cheers over clinking glasses or cans with the party people over on Western. I didn't want life to be real. But this shit right here, right now, this was the *realest* shit there ever could be. I wanted nothing to do with it.

I was twenty-five years old. I craved light-hearted discussions on fleeting topics, reading, computer games, alcohol, and camaraderie. I wanted to ignore what had trapped us up here, I didn't want to sit and dwell on it. I'd rather be out on the roof experiencing the moment than huddled in a tiny room with crying women and a whimpering dog, resenting it.

Dolja presented a problem. We stored his food in a repurposed trash can by the garage. He drank water from a bowl. We had access to neither. He could lap water from my hand until we ran out, but his food was totally submerged. I felt bad feeding him spicy Doritos, but it was the only thing we had to eat.

No one said anything, the silence intermittently broken by a sniffle or a silent sob. The still air, the stale smell of the items stored in the attic, and the profound sadness were drowning me, as surely as the waters outside would have. Something had to give.

"Should we check the radio?" I asked the room, directing my question at no one in particular. No one replied. Then, I understood that each one of them felt the same way. Isolated from the world. Trapped in that attic room, trapped in the suffocating silence of their tormenting mental dialogues. The radio promised answers, information, a distraction, anything but this.

Working my way forward on the dial by miniscule increments, all I heard was static on the Walkman. I switched from AM to FM. Uncle G produced a little pocket torch. Other than a single candle burning in the corner of the attic room on the bureau, Uncle G's tiny spotlight focused on my thumb was the only light in the pitch-black room. The wind outside swayed the thin curtain over the window I'd climbed through. You could cut the tension with a knife. The early numbers on the dial, the late 80s and early 90s, nothing. As I passed what I remember was 99.5 WRNO—the "Rock" of New Orleans—we heard voices, then more static.

"Go back, go back," all three of them shouted.

I tuned in the signal. And what did we hear? Not answers. What we heard was three, maybe four, men broadcasting from what could have been another attic like the one we were in. Of course, these people were in a studio somewhere, but they sounded every bit as shaken and confused as the three people I was looking at.

The words made no sense. Even at the time, I wished I'd had some way to record the ludicrous things being said. I wish could remember more of it. I wish I could, in good faith, add quotation marks to what I'm about to write, but through the muddle, I ascertained that St. Bernard Parish had ceased to exist. There were several reports of people being seen clinging to scraps of floating debris, fighting to stay above water.

Mostly, they shared individual reports, people calling in and emailing from smartphones or laptops. A family stranded on their roof in New Orleans East, another trapped in their attic in Chalmette. People in the Ninth Ward claiming widespread fires and flooding. Chaos and hearsay ruled the airwaves. The men doing the talking had *the fear* in their voices. These men were afraid of the water, just like us.

Many calls had to do with bashing Aaron Broussard, the Jefferson Parish President. People wanted to know when the pumps would turn on. Some said the pump operators had been sent home.

Uncle Gene tried to calm Jimena, telling her that these were Jefferson Parish workers they were talking about. Orleans Parish surely had their shit together. Nothing added up. I surmised that these fellas, despite their best intentions, had no real information to share. I only wish that somewhere, and I admit I haven't tried looking too hard, I could find an archive of this broadcast. To have been able to record an hour, or just ten minutes, of all this nonsense would really add relevance to the mindset of frightened citizens like us. We were scared to begin with, before we started to realize our own mortality was at stake.

These guys were further terrifying my people, exciting them into a frenzy of tears. I've tried to put myself in their position in an attempt to better understand. They were the only emergency station. The only people broadcasting. It was their job, their duty, to keep broadcasting, to stay on the air. Thirty minutes in and most of what they were saying was pure repetition. Inside the Walkman was a copy of Led Zeppelin's *Houses of the Holy* on audiocassette, but to change over from the radio to listen to "The Crunge" would be too much for everyone around me. Mother probably would've dug it. She loves that song. But she wasn't operating at one hundred percent Cecilia. Uncle G was probably the biggest Zepp fan of us all, but he wasn't himself either. Jimena surely had no idea who the hell they even were, despite the fact that they'd sold fifty million albums worldwide. Now was not the time, not even for "No Quarter," a song more suited in tenor to our predicament. The voices coming out of the tiny black speakers had mesmerized them. I couldn't believe a word being said. It was time for me to make an exit.

I excused myself to leave and was met by a chorus of protest from Mother and Jimena. They were begging me to stay inside with them, asking, "Don't you want to listen to the radio?" I tried to tell them that every twenty minutes the announcers were repeating the same things. The air outside was cool and fresh, the room close and hot.

"I'll be fine, if you need anything, just shout." Climbing out of that depressing oven and back into the winds enlivened my senses and titillated my skin. The musty scent of the attic was swept from my nostrils by the delightful breeze swirling around out on the roof, which still gusted in gales.

Now, anyone who's been outdoors on a late August night in New Orleans may have trouble believing this, but it was cold that night. Honestly, truthfully, no shit, cold. I'd estimate the temperature to be about seventy degrees. Factor in the wind chill and it felt like fifty out on the flat roof. The clothing I had on wasn't going to be enough for the winds, yet this outfit would have to stand up to much worse over the next six days. I had on a faded gray t-shirt. For the life of me, I can't recall the design on the shirt, or even if there was one to begin with. A pair of boxer shorts under a well-worn pair of Dickies brand carpenter jeans were held in place by a 60-inch long Army surplus web belt. Even without a cataclysmic natural disaster, I'd probably have been wearing something similar for the next six days.

Most important were my shoes.

A pair of woodland camo-patterned house slippers with green rubber soles. The insides were soft synthetic flannel. The very thought of woodland camo on a pair of slippers is so absurd that when I saw them on a shelf about a year before, I knew I had to have them. I wore the hell out of these things, out to bars, to the store, to hang out with friends, everywhere. The insides weren't soft anymore. Most of the lining had started to rip. I really didn't wear them out of the house anymore, but that's what I had up on the roof, no socks.

The chilly wind was too much for me. I stuck my head back in the attic window and asked if they had a blanket I could take with me.

"What's wrong?" Mother asked, her voice thick with radio-induced paranoia.

I said that it was chilly out there with the wind still blowing so strongly. The three people sitting in the suffocating attic room looked perplexed. They were burning up in that tight little room. Through the window, they handed me two long hospital examination gowns, size triple X. Why the gowns were in a drawer in the attic only God knows. No one in my family had been seriously ill, but my grandmother is kind of a kleptomaniac when it comes to hospitals and doctors' offices and fast-food napkins, a phenomenon not uncommon to people who came of age during tougher times. Each of the gowns was the size of a small bed sheet. Thus equipped, I went back to my spot on the flat roof and lay down on a spread-out gown, covering myself with the other.

I looked up and could see a million stars twinkling. The sky was clear, except for the occasional small, dark cloud racing by. Without the normal glow of the City's light pollution, the sky looked like one of those nature shows shot in the desert. I wished I knew more about constellations, because they were all there right in front of me. That night I counted seven shooting stars.

But the stars and the clouds weren't alone up there. At any one time I could see a dozen helicopters flying around, most with searchlights. I assumed they were news copters, cameramen, and reporters on board. Those were the smaller ones, but others were larger and blacked out—military equipage. I decided I'd make it my mission to communicate with one. I had nothing else to do. I have no knowledge of Morse code, but my Army surplus flashlight had a button on it to send signals. I chose a sequence and flashed it at all of the choppers that came close enough. One after another, I'd flash them my signal, and one after another, they just kept on flying. Maybe they weren't seeing the light, or maybe they were just too busy.

What I'd started as a game quickly became a desperate attempt to be seen, to be recognized, to have someone else know that I was alive down there on the roof. I kept on clicking. The helicopters were everywhere, flying in all directions. I climbed to the point of the roof and, looking toward the City, I could see dozens of them. Surely one of them should notice a flashing white light beaming up from a pitch-black City. Finally, one did.

I flashed as it cruised by. As it slowed and turned, I continued to steadily flash my sequence. I could have been saying something crude or offensive, but more likely it was transmitting downright gibberish. The helicopter turned and shined its spotlight directly on me. I stopped flashing my light and began flapping my arms.

As young teenagers, we'd hang out by the train tracks and when a train came by, we'd wave our arms and shout, "Water!" Most of the time, the trains would rumble past. Maybe they'd blow their horn at us, but there were several times where they'd throw us these little plastic bottles with foil on top, like you see kids drinking blue, green, and red punch from, but these were bottles of water. Just a few bottles, or a bag full of them. On more than one occasion, the engineers dropped us a whole case. I remember one time when the water bottles they dropped were cold from ice chests, cool beads of condensation running down the sides. That was special.

The memory of those bottles of cold water was on my mind as I flapped my arms at the flying machine, which had me blinded in its spotlight. Someone was up there, looking at me. Then it spoke . . .

"Are you alone?" asked the helicopter.

I shouted "NO," but whether they heard me or not, I was shaking my head.

"How many are in there?"

"Four and a dog!" I held up five fingers. I flashed my light at him five times. The chopper held me there in focus for another few seconds and then flew away. Not even a single bottle of water for lil Brucey.

I gave up on the helicopters and laid myself down under the stars. I tried to relax, to slow down and maybe get some sleep. Tomorrow would be a long day. Just get a little sleep and let those pumps kick in. I'd wake up and most of the water would be gone, and we could find something good to eat. I wrapped myself in both gowns, trying in vain to keep the wind off of me. The gowns were made of very thin material. I closed my eyes and the stars disappeared. The water underneath and all around had come to life, an endless, gentle sound to fill the silence, like a soothing audiotherapy tape you'd buy at a health and wellness store.

In this instance, the sound of the water underneath and all around was anything but soothing. It was terrifying. What would happen next? What the hell were we going to do? What was Simone doing? God, I hoped she was okay. I hoped we would be okay. I wanted to take a shower and crawl into bed with Dolja on one side and my bad right knee elevated on Klaus the hippo, the way I normally slept. I wanted a combo meal with large fries.

If I had to be up on a roof, I wanted Simone to be up there with me, lying next to me, shivering underneath a hospital gown. We'd been through some tough spots together and I needed a partner right then—a tried and true companion to lean on, because every heartbeat was now another tick further into the unknown. The water may disappear, but we'd have a big-time mess to clean up. No electricity for a while, our vehicles likely ruined, no running water either. Certainly it wouldn't be safe to drink. Hopefully the gas would still be on so we could boil the water. I opened my eyes, the stars were still there. Simone still wasn't. And the water continued to sing gentle songs. I felt so tired. I tried to breathe calmly and hold in the tears. It was lonely up there on the roof. In time, sleep must have taken me.

Crash!

Boom!

I might have been asleep for ten minutes or two hours, I don't know. It was still dark, save for the stars.

Crash!

Crack!

The sound of breaking wood and glass, of nails being pulled out of place. And then, SPLOOSH!

My God, I thought, *There's something in the water!* No person in their right mind would be going out for a late night swim. It can't be human. I was on my feet, flashlight in hand, running to the edge of the roof. What the hell was that sound? Maybe an alligator or some kind of man-sized sewer rat mutated by the flood waters. That would be fucked up!

I shined my light and saw a Rottweiler. Splash, sploosh, splash, splash, the big black dog churned up the water. Not the smooth doggie paddle of a trained Labrador, but desperate, searching kicks. Each paw that went down was trying to find solid ground.

Sploosh, splash, splash.

I shined my light at a porch across the street. The dog had broken through the door of the front porch. Like on our house, the outermost door was constructed from a wooden frame and glass slats you could raise and lower, a screen of mesh behind that. The decades-old glass panes could not be expected to contain a determined, frightened animal weighing more than ninety pounds. Rottweilers are all muscle, which may be why the dog seemed to be having so much trouble staying afloat.

Sploosh, splash, splash, splash.

In the beam of my light, I could see the big black head fighting hard to stay above the water line. The ripples chasing across the surface carried the light waves off down the street into blackness. The struggling animal saw my light and began to swim toward me, or my light. The swollen, flooded streets meant that this was a swim of more than fifty feet, and no purchase to show for it. *Go back, dog. Don't come this way, I said to myself. Just go back, there's nowhere to stand here.* I pointed my light back toward the house that it had come from.

Sploosh, splash, splash.

Another beam of light swept across the water and then that voice, "Annie . . . Annie . . ."

Splash, splash, splash. "Annie!"

I couldn't get a good look at the man across the street, but he had on eyeglasses and his voice sounded tired. The farthest out he ventured was the first step down from his porch, the water reaching well up his thighs.

"Annie."

I pointed the light at the dog and shouted across the abyss. "She's swimming toward my light. I'll turn mine off, you keep yours on her, and maybe she'll swim back." I'd never met this man before on the street, never waved hello, and certainly hadn't known that he and possibly others were in that house, maybe even in the attic, like my people. If they were in the attic, they would have been stuck in there. That house, always a rental, hadn't been added onto like ours. They didn't have roof access like I did. And here I am barking orders at this poor, wet, miserable guy.

He said, "Alright. Anniiie . . ."

Splash, splash, sploosh.

After staring into the blackness for a while longer with my fingers crossed, I lay back down. I was really pulling for Annie the Rottweiler, but I needed to rest some more while it was still dark. I don't know what time it was, but it felt early. I closed my eyes.

The desperation in the man's voice became more emphatic with each cry of "Annie!"

Annie's only reply was more:

Sploosh, splash, splash, splash, sploosh, splash, splash.

I opened my eyes. The sky was pink and the world was silent. The wind had stopped blowing entirely. All was still. I could hear the water beneath me and all around lapping at the cars and walls, and the entire world. I felt terribly thirsty. My body was stiff from lying on the roof.

The stillness was broken by the voice—flat and obligatory—calling, "Annie?" Annie must have swum until she couldn't any longer.

TUESDAY
AUGUST 30TH, 2005

DAWN

END OF THE COMMON ERA

As dawn broke on me and the City of New Orleans, the water was just as high as it had ever been. The pumps hadn't come on. I knew we were fucked. If a big strong dog couldn't make it out there on the high seas, what chance did my sedentary mother have? We'd have to stay with the house. Maybe the helicopter I'd signaled the night before was mapping out stranded people. Maybe they'd send supplies or get us out of here by air. That would be cool. Heck, they— whoever *they* were—owed me a helicopter ride for all this mess. I gathered up my robes and stuck my head in the attic window.

The sad scene had changed very little. Mother was resting on the bed, Uncle G consoling Jimena. They'd also been hoping that this new day would dawn on a much drier City. Our precious water supply was becoming frighteningly low, less than a gallon remained in the jug. And what promised to be a brutally hot day was beginning outside. Four grown people and a small dog, less than a gallon of water between us. The old Pepsi thermometer nailed to the overhead beam read eighty-seven degrees. It wasn't yet seven in the morning. On hand for breakfast we had a family-size bag of "Spicy Nacho" flavored Doritos chips, the perfect salty and spicy snack for dehydrated disaster victims. We also had a tub of sugar-free meringue cookies. One bite of these things and all of the saliva was immediately sucked out of your mouth. A foul-tasting piece of plaster or a tongue-burning tortilla chip. Those were the options. Also, Jimena had a twenty- ounce bottle of Sprite for her personal consumption, and Uncle G produced a three-quarters full, two-liter bottle of Diet Coke—not the most hydrating beverage, but at least it was wet.

None of us wanted to go sloshing around downstairs to search for additional supplies. Peering down from the attic, it was difficult to judge the water's depth. Our water jugs were submerged. We knew that much. And there was no way we could trust the water that might come out of the tap. Getting wet in that muck wasn't worth a can of corn or a bag of flour. Not yet. For now, we would try to make do with what we had.

I nibbled at a little of each food item, the chips and the cookies, and took a drink of warm water, washed it down with a swig of Diet Coke, and spent the next half-hour trying to brush as much seasoning off of a couple chips as I could to feed to Dolja. He was starting to unravel. His patience for all of this madness had come to an end. He was as thirsty and tired as the rest of us. He ate the chips and lapped some water from a teacup saucer that had served to hold our single candle stick. He drank his water and looked eager for more, but I had to deny him; we were trying to ration our supplies. Mother forced me to take her spot on the mattress. She sat on the floor with the dog. There were no pillows on the bed, but luckily I had Klaus the hippo with us and he served as a fine pillow. I could feel a second near-sleepless night weighing on me heavily. After our little breakfast, I tried to get comfortable as best I could. By 8:30 in the morning the temperature in the attic was up to ninety-four degrees.

Who were we kidding? How long did we really think we could make it? With the amount of water we had, we couldn't survive for three days at those temperatures. Probably less than that. Every trickle of sweat would bring us closer to the end. The gravity of our predicament consumed my every thought.

What were we going to have to do?

What choices, hard choices, lay ahead of us?

How long do we let ourselves suffer? How long do we let the dog suffer?

How long do we wait?

How weak do we let ourselves become before we try to make it out of there and try our luck on the brown ocean?

The six-foot wooden privacy fence around the patio was almost completely submerged—less than an inch of the top was exposed to daylight. At 5'10" I was far and away the tallest person in the attic, but even I would be over my head in water. From my vantage point on the roof, I could see nothing but water in all directions. Swimming out of there would mean swimming blind, to no destination foreseeably better than where we were. The mercury continued to rise and the water wasn't going down. We were trapped. Someone would find our dried-out corpses in this attic. We were going to die in here. One by one we would die of thirst up in this sweltering little attic room. The room where my grandparents had cuddled and watched telenovelas after Thanksgiving dinner. The room where Simone had lived for a few months after she decided cohabitating with me and my puppy love attraction was too stressful. I pushed her away then, and now I would never get to see her again. I'd never get to apologize, to say *thank you*, to say *I love you*, ever again. Because I was going die in my attic.

Already, Mother was encouraging me to drink her share of water. I told her she needed to drink or I would have to rough her up.

I had this vision in my head of all of us drying out like leather. Of course, in this vision I am the last to die. I'd listen to all of their goodbyes. One by one, I'd get to see them expire. First would probably be the dog, then Mother, then Uncle G and Jimena. I'd be trapped in the attic alone with their lifeless bodies, sipping the last capfuls of Diet Coke. Maybe someone would find me in there, and maybe they wouldn't. Maybe the water would go down eventually, and maybe it wouldn't. If the water stayed at its present level indefinitely, we were goners. If only for a week, we were just as dead. I laid myself down on the musty twin mattress and threw my arm around my hippo. He'd outlive us all. He didn't need food or water. When archaeologists, or whoever, discovered our final resting place, it would be up to Klaus to do the explaining.

All of these thoughts swam through my mind as I lay there with my eyes closed. I could hear Mother weeping softly as she stroked Dolja's fur. I could hear Jimena weeping, too, as my Uncle stroked her hair. I shut my eyes tighter and fought down the tears. Again, I felt myself leave the world as sleep swallowed me up. I don't remember dreaming, but if I did, I hope that I dreamt about somewhere cool and clean, and that I had a tall drink with plenty of ice in it.

I woke to Mother shaking my arm and saying my name in a hushed voice. I've always thought it to be one of my best and favorite attributes, that I can *wake up* all at once. Unless I wake confused from a vivid dream, I'm usually fully coherent immediately.

She whispered, "Bruce, Bruce." There was an urgency in her tone. The dog was barking.

Uncle Gene and Jimena were laying down on the floor, trying to keep themselves hidden. Uncle G spoke in a whisper, "Bruce, people . . ."

Quiet as everyone tried to be, Dolja had blown our cover. Then, he lost it. He was as overheated as us, and we weren't wearing fur coats like him. "Arf, arf, arf! Grrrrrrrrr. Arf!"

"What time is it?" I asked, sitting up on the bed.

"You've been asleep about an hour," Mother replied. The dog kept barking. Then I heard a booming voice come through the attic window.

"Anyone in there?" the mysterious voice called out. Through the open attic window, we heard them loud and clear.

"Just be quiet," said Uncle Gene, his face bright red and his breathing ragged.

"Just be quiet," said Mother.

"RrAaaarf! Arf! Warf!" said Dolja.

I could hear indiscernible voices, several of them, and again the bellowing voice. "Is there anyone in there?"

"Just be quiet . . ."

"Raaarf Rrruff ruff wuff"

The voice and the murmuring were coming closer, water dripping, a buzzing, humming sound. "Hello! Is anyone in the attic?"

"They're talking to us!" I said, a little too loudly for the taste of my companions.

"Shhh . . ."

"Shhh..."

"*Callate niño . . .*"

"Hello?" said a distinctly different, distinctly younger, voice. "We're neighbors. Don't worry. Come out, if you're in there. We want to help."

"Shhh, no baby, don't . . ." Mother whispered, shaking her head. I couldn't take it any longer. I taught myself in just a few hours to hate that attic room. I wasn't going to die of thirst in my attic. I'd rather die on the streets.

"YEAH," I shouted.

"Bruce, no! What are you doing?" said Uncle G.

"Hey? We hear the dog. We been shoutin'! You in there or not?" The voice asked again.

"Yeah! Hold on a second." I said.

"Rowoof. Arf. Awoof." Dolja added.

It was done. I'd spilled the beans. They couldn't protest anymore. My family gave up their efforts at concealment and sat up straighter, all eyes on me. I hoped I was doing the right thing. I waved my hand outside the window.

"Kill the motor."

"Grab hold of that fence."

"You in there?"

I stuck my head out of the window and was blinded for a moment by the bright sunlight. I said something like, "Hey, how's it going?" As my eyes adjusted I could see a man's head peering over the edge of the patio roof.

"How many of you are in there?"

"Four…and a dog."

Again, I heard the muttering of several voices, the booming one then said, "You want out?" Three words, three syllables, those three simple words. "You want out?"

A million thoughts raced through my mind.

The plastic train I'd ride around and around in circles on the patio as a toddler—that morning I'd found a section of the track in the attic. The time my great-grandmother, Papi's mother, busted my friends and me smoking cigarettes in the backyard. When I saw her face in the window, I was so scared. She didn't rat me out. I thought of how my grandparents would always give me this ENORMOUS box of Raisin Bran every Christmas. Maybe they were concerned about the amount of fiber I was getting. I thought about the couch that my friend Gary bought for Mother on her birthday, because he thought the one she'd been sleeping on wasn't comfortable enough for her. I thought of my other friends and all the times we'd had in both my apartment and the main house. I thought of us playing the first *novice-core* thrash songs I ever wrote, and my Abuelita suggesting our band name be *Los Idiotas*. No matter how loud we played, it was always just, "Oh, the children . . . the crazy children." I thought of playing Tecmo football literally for weeks straight. I even thought of the night I'd stayed home to play some music while Simone went out for drinks. She came home and passed out on the couch in a miniskirt. I'd stared at her thighs for hours.

And in the same moment, I thought of my mother and uncle, and their memories, stretching back decades past my own. I thought of my grandparents. My Papi singing love ballads while he did just about anything at any time of day. I'd wake up nearly every morning to the sound of him singing. The man does have a brilliant voice.

I thought of my grandmother, clad head to toe in white, wearing a wide straw hat, tending her roses on a balmy summer's day. Her garden, now five feet under the brown water, was the floor of this grotesque aquarium. I thought of the smiles on their brown faces.

The question resounded in my ears, "You want out?"

Uncle G and Jimena's faces were bright red. Mother's looked three shades paler than normal. Her breathing sounded unsteady and shallow. None of them were sweating anymore.

"Grrrrrr. Row Row Row Row Row Rooooowww," Dolja said, his tongue hanging long and far out of his mouth, weighted with thirst.

The Pepsi thermometer read One Hundred Six degrees. It was barely eleven in the morning. An unknown number of scorching days in the attic lay ahead of us. Circumstances had gotten well out of our control. We'd failed in our mission to protect the house. At this point, it wasn't worth dying for.

"Yeah, we want to get out. Hold on a second. I'm coming out."

"Bruce, no. Bruce, you don't know these people," Jimena said in her heavy-laden accent. Her vocabulary and grammar had come a long way in a short time, but her accent was still super thick.

"We have to go, y'all. It's too hot in here for us to just sit with no water." I said.

"Gene, go with him," Mother nodded at me.

"Genie, no . . ." Jimena began to cry again.

"Baby, I gotta look out for Brucey. We'll be right outside the window."

I waited until Uncle Gene was out of the window and together we stepped down the slanted patio roof. Before us were a dozen unhappy people in an eighteen-foot fishing boat. In the front of the boat, standing, was a muscular, lighter-skinned black guy wearing a collared navy blue golf shirt, a size too small, so it really showed off his beefy biceps. He wore swim trunks and no shoes. Sitting at his feet was a teenaged white boy, stocky and awkward. Naked but for a pair of red swim trunks, he was stretched over the side gripping the top of our fence. Definitely the younger voice I'd heard. What I assumed to be the boy's father sat silently behind the wheel, wearing a Gilligan hat and sunglasses. The other eight or so people in the boat had obviously just had as uncomfortable a night as we'd had.

The black guy did all the talking. "You said there are four of you?"

"Four and a dog."

He cocked his head to the side, pursed his lips, "I can hear the dog. What kind of dog you got?"

"He's little, a Miniature Pinscher."

"A Doberman Pinscher?"

"No, a little one. He doesn't even weigh twenty pounds."

"Barks like a big dog." I was very proud of my Dolja when he said that.

"Look, we don't have room for four people." My heart sank, but he continued,

"We're gonna drop off these folks, and we'll come back for you. Give us twenty, thirty minutes.

"You're going to come back . . ." I could hear the trepidation in my voice.

"We'll be back. Forty minutes."

"Please come back. Don't leave us up here."

"We'll be back, man. Y'all be ready."

"There are people all over," said the teenage boy.

I had to ask. I spoke in the direction of the skipper behind the wheel, "Did the helicopter guys tell you where to find us?"

Under his mustache I could see him pull up one corner of his mouth into a half-smile. "Another one. Push us off."

He opened the throttle and off they went down Mirabeau Avenue and then made a left on Marigny, the next street up. Once out of sight I turned to my uncle and said, "Did you see that dude's arms in that little shirt?"

My attempt at humor was lost on him. Eugene had been swallowed up by the moment. "G, we gotta be ready to leave here in twenty minutes. We want to be ready when they come back. C'mon."

"It's Papi's house, Bruce Juan. We're supposed to stay with it and protect it. Somebody could break in if we leave."

I said, "Yes, they could. But the house has four feet of water in it, G. At this point, what do you think would upset Abuelita worse, some broken glass or them rushing out here from Florida to drag our bodies out of the attic? We don't have the supplies to stay here. Papi and Abuelita will understand that we had to leave. I know this is hard." I embraced my uncle as we stood on the patio roof, two worn-out, dehydrated men with a huge weight on our shoulders. When we ended our hug, I said, "C'mon. We've gotta get the girls ready to move."

We climbed back into the attic window. Coming in from the powerful, naked sunlight to the dark, the still room sucked the vision from my eyes, leaving blackness. For a minute or two we explained what had been said outside. I held my eyes closed tightly, allowing them to adjust.

The time of decision. We were going to abandon the house. But we weren't prepared to walk away. Not yet, at least. Before getting down to the business at hand, we agreed to each take a good swig of water to fortify ourselves. First, we had to answer a question. Where the hell were we going? The boat would get us off of the roof, but where would we go from there?

The answer to that was simple. We were going to the Superdome. After all, that was the designated emergency shelter for the City during these big storms. And now that a *real* disaster had occurred, the Superdome would be the safest place to stay. They'd have water, food, and security—all things we sorely lacked in the attic. Even if the helicopter that shined its lights on me had dropped supplies, they wouldn't have lasted forever. They'd eventually run out, just prolonging our deaths, not preventing them. We needed to be where people had things set up and taken care of. So, we all agreed that the Superdome would be our destination. Now to make sure that we'd be able to get there. We estimated the distance to the Superdome at about six miles. In reality, the distance is just over four miles, but like so many things right then, this was just another unknown. Life was a big math problem. And this distance added another variable to the equation, something like: sweltering hot temperature plus x number feet of brown water multiplied by six miles and divided by us.

Six miles on foot, and I was wearing my house slippers. Given the circumstances, I was fine with that. Jimena and Uncle G were well shod. They both had sturdy sneakers and clean socks on their feet. The real problem was Mother. She'd climbed the attic ladder in a pair of broken down flip-flop sandals. One had slipped off of her foot during the climb and fallen into the water and floated away. There was no way she could make six miles barefoot. We dug around the attic and Uncle G found a pair of beaten down, dirty running shoes in the large sea chest that my grandmother had previously used for gardening. The shoes had been left up in the attic who knows how long ago. They were musty smelling and filthy all over. She tried them on. They were a size too small, but she said it would be okay. Cecilia's a trooper, if nothing else. I wouldn't have put those things on my bare feet if my life depended on it.

However, her life did depend on them. She pulled them on with no complaint.

The next problem would be the dog. If we were going to leave this house, we were going to bring him with us. There was no alternative. We weren't going to leave him up in the attic until he went mad with thirst. It would be kinder just to kill him right then, but that wasn't going to happen. Dolja was family. He was getting on that boat with us. There was no alternative.

We'd carried him into the attic. We'd be carrying him all over the City unless we produced some kind of leash for him. Of the plethora of household items all around us—furniture, telephone, television, and the like—aside from Uncle G's watch and my flashlight, there was very little of practical survival use. No long strands of good, thin rope—or better yet, a spare dog leash—to be had. I pulled down the sheer mesh curtain from the window. I thought I could tear it into strips and maybe braid them into a stronger rope like I've seen people do in movies.

Necessity is a motherfucker, but it is also the greatest motivator, the mother of invention.

Had I not stood up to pull down that curtain, I wouldn't have seen the cord from the back of the telephone snaking behind the old sea chest. I slid the clip out of the back of the phone and began taking up the wire with my hands. At about four feet, I came to the end. The rest of the wire's length had been fed through the floor of the attic to a plug God knows where. I considered the damage I might do to other wiring, but still decided it was the best material I could find at the time. Slowly and steadily, I continued drawing up the phone wire. I drew out another foot or so and could feel that I had drawn out as much as I was going to get. I asked if anyone had a knife or scissors. In the cabinet underneath the television set, we found an enormous pair of sewing scissors, rusty from want of oiling. I snipped the cord and went to work knotting one end to Dolja's collar. The cord, like most other wiring in the house, was old and worn out. It made a less than ideal tether, but in this nightmare we were living, it would have to work.

Over on the bed lay Klaus the hippo, my best friend second only to Dolja. I couldn't allow that awful prophecy to be fulfilled. Klaus represented fifty percent of the promise I'd made to myself so long ago; if the house were burning, I'd run in to save my grandfather's guitar and my hippopotamus. My Paw-Paw's guitar and everything else below us was ruined. The entire house lost. What if the house did somehow burn down after we'd made our escape? The loss of Klaus and the guitar would be too much to bear. I'd carried him with me into the attic. I'd brought him this far. I was uncertain whether or not I'd see the inside of this house ever again, and within it so many other favorite possessions completely destroyed. I hated the thought of leaving behind one so, so special, especially since Klaus was right there in front of me, not submerged and not destroyed. He was right there on the bed in the attic, looking at me.

Klaus is a large animal, about two feet long, a foot tall; he weighs about six pounds. His soft grayish-black fur is stretched around a whole bunch of plush. Klaus is far too large and dense for the washing machine. Other than spot cleaning, he's never been wet. He wasn't constructed for life on the high seas. Desperately, I went in search of something waterproof to wrap him in.

From behind the false wall partition, I dug out a black, plastic garbage bag with an ancient couch cushion inside. It makes perfect sense that my grandparents would save a single cushion from a long-discarded couch. And better still, they took precautions to protect this anomalous cushion from the elements by preserving it in a plastic sack. The bag looked beaten to death. It was covered with wear and riddled with tiny holes. However, the cushion inside looked perfect. I threw it aside and dropped Klaus in rump first. He wouldn't be totally waterproof in there, but it was better than nothing.

Mother and I were sitting together on the bed while I tied up the plastic bag. Jimena had gone down the attic ladder to inspect a small utility shelf underneath the attic stairs. The top shelf normally held some canned goods, overflow from the kitchen cupboard. She'd found a can of brown gravy and two cans of evaporated milk, not exactly the bounteous feast she'd hoped for. When she saw that we were wrapping the hippo in plastic, obviously for the journey ahead, Jimena began spouting off in rapid-fire Spanish. She wasn't shy about directing it toward me. I couldn't interpret everything she was saying, but more than enough to get the gist.

Mother fired back, "And what the fuck business is it of yours?"

"Ces!" Uncle G shouted. He'd been sitting at the window keeping watch for our rescuers.

"Nuh-uh," Mother continued. "The *piece of trash* in this bag is important to Bruce and me. She needs to quit with that shit."

Again the heavy accent-laden English, "Brucey, it is stupid toy, you . . ."

"You're right," I fired back. "But this *stupid toy* is the only thing I own that's not under water." I turned to Uncle G and said, "No one's asking her to carry this bag. I'll carry it."

Another burst of protest in Spanish followed, but Uncle Gene cooled the situation, saying, "If he wants to carry a stuffed animal in a bag all through the City and to the Superdome, just let him, baby. You know they're crazy about that thing."

This was just round one of several arguments between Mother and Jimena over the next couple of days. The two of them were expressing the stress they were feeling over the situation in a very unconstructive manner. Words would be said, but I knew and they knew that no matter what lie ahead, sticking together is what would get us through.

Personally, I was bouncing off the walls. I was so anxious to get our journey underway. With the hippo issue behind us, I thought it might be best to get a jump on the business at hand. "Looks like we've gotten together everything we're taking with us. Should we go out onto the roof?"

Everyone agreed that we might as well. It couldn't possibly be hotter out there than the one hundred twenty degree oven we were sitting in. That's an estimate. The old Pepsi thermometer had maxed out at one hundred ten.

Before we went outside, we decided we should consolidate our supplies and have a snack. We didn't know when we would get another chance. Jimena had been drinking from a now-empty Sprite bottle. We filled it with our remaining water and passed the jug around to finish off what was left. After that, we drank the last sips of Diet Coke and ate some Doritos. After our noontime meal, we passed around a little bottle of hand sanitizer and, one-by-one, started climbing out of the attic window. Uncle G and I were professionals at this maneuver. Mother hadn't been out there in decades; Jimena, possibly never.

I was out first. Uncle G handed me the two backpacks, the hippo, and the dog through the window. He was next out, and then aided Jimena. Unfortunately, she had beginner's fear and became deathly afraid that her leading foot would never find the roof. She yelped and began to wail Spanish expletives at Gene and me. Teetering on the ledge, with her foot only four inches from touching down, Uncle G grabbed her waist, she let out another screech of terror, and he pulled her down to safety.

Next, I helped Mother climb through. She'd spent months laid up on the couch recovering from her recent operations, and it really showed as her body was forced to extend and bend. But a little patience and a few grunts and Cecilia had two filthy, ragged shoes planted on the patio roof of 4899 Mandeville Street.

The first thing she said was, "Look out, y'all. Mama's gotta take a leak, ya heard me?"

I guided her over to the section of flat roof and instructed her to just squat and go where she had solid footing, not over the side. I turned my back until she was done and then helped her back to where the others were seated, waiting for the boat to return. Uncle G handed me Dolja's phone cord leash and guided Jimena over to the same spot. I don't remember any of the three of them using the restroom the entire time they were in the attic. Mother told me that her *pee was all yellow*. Normally, she'd drink close to two gallons of water a day. Mother had consumed maybe ten or twelve ounces in the past twenty-four hours, and spent the night in the sweltering attic. The dog lifted a leg and let go. Dolja's urine trickled down the roof a rich, golden yellow. We couldn't keep this up forever. Dehydration was quickly becoming a serious threat. I could still feel the spicy nacho chips burning my mouth. Everyone had drained themselves of bodily fluids, and there was very little water left to go around. We couldn't do anything about that right now. We simply sat down to await the return of our rescuers.

With patches of clouds dotting the bright blue sky, it was mostly sunny. The air was saturated with humidity. The sunlight's glare reflected powerfully off of the water's surface. We tried our best to cover our eyes with our hands. It was impossible not to squint. We sat, and we waited. We amused ourselves by making comments on how unnaturally the dog was walking on the slanted roof. Though he looked uneasy, he wouldn't come sit by any of us, like he'd made a game out of tip-toeing around. Either that or he was losing his little doggy mind.

For Mother and Uncle G, this was their first rooftop view of the extent of the flooding in the neighborhood.

"Oh no . . . look at Miss Edith's old place."

"Did you see Michelle and her family's house?"

"And Ahmed's place, it's up over the tops of the windows."

"Ahmed's house is on a slab, it's not raised like the others."

Really, it wasn't a bad way to pass the time while waiting to be rescued from certain death.

"And down there, where the Sanchez's kids . . ."

"Uhh." "Oh shit." "Whoa." We exclaimed individually and in unison, our conversation immediately cut short. A large, friendly, slow-moving cloud floating above us had moved, exposing us to the unfiltered fury of the broiling sun above. Totally naked before the magnificence of our star's light, we hunkered over and put our hands behind our heads to shield our overheated brains from the brilliant rays. Now this was truly torture. I grabbed the plastic bag with the hippo inside and urged Mother to sit under the tiny amount of shade Klaus provided. Uncle G and Jimena also lifted their bags over their heads. The intense light created an intense glare. I closed my eyes. Red was all I saw. I tried to tune out the world and wait.

I heard the sound of metal popping, and opened my eyes again. Several long minutes had passed. I'd gotten a little more used to the sun. Maybe we were under another cloud. I couldn't tell, and I wasn't about to look up and see if we were. Jimena had a little Boy Scout-type can opener on her keychain. She opened one of the cans of evaporated milk. Just the thought of one hundred-degree dairy from a can made me want to hurl. I tried to stop her. "Jimmy, don't drink that. It's too hot out here."

"She's thirsty, Bruce," replied Uncle G in a thin, almost maternal tone.

"She's got an empty stomach, she'll get sick," I said.

She held the can to her lips and drank deeply, swallowing down about half of the eight ounce can of warm, evaporated milk. In less than one hundred twenty seconds, she was retching over the side of the roof, plop plop plopping down into the brown sea below. Her retching was not as smooth as the easy regurgitation from the gallon challenge a few nights prior. Even a glass of the coldest, freshest, most delicious milk on Earth would likely turn to rot in a person's guts in that heat, let alone a boiling hot can of evaporated freakin' milk. Granted, I am not and never have been a dairy person, but it just wasn't a good idea from the start. Evaporated milk.

I held the hippo over us again, and the dog joined us in the hippo's shadow, sitting in Mother's lap. I closed my eyes. Everything was so still and quiet. No screaming party people, no helicopters, no swimming dogs, just the quiet lapping of the water layered on top of complete and utter silence. The fierce red of my own blood visible through my eyelids, the broiling sun beating me to pieces. My head throbbed with each beat of my heart, and blood pounded in my ears. Though I was sitting, I felt like I could fall over. And it's odd, but it also felt like when I fell, it would be from at least standing height, if not higher. My head was full of hot air. I couldn't think straight. I felt dizzy, my legs were all pins and needles. I dared to open my eyes to check on Mother. The light and glare were blinding. She sat open-mouthed, thousand-yard staring at the house across the street.

"Mother!" I grabbed her hand and squeezed it.

"Whuuu. Wha What's wrong?"

"You alright?" I asked her.

"Yeah baby, how's Klausie?" she said as if in a dream. She used to sleepwalk and talk all the time, but not for at least a year. This was exactly how she used to talk during her episodes of somnambulism.

"He's hot. Mother!" I gave her arm a shake.

She fluttered her eyelids as her eyes rolled backward. I put my arm around her shoulders, swaying her gently from side to side.

"Mother . . . Mother . . ."

"Hmmm . . ." she smiled real big.

"Hey!"

"Bbwwuuh, huh, huh, what? What's wrong?"

"You fell asleep."

"No shit? Did I?"

"Yeah, c'mon, wake up. We gotta be ready for the boat."

Spells like this used to be very common for her, but she hadn't had one in a long while, definitely not since her gamma knife surgery. I found it very unsettling that this old problem should flare up again right now. She looked as though she was about to start one of her shaking seizures. These episodes could be extremely frightening and hard to deal with, until she got a prescription for some miracle pill that would dissolve in her mouth. When I shoved one in there, the shaking fit would stop in a matter of seconds. Of course, these pills were floating around somewhere down in the apartment. "Hang in there, Mama," I told her as I rubbed her shoulders.

"Why are they taking so long?"

"What if they don't come back?"

"We've been out here for over an hour."

I was beginning to have my own doubts. I suggested we at least go back into the attic to get out of the sun. Everyone agreed to this. But it felt like an admission of defeat, nevertheless. How long could we possibly stay in there now that we were down to a meager twenty ounces of potable water between the four and a half of us? At these temperatures, not for long.

Fortunately, our liberators hadn't forgotten us. Uncle G had one foot in the window when the silence broke.

Bruuh Bruuh Bruuh Bruuh Bruuh

Not the quiet electric motor I'd heard before, but the rumble of an outboard engine.

"The boat!"

The wake they were creating sent waves slapping into the sides of the houses as they glided up the street toward us. They stopped and the teenager in the red swimming shorts held the fence. So this was it. We'd get into the boat and putt putt away into the unknown. But . . . how do we get into the boat?

While we were waiting, I'd worked out a solution—a solution that proved much more practicable in theory than in reality. The plan was a simple one. We'd just slide off of the roof and stand on top of the fence below. The drop was, I don't know, less than two feet?

The big, muscular black guy was standing at the bow, mustache man at the helm, and a half dozen different grumpy, tired-looking people were squeezed into the seats. I surmised that these guys manning the boat were good people. People being *neighborly* in the truest sense of the word. Ferrying marooned men and women from their flooded homes and at least giving them a chance at survival. Death's hand would have eventually found us in that attic. Before that, we'd have likely tried to swim out and save ourselves. We might have made it.

And then again, maybe not.

So, I'd just slide off of the roof and step from the fence into the boat, nothing to it. And yet, this simple bit of maneuvering from house to boat meant so much. I walked to the edge of the roof and sat down. A hundred thousand memories flashed across my mind. This was it. This was the moment. I, we, were going to abandon the house to save our own skins, like rats jumping from a sinking ship. We were abandoning our lives. We were going to abandon my grandfather's and my grandmother's entire life's work. This house was our family home, and we were going to leave it behind for a mere chance. This boat represented a great unknown. Only God knew what else was out there, because I sure as hell didn't. I scooted myself closer to the edge and let my feet drop over the side. The people in front of me looked impatient. They looked like they wanted to be wherever this boat was going to take them and not in the boat any longer than they had to be. They'd already embraced the unknown. I was staring it in the face. The ridge of fence I could see sticking out above the water's surface looked tiny, thin, and terribly far away. Closer to the edge now. *"Embrace the unknown, Bruce,"* the voice—my voice—said inside my head. *"But everything I know is right here,"* the voice replied.

"And from now own, nothing will ever be the same." I said aloud.

"The B.C./A.D. moment of my life. Nothing will ever be the same." My feet dangled over the side, searching for the fence. I slid my rump off of the roof.

Abort!

But I'd passed the point of no return. Where's the fucking fence? I dug my fingernails into the gritty roof shingles, the rain gutter bending under me, straining the nails that held it out of place, intoning a piercing, shrill sound of metal on wood. The ribs of my left side grinding across the shingles, ripping across the gutter, continuing up my side to my underarm and then . . . open space. Freefall. Over six feet of shitty brown water waiting to swallow me up. I didn't hear my mother screaming. I didn't hear anything. I didn't know anything. The instant gravity took control of my body, everything simply went white. I hope I never experience that sensation again in my life. Total fear–pure, human, and beautiful.

But the water didn't swallow me. I couldn't breathe. I was hovering, suspended in open space.

Since when could I levitate? The angels had come to lift me up and keep me dry. I could hear the angel speaking to me. "Put your feet under you, bra. C'mon man, you ain't going nowhere. Now find your feet, man. I got you. Find your feet. You're not gonna fall. I got you, man. I'm not gonna let you fall."

The world came rushing back to me. The big, muscular guy had caught me in a strong-armed bear hug. He just caught my two-hundred pounds like a sack of laundry. I could feel the texture of the weathered peaks of the wooden fence through the thin, worn soles of my camouflage house slippers. My jeans were wet to the shin, my shoes soaked, but the brown water hadn't swallowed me. I was standing on top of the fence, less than an inch above the surface of the brown water, holding hands with a neighbor I'd never met before. The man probably lived a block away from me for the past ten years. It's funny what it sometimes takes to bring people together. He is the angel who caught me from out of the sky, an angel then and now. For the life of me, I can't remember his name. Maybe that's appropriate for an angel.

The world looked far different from down below. The distance between the roof and the fence was more than three feet vertically, and also eighteen inches outward horizontally. My simple plan had proved too simple. Using the roof to make our exit had been a really bad idea. There was no way Mother was going to attempt that drop. They would go back into the attic and down into the flooded house. They were going to come out of the front door.

A quick flash of jealousy hit me. They were going to walk the length of the house waist-deep in water to meet us at the front door. They were going to see everything, room by room, in that condition. Now that I had been "rescued" and was on the boat, I was unable to see it for myself.

Uncle G handed the backpacks down to me and I handed them to the teenage boy in the boat. Then the hippo in his weathered, black garbage bag, and finally he handed Dolja to me. That's a photo I wish I had.

Dog in arm, I raised one foot into the boat. The angel gripped my shoulder, and then two feet, fingers of my free hand released from the rain gutter I'd been holding on to, and I was clear. Dolja and I had escaped from 4899 Mandeville Street.

Uncle Gene helped Mother and Jimena back into the window, and then they were out of sight. Using the small, electric motor at the bow, the angel and the shirtless kid were in control of the boat now. I piled our bags on top of myself after sitting on the fiberglass bench, trying to contain Dolja's squirming. The hippo proved a much more sedate shipmate.

A hispanic family of four huddled at the rear of the boat next to the Captain. A mom and dad, a daughter I guessed to be seventeen, and a boy around twelve wearing a life vest. Across from me sat an elderly white couple. The man had clear tubes in his nostrils, a small green oxygen tank at his side. The lady had a yellowish hue to her wanton skin. The two of them were stacked with plastic bags full of what I guessed to be dialysis fluid, or something like that. I know that some medical drugs, like insulin, require refrigeration. Whatever this clear fluid was—and quite possibly these people were counting on this fluid to keep them alive—must now measure more than ninety degrees. Later, I heard that these two had spent the previous night standing on their kitchen table neck-deep in water. Neither one of them could have been a day under seventy-five. I could only assume that my angel had saved them, too.

I began doing some addition in my head. Family of four plus two septuagenarians, the three-man crew, and now us four coming aboard. Thirteen souls. Thirteen souls on a craft that couldn't possibly be designed to exceed eight.

Luckily, these weren't the *open seas*; this was Gentilly.

The sunlight blasted the open boat just as intensely as it had pounded the rooftop. The vibe I got from the crew was one of glowering impatience. Apprehension on the faces of the Latino family. The old lady really wanted to get her husband into the shade. Like the rest of us, the brutal sun was roasting him. To me, the old man looked like he was struggling just to stay alive with every labored breath. His eyes were glazed, strands of silver hair hung limply from his probably once-perfect barber shop part. He showed no signs that he was making his peace with God. No calm acceptance of the end. He was a fighter. Though he was struggling, he wasn't done struggling.

Time passed achingly slowly on the surface of the still, brown water. Dolja wouldn't stop growling and barking, and trying to squirm out of my grasp. I figured out what the trouble was and allowed him to lap a few sips from the brown sea. That's how thirsty he'd become. I couldn't deny him. He didn't understand the difference between clean water and this brackish sewer water anyway. He didn't go back for more; I will say that. When I pulled him back, he rested his head calmly on my knee. He just needed to wet his whistle. After about five minutes, the old lady startled me by shaking my knee. I'd kind of zoned out.

"What's taking them so long?" Her face contorted into a pained expression, every anguished wrinkle twisted.

"I don't know. My mother is sick and doesn't see well," I said.

"She slowin' everybody down," the angel said to the Captain. Despite his mirrored shades, I knew he was glaring at me.

"They're coming," was all I could say.

Dolja began to bark again, softly echoing around the still silence of the flooded neighborhood. The Captain huffed aloud and crossed his arms. My burning face flushed with embarrassment, but then I thought, *You know what? To hell with these people.* We had as much right to have our lives saved as anyone else in this boat. If this poor old guy were to die right this moment, it wouldn't be because Mother is nearly blind and is probably being led through the length of our blacked-out house one step at a time. This guy has what are called preexisting conditions. I hadn't considered the darkness and Mother's vision when they were going back into the attic. My flashlight was stuffed in Uncle G's bag sitting between my feet.

The boat floated in six feet of water over our front yard, waiting. A few minutes later, I heard the locks turning on the iron door leading to the porch, the same door we'd stuffed with pillows and cushions as we made our last stand against the rising waters the previous afternoon. There were voices now and swishing water as they waded onto the porch. True to form, I heard the lock turn again, securing the door. Uncle G seemed to have trouble opening the front door in the waist-deep water, but after a little wiggling, he had it open enough for them to slip through. Mother recoiled from the sunlight as she descended the first step off of the porch. Uncle G forced the door closed. Mother required a hoist to get up into the boat, but one by one, they climbed aboard. We'd all escaped the house and were headed toward our uncertain future.

Can Everybody Swim?

The kid in the front used the electric motor to maneuver us out of the front yard. Once we were out in the street again, the Captain kicked on the motor and pushed the throttle forward. Away we went, cruising westbound on Mirabeau Avenue, the thirteen and a half of us. It's a good thing we had the dog, thirteen is an unlucky number at sea.

We weren't traveling very fast, maybe ten miles per hour. What's that, like twelve knots? Even at that slow speed, the boat created quite a wake. Waves smashed against the exterior walls of the houses on either side of the street, splashing high up the sides upon contact. Jimena said they should slow down and not push waves into people's homes. She had a point, of course, but these houses were all ruined anyway. Some movement in the water wasn't going to make any of the damage significantly worse.

At the intersection of Mirabeau and Elysian Fields, we slowed to avoid some fallen, submerged trees. The water stretched on as far as I could see in any direction; a busy metropolitan thoroughfare now the surface of a shimmering lagoon. The Captain turned the boat to the left at the intersection, southbound onto Elysian Fields, three blocks until the next major intersection at Gentilly Boulevard.

The boat puttered up Elysian Fields, passing homes I'd driven past a thousand times. Soon, to our left, we were passing the submerged campus of Brother Martin High School, established in 1869. To our right, a small cemetery set behind a lattice-work fence made of wrought iron. The tops of crosses and tips of angels' wings crowning the tombs broke the water's surface. The tranquility of the flooded graveyard sharply contrasted the human drama playing out on the fishing boat. I wondered if the water had seeped into the vaults and if the coffins were floating in their crypts. I pushed the thought from my mind. The next block ahead touches Gentilly Boulevard.

The boat began to slow. The Captain raised the outboard motor as we approached noticeably shallower water. Ahead, I could see black asphalt shining like a golden ribbon in the sunlight. Gentilly Boulevard was completely dry. I couldn't believe my eyes. Dry land! And I mean bone dry. I could see the heat rippling from the road surface. The big teenage kid in the red swim trunks extended his legs over the edge and jumped into the water as if it were the swimming pool in his backyard. Barefoot, by the way. To my total amazement, just like the guy in the canoe, his legs didn't begin melting off when his skin contacted the water. This possibility still worried me, though I'd seen several people, including my own family, make contact with the brown stuff. I'd gotten my feet wet and even let the dog lap the water. He seemed fine, and had started squirming again trying to get more. This time, I held him back. The kid walked the boat over the neutral ground, or median if you're a non-New Orleanian, and pulled the boat until we heard the first scrape from somewhere down below. End of the line.

The boat had brought us to Harold's Hardware Store, a little neighborhood hardware store sandwiched between a sno-ball stand and a hair salon. There were a couple of dozen people milling around in front of the store. The door was wide open, the employees and family of the owners were standing in a row in front of the place handing out bottles of water. There was a port-a-potty set up in the little parking lot and a long line of the dispossessed waiting to use the chemical toilet. A large warehouse fan was blowing toward the crowd. I could hear several generators humming.

The Captain began shouting to the people standing at the store's entrance, explaining the dangerous condition of the old man with the oxygen tank. The rest of us disembarked and got in line for some water. They gave us two bottles of deliciously cold seventy degree water, a blazing hot bottle of Diet Sprite, and a bag of cold popcorn for the four and a half of us to split. We squeezed ourselves into a small patch of shade and passed the bottles. It was wonderful. Even Dolja got his fill, one palmful at a time. I could feel my body cooling, the pounding in my head began to subside. I was so grateful right then, to feel almost normal again.

Jimena struck up a conversation with the hispanic family we'd met on the boat. They approached us after they'd gotten their water from the hardware store workers. The conversation was in Spanish, but I could get the gist of what they were saying. When Uncle G blurted out, "Superdome," I knew they were asking if we could stick together. An example of natural disaster osmosis, our group expanded from four to eight. We'd get moving soon enough, but it sure felt nice to sit down in a patch of shade with the big fan blowing. Our new companions sat with us. Their names, respectively, were: Stefan (father), Maria (mother), Inez (daughter), and Stefanito (son). The lot of them referred to the kid as *Fanito*.

There was some passing small talk between the other people hanging around the storefront, right there on the new shore of the Gulf of Mexico. I started asking around if they knew how deep the water was leading to the Interstate. Could we walk it? The consensus was a big "I don't know." Poor intelligence for such vital information. A couple people said it was fine, others *deep*, but all of the people had been rescued from homes on the northern side of Gentilly Boulevard, like us. Gentilly stretched high and dry as far as the eye could see before the road bends, heading east. Looking down toward the west, toward City Park and Mid-City, the water swallowed up the asphalt in the distance. This course would be a long, indirect, winding route toward downtown. We needed the shortest route possible, and that was straight down Elysian Fields to the Interstate. Nearly all of the Interstate system that runs through New Orleans is raised fifteen to twenty feet above street level to minimize the noise. This raised roadway was our best bet to get us into the City high and dry. Walking for six miles sounded daunting enough, swimming for six miles: impossible. Rising from the water a mile ahead of us was Interstate 610, a bypass on which travelers and commuters can avoid swooping in a great arc through the central City and take a straight line through the suburban sections of town. Interstate 610 splits from the I-10 right near the Jefferson Parish line to the west and reconnects with the I-10 just before the Franklin Avenue exit, about a half a mile to the east. This was important because we'd need to backtrack eastward to get to the I-10 proper in order to make our way downtown to the Superdome. The highway runs right alongside the stadium.

Before any of that, we had to get ourselves to the Elysian Fields on-ramp.

We had no idea how deep the water was ahead of us, but we accepted that regardless of depth, we'd be getting wet. We passed around the bag of Spicy Nacho Doritos and drank some warm Diet Sprite. There was plenty of daylight left and the summer sun shone as powerfully as ever. I'd walked away from my group to mingle with the other evacuees, and at one point left the herd altogether to scope out the corner store I somehow found myself in at least once a day. It was completely dry there, maybe they were open.

Despite my best efforts, my feet got wet as I crossed the little side street. The store was locked up tight, all of the windows were boarded over with plywood. I noticed two kind of rough-looking older white guys talking and laughing with two young black boys, maybe ten and twelve years old, respectively. I shouted a "hello" and walked over to see what was so interesting.

One of the older guys looked at me and said, "He's all talk. That boy ain't gonna get that machine to open."

"Machine?" I asked.

The man replied, "They been bustin' open ATM machines, or at least they say they have. Ain't that right?" he shouted.

The older boy wielded two short screwdrivers, and the younger one held a big long one. I didn't see how they did it, but they had that machine open in less than twenty seconds. The younger boy reached his hand inside and removed a stack of twenty dollar bills two inches thick. He divided the stack roughly in half, and handed it to his accomplice. The older boy then added these bills to the ones he'd already liberated. The kid held up a stack of twenties five inches tall, smiled real big, and said, "I love Hurricane Katrina."

It was the largest single stack of cash I've ever seen in my entire life. I wanted that cash. I didn't have a single dollar on me, but in reality, all of that cash was useless right now. I would have been better served by a huge jug of cold water, a pack of cigarettes, and maybe a fat club sandwich.

The boys ran off to find another machine, and the two guys and I walked back toward the hardware store. The boat returned around this time, and another load of rescued individuals began to disembark. I'd wandered near enough to the line of employees to overhear one say something to the effect of, ". . . and more keep coming, not a one of them are leaving, what are they waiting for? Chicken and burgers?"

I know I wasn't supposed to hear that. But I took his words to heart. These people were doing all they could for their neighbors, but they weren't a refugee center, and when their supplies ran out, that would be it. I don't begrudge them in the least. They'd helped us immensely, possibly saved our lives with the well-timed hydration, but we couldn't depend on them to get us through the disaster.

I thought of the sorry condition of the garbage bag Klaus the hippo was in. Maybe these hardware store folks wouldn't mind giving me a strong new one, but after the burgers and chicken comment, I decided against it. I didn't want to take anything else from these people, even if it was for the safety and benefit of my most huggable friend. If I had known what we were about to get ourselves into, I would have swallowed my pride and asked anyway.

I saw a couple of guys load the sick, old man and his wife into a golf cart, and they rode off together to an unknown destination.

A couple of years later, Mother and I would be back inside this hardware store to get some keys made. We would talk with one of the clerks who knew Cecilia from way back, growing up in the neighborhood. We mentioned that we'd spent a couple of hours at the store during the flood and I asked if he knew anything about what happened to that old guy. He said that he remembered the silver-haired man and told us that they'd loaded him onto that golf cart and driven him to Brother Martin's football practice field on the block directly behind the store. Using a CB radio, they contacted some medical personnel and a helicopter was sent to pick up the old man and his wife. He was too far gone and died a couple of days after in a hospital near Baton Rouge. From what I saw of him, I know he fought to the very last breath. Another mortal wound inflicted by this bitch of a storm.

I returned to our expanded group and explained what I'd overheard about the chicken and burgers. It was a little after one in the afternoon and time for us to move on. Everyone at the store had been wonderfully gracious, but I didn't want to stick around to see what happened when supplies ran out. Regardless, I still should have asked for a new garbage bag.

We gathered our things and headed south on Elysian Fields. It was kind of nice having the family along with us. Even better since they separated Mother and Jimena from further squabbling. The two young people added a feeling of vitality to our group that had been missing. Twelve-year-old Stefanito was impetuous and full of energy. Nothing about our situation seemed to bother him at all. I admired that about him. Inez was a senior in high school, courteous, and outwardly shy. After talking to her some, I decided this was an act she'd perfected over years of dealing with her strict parents. She was as down-to-earth and carefree as the next teenage girl, but she hid behind her manners when her mother and father were present. I know this sounds terrible because she was seventeen and I was twenty-five, but I took comfort in knowing that if this was the *end of the world*, by default, I'd at least be near the front of the *most eligible last men on Earth* line. No one wants to die alone.

Not knowing what we were in for, we decided to divide the labor. Mother would carry Klaus the hippo and I would take care of the dog. Jimena and Uncle G each had their bags and, as for the family, only the dad had a small backpack on his shoulders. I looked longingly at the gas station on the corner of Gentilly and Elysian Fields, my cigarette stop for the previous several years. I'd been out since the day before, and Jimena's last had gone up in smoke after we'd left the boat. Wandering into the unknown was scary enough. Doing so with no cigarettes was downright terrifying.

We crossed Gentilly Boulevard, ahead in the wide roadway was a small shelter for bus passengers. On a bench we saw a white man, kind of fat with a mustache, about forty years old. He had a grocery cart stuffed with assorted sundries. He asked where we were headed and shook his head when we responded, ". . . to the Interstate."

"Gets deep down there."

He offered us a place under the bus shelter with him. We declined. The man wished us good luck and gave us two quart-size bottles of Powerade–one red, one blue. He'd procured the drinks from the drug store around the corner. He said the place was wide open, but not a whole lot was left. As much as I wanted a pack of cigarettes, I wasn't ready to begin my career in looting. He said something about the old man that I couldn't understand. The guy was weird and he laughed at himself after everything he said. I hate that. The eight of us pressed on, the crazy guy still attempting to talk to us. We walked past the back side of the drugstore. I could see broken glass around the entrance and several people milling around. I tried not to stare.

Dolja had been walking with us, me leading him on his phone cord leash. As we crossed the first street past Gentilly, the water was there to meet us. The brown sea stretched for blocks ahead. The street looked so much wider, the water stretched from house to house, across front yards, the traffic lanes and neutral ground. One great sheet, reflecting the blue sky above.

Undaunted, we stepped in, Dolja leading the way. Gradually, the water got a little higher, first over our shoes, then ankles, and then up to calves. I picked up the dog, the eight of us sloshing around. By the end of the block, I was in to my knees. It's misleading to describe this progression as the water was getting higher. Despite an occasional ripple, it was a perfect sheet of glass. The water wasn't getting higher, the ground was sloping downward beneath us. In all my life, I never noticed the variation of the grade. We were certainly noticing it now. Only three blocks to go.

A third of the way through the next block, I just busted out laughing. Everyone looked at me like I was crazy, like I might have started cracking up out there with my little dog.

"What? Nothing, I'm fine."

I'd remembered a line from a British adult film I'd seen years before. As the girls slip into a hot tub, the guy filming says, "Aah, they got their knickers all wet." I continued chuckling as the water crept up over my belt. Around this point, we paused for a discussion, or rather two discussions. The parents, Stefano and Maria, spoke in Spanish to Uncle G, Jimena, and Mother, while I made sarcastic small talk with the kids in English. We'd started in on the second to last block before the on-ramp. So close to our destination, but with water to my belly button and a squirming pup in my arms, we needed things to level off soon.

Ahead of us in the water was a head. A human head facing the Interstate.

"What the hell is that?" Mother said.

"Hello?" another shouted.

The head turned to the side and spoke. It had on sunglasses. "How ya doin' there?"

"How are you? You alright?" Inez shouted, translating her mother's question.

"Oh, I'm just fine. Battery crapped out on me."

In the water was an older white man, mid-fifties, stuck in an electric wheelchair up to his shoulders in water.

"Can we do anything to help you?" we were asking him over and over.

"Nope, I'm just fine. Just waitin' here for my wife."

"Your wife is coming to get you?"

"Oh, yeah. She's on her way. Any minute now."

I thought the guy had lost his mind. Maybe his wife died decades ago and this was a suicide thing. I didn't know, but he sure was friendly about it, which made things even more disturbing. After a while, we gave up.

"Okay, sir. Good luck to ya. I hope you find your wife."

"Good luck to you folks. She gone to get my other chair, damn battery went out on dis one. She ain't gonna leave me out here." He got a good laugh out of that one.

We continued up the block, the stop signs and street signs our only indication that we were nearing the next intersection. Time and again, I would sweep my hand across the surface of the water to break up the iridescent sheen of motor oil and other pollutants. I felt something thump against my left knee. Instinctively, I raised my foot to rub the point of contact to test the area for pain. Balancing on one foot, with a little black dog pressed against my chest, nipple-deep in water.

Then the unthinkable happened. The camouflage loafer on my foot slid off! Oh, fuck! Oh, God, don't leave me out here in the middle of the ocean with only one shoe! Please, NO! I panicked and half-dunked the dog into the water. I was feeling around down by my legs hoping to catch it before it drifted away, or whatever shoes do when they're not on feet. Terror gripped me. I could see nothing down there. My hands disappeared completely only a few inches deep in the thick murky water. I splashed around. Still nothing. Mother asked if I was okay. I said, "I lost my . . ." THUMP.

A woodland camouflage patterned house slipper hit me in the chin as it floated up on its way to the surface. Joyously, I slid the sodden slipper back on my naked foot. That was a close one, y'all. We'd almost made it to 610, and then we'd have to walk of several miles after that. I couldn't imagine having to walk that distance with only one shoe. I have never been so grateful over getting knocked in the chin as when my shoe came back to me that day.

We resumed our progress, but only for another dozen yards or so. The water reached to our shoulders. Being the tallest person there, I stepped several paces farther, turned back to the group and shook my head. The ground continued to drop, and one more block separated us from the on-ramp. Any farther and we'd be swimming. Uncle Gene and Jimena's backpacks, Klaus the hippo, and Dolja the dog, all balanced atop our heads. We stood there for a moment with no one saying a word. This was going to be a big challenge. We would have to swim fifty to seventy yards, maybe more, with nothing below us until we got to the on-ramp. After some discussion, it was agreed that we should go for it. It was the only way, but no one seemed in a big hurry to lose their grip on solid ground.

"Listen!" shouted the son. "Listen!"

"*Callate*, Fanito," his sister scolded.

We all strained to hear the sound.

Drip Drip Drip Sploosh

Drip Drip Drip Sploosh

Slow and steady. Ahead of us, on the far side of the overpass, we saw a small, green, flat boat pushing its way through the water. When it came fully into sight we saw two people aboard, one of them rowing with a pair of oars. The flat boat turned in our direction. More angels.

"Help!"

"Help us."

"*Ayuda*."

"Help us, please!"

We shouted and shouted. I suggested we backtrack a few steps. The boat was coming toward us, no need to swim toward it. As we started wading back toward the floating head in the wheelchair, our low spirits rebounded high as the sky. We waved our free arms and made a big splash. In the boat were two people, a man rowing and a muscular woman at the bow. I heard her shout back to the rower, "There he is." Both wore boots, cargo shorts, and wide belts, tucked into which were navy blue t-shirts with the NOPD insignia on the breast. Both wore blacked-out sunglasses. I could see that the rower was armed with a pistol.

She even spoke like a cop. "Yes, people, we can get you to the highway, but not all at once. The watercraft is too small for everyone. Just be patient for a moment. Please help hold the boat still for a moment, sir."

Uncle G grabbed the boat with one hand, holding his backpack with the other, and just like that, she was in the water with us. Shpluum!

"Thank you, sir." She grabbed the side of the boat and walked it toward the old guy in the electric wheelchair. She looked awful young and cop-like to be his wife.

"Mr. Reynolds?"

"Oh yeah, that's me."

My jaw dropped. This guy had pull. We gathered around, navel-deep in water. She helped unbuckle a shoulder strap for him and started to lift him up when he shouted, "No! No. My battery!" On his lap, submerged and out of sight, rested a large black battery, far too small for a car. "I need this for my chair."

I was confused. His chair looked pretty well ruined to me, but he insisted on bringing his battery. The rower finally spoke. "Better berth over by those steps."

"I can swim him over; let's get the women on right here."

The old man sat patiently in his chair while we loaded the bags and Inez onto the boat. Next Maria, and then Jimena.

"C'mon, ma'am, you're next," the officer said to Mother.

Her face split into tears, "Take Bruce. Let Bruce on first."

"Oh man, just get on the boat, Mother."

"No, you first, baby."

The officer handled the situation perfectly. "Ma'am, I'm going to stay here with him, my partner is not going to leave me. Now, let's get you on the boat."

With a little bit of teamwork, we hoisted her up and in. She wrapped her dripping wet arm around the black bag with the hippo inside and said, "We'll be waiting for you."

The rower instructed everyone to stay low as he started working the oars. She never took her eyes off me as the boat rowed away, long after the female officer had taken charge.

"Gentlemen, can everybody swim?" she asked.

Everyone except the old guy in the chair replied in the affirmative. We set our sights on a modest-sized Protestant church sitting on the street corner, one block before the Interstate. I'm not sure the denomination that worships there, but I knew the building. The brick church sat on top of a high, grass-covered mound. The round, stained-glass window above the main entrance had been shattered by the winds. A pathway of graded stairs with several flat landings ascended from street level to the front door. The water level was near the topmost landing, easily ten feet deep at that point. The two Stephens swam off together, joking and laughing as if this were an everyday bit of father-son recreation.

The female officer tried to lift the man from his chair. "Wait, my battery." The boat was far away now and he hadn't thought to remind us about putting it on board.

"I'll need to swim with him; can one of you transport this battery?"

For real? "Transport" a ten pound brick across forty yards of bottomless water? Uncle G turned white. I volunteered. I'm not a very strong swimmer, but I'm definitely buoyant. If I were to drop the battery, it's not like the old guy could really be too angry with me. Look at the situation he'd put me in. Swimming with your ten pound brick in opaque brown water? That's a tall order for any stranger.

"Keep your mouth closed, Brucey. You don't want to swallow any of this junk," Uncle Gene advised me.

I slid the slippers off my feet and stuffed them down into the pockets of my carpenter jeans. I wasn't going to risk kicking one of them off. While there was still ground to stand on beneath me, I practiced a little trial and error to determine the best way to swim with the battery. I floated on my back like a log. The battery came with me. I wasn't floating quite as high as I normally would have in a swimming pool, but this would work. Doing a lazy backstroke and kicking gently, I overtook Uncle G, who was struggling to doggy paddle toward the steps, but he was making it, too. I rolled my head around to see behind me, and in no time I was over the steps. A few more kicks and I set my feet down, battery and all. Uncle Gene breathed heavily as he approached the landing. He opened his mouth to draw a big breath as he made his final lunge toward the steps. The splash he created rebounded off the steps, and a small wave hit him in the face while his mouth was open. Promptly, he spit the water back out.

We'd all made it: the Stephens, the lady cop, the old white guy, Uncle G, me, and the battery for the useless, sunken chair. Never before had I measured the distance of a swim in blocks. We weren't there very long—less than ten minutes—when the boat reappeared, the same guy rowing. Together, the two officers lifted and laid the man down in the boat.

"I can take two more," the rower said.

"Take these men. I will wait with my son," Stefano said in slow, heavily accented English. He repeated, "Let these two men go, I will stay here with my son. Maria and Inez are together. Stay with them; the boat will come back for Fanito and me."

Uncle G and I climbed aboard and the lady cop shoved us off. She was staying behind with the Stefanos. The officer rowed us out onto Elysian Fields and underneath the roadway. The water played with the sunlight as it reflected upon the underbelly of the raised overpass. The boat halted at the shoreline created by the eastbound 610 Elysian Fields off-ramp. Uncle G and I scrambled ashore, and to my amazement, so did the old man we'd plucked from the wheelchair. He just stood up and, with waddling little penguin steps, he began marching up the ramp to the main road surface. I was so stunned that I even agreed to carry his battery again. Uncle G gave the boat a shove and the lone officer rowed away.

We made our way up the ramp, which doesn't seem very long when you're exiting at fifty miles an hour, but walking uphill on the slanted off-ramp for the equivalent of two blocks really got the muscles in my legs aching. And after the swim, I was super thirsty. Despite the cramps in my calves, Uncle G and I easily outpaced the little, waddling man. Once again, he refused any assistance except that I continue to carry his battery.

TUESDAY,
AUGUST 30TH, 2005

CONTINUED . . .

Sorrow on the 610

Once we'd fully ascended the ramp to the roadway, it wasn't long before we spotted the women of our group talking to a black couple nearby. There were two dozen people sitting and standing on the section above Elysian Fields. Many more formed a steady stream walking west. Looking down the shimmering highway surface, I could see scores more people walking from the east toward the City.

These people the ladies met said they'd been up on the road since first light. They swam from their house, which wasn't far from the highway. I saw that they were smoking, so I asked them if they had a cigarette they could spare. The lady dug in her purse and tossed me a full pack of generic, off-brand menthols. At first, I was really excited, but I saw that they'd gotten wet. Dismayed, I opened the box and could see that most of them were ruined, all brown and soggy, but a handful in the middle row were perfect, except at their tips. I slid out the good ones and passed them around, and we enjoyed a moist cigarette up there under the sun.

Despite all of the water and the refugees marching westward, I couldn't help but remember the unseen party people I'd heard from the roof, and I couldn't shake the fact that I am a New Orleanian and that nearly every situation is an excuse for a party waiting to start. And at that moment, I sure could use some loosening up. The whole water-up-to-my-neck thing had been pretty heavy. So when the guy Mother had been talking to offered me a beer, I couldn't help myself. It wasn't an immediate response, but I said yes.

I gave myself a moment, to weigh how this might alter our situation. I no longer felt the broiling heat as acutely as when we were up on the roof or in the attic. My body had been cooled by our wade up Elysian Fields. Though I'd air dried off some from our swim, in the late summer sun my damp clothing felt nice on my skin. Also, I thought of how dehydrated I might have been. Alcohol is supposed to be dehydrating, but I'd just drunk some blue Powerade and some actual water at the hardware store before that. All in all, I felt pretty good, and we'd scored five decent cigarettes out of the pack the lady gave us. Perfect. When you're a smoker, and you're talking about having a drink, you have to have a cigarette close by. No way around it.

The guy offering the beer pointed me to a common, blue plastic storage bin next to some other assorted belongings stacked over by the guardrail. "In there, young man," he said. "Get you two."

As I walked toward this inauspicious storage bin, I fantasized about opening a big ice chest stacked to the brim with frosty Bud Lights submerged in ice and cold water. Those silly lizards and frogs from the old commercials, you remember, and big-titted girls in bikinis playing volleyball in the sand. The whole *shebang*.

Inside, I found four sweaty cans of Miller Lite and about a dozen Milwaukee's Best Ice. I picked up a Miller Lite. It felt cool to the touch. Nowhere near cold, but cooler than the hundred-degree world around us. Just being in the shade and in the box away from the hot air kept these cans twenty degrees cooler than the space around them. (A factoid of sans-refrigeration thermodynamics that would pay off for us big time in another couple of days, as the heat and sun nearly destroyed us in front of the Army barricades trapping us in the Superdome.)

I popped the Miller Lite open, thanked the man, and took a swig. The warm beer hit my tongue like carbonated battery acid. Instantaneously, I could feel every taste bud in my mouth recoil in horror. It was awful. I drank more.

My mother told me I was crazy, but after a few sips my body started to remember, and the thing in my hand began to taste like beer, that wonderful beverage I love so much. Mother, Jimena, and I lit a menthol cigarette a piece, thanked our new friends for their generosity, and walked toward where Maria and Inez were standing across the roadway, along the opposite guardrail. However, not before I took the man up on his offer and snagged a second can of beer.

They stood by the guardrail, waving at the Stefanos, when one of the weirdest events I've ever witnessed occurred. Driving from the west, heading toward us at high speed, came a loaded dually pickup truck with a full extended crew cab and bed. I think it may have been a Ford F-350. Standing in the bed were three black teenage boys, the oldest maybe twenty years of age. The interior of the cab held about a dozen other younger black children of varying ages and sexes. Three teenage girls rode in the front seat. A woman around forty sat behind the wheel. The truck slowed as it approached us and stopped. I couldn't help but think of the Beverly Hillbillies. They were crammed in there so tightly. I had to laugh.

The woman driving the truck stepped down from behind the wheel and shouted, "Oh, there he is!" A couple of the smaller children were shouting, "Daddy! Daddy! Look, it's Daddy!" This stocky, short black woman ran up to the old white guy we'd discovered neck-deep in water on Elysian Fields Avenue and embraced him. "My husband!" she exclaimed. The girls in the front seat ran out to hug him, too, and helped him up into the cab of the truck. Two of the older girls were headed back to join the boys standing in the bed of the truck. The girl still seated in the middle beamed as the man they'd been searching for climbed into the passenger seat.

"Wait, wait, wait!" he shouted, then looked at me and asked, "Where's my battery?"

I'd forgotten all about the damn thing and was already dazed and speechless over the scene playing out in front of me. I was starting to feel a little buzz from the hot beer. I'd chucked the first can into the brown water and started on the second. Shortly after opening the second one, I started to feel a mean headache coming on. The sun and my level of dehydration were kicking in. I pointed at the guardrail where I'd set it down, and the battery was scooped up quickly by one of the boys from the back of the truck. The old man thanked me for carrying it for him, as his wife turned the truck around to head back west. As they drove off, I saw another electric wheelchair strapped to the tailgate. In a puff of gray exhaust they were gone, tearing ass down Interstate 610. It felt good that I'd carried his battery for him, but I also felt a little let down. Wherever they were going, they were gonna get there a hell of a lot quicker than we would get to the Superdome on foot.

It was late afternoon in late summer, past five o'clock. We still had a couple hours of daylight left, but time would be a serious factor if we were going to get to the stadium before nightfall. I heard panicked shouts from across the road where Maria and Inez were keeping a vigil on the Stefanos waiting on the church steps. When I looked over the railing of the Interstate, I saw that a second boat with an outboard motor had joined the rowboat. Using a rope, the motor boat now towed the rowboat. In tandem, the two boats were cruising eastbound on a flooded side street parallel to the highway. We could only watch as Stefano Sr. pointed toward his family, pleading to be let off at the on-ramp. The officers didn't pay him any attention. And as the raised roadway curved ahead of us, we lost sight of Fanito and Stefan.

Understandably, Maria and Inez were wrecks. The emotion contagiously passed to Jimena and she began to cry along with the mother and daughter. As nicely as possible, Uncle G, Mother, and I tried to calm everyone down and make practical suggestions of what we needed to do. And though the Superdome is situated west-southwest of where we were on the 610, there was only one thing we could do, the six and a half of us there in the fading daylight. We were going to chase those boats. We were marching east.

We gathered our bags, dog, and hippo and started toward the Franklin Avenue exit.

We were definitely walking against traffic, foot traffic that is. For every person walking east—and there were six of us—there were fifty people walking west. Dirty, tired, grumpy-looking people transporting assorted items and assorted persons by all means of conveyance. A grocery cart being pushed with an elderly woman inside, a baby stroller full of clothing and water jugs, a Radio Flyer wagon with several children on board. Most carried black garbage bags slung over one shoulder. The ramshackle procession seemed endless as we walked eastward. Mother and Uncle Gene spotted the house of some lifelong family friends. It was submerged to the rain gutters.

When we'd made it about a half mile or more from the Elysian Fields exit, we were approaching the juncture point—or separation point, depending on which direction you're traveling—of the 610 and the I-10. It's a complex clover of flying merge lanes. People were literally stacked on the interchange. Some upon a high, curving merge lane, others on a sloping down-ramp that brought them to the water's edge, only to have to turn back and seek a different route.

Ahead of us, I spotted a shirtless black man, about twenty-five, wearing a backpack, a ball cap, and a pair of baggy jean shorts. I noticed him because he kept yelling at everything around him. He walked alone. He was walking above us, coming down a ramp about a hundred yards ahead of us. Our respective trajectories brought us closer with every step. As his arm of road descended, he passed under another lane curving above. He continued to shout, "Mutha Fuck all this fuckin' walkin'. I'm sick of all this fuckin' walkin'!" The same things he'd been shouting repeatedly *ad nauseam* since I could discern his words. As his voice blasted out another good "Fuck all this walkin'," a handful of pigeons took flight, swooping from the underside of the roadway above him. In the blink of an eye, he pulled out a pistol and fired three wild shots at the passing birds.

Bam Bam Bam

There are people walking in EVERY possible spherical direction from where he stood and fired.

"Fuck these mutha fuckin' birds!" he kept on as empty shell casings bounced and clattered on the pavement around him. Luckily, no one was hit, not even a pigeon.

This episode shook us up. If this frustrated guy had become frustrated enough to start shooting live ammunition while surrounded on all sides by men, women, and children—and oddly, very few of these men, women, and children seemed affected by his behavior—then it might not be too much longer before others decided to unleash their anger in other, even more dangerous, ways. With night approaching, I didn't want to be out on the road to find out. We kept walking, the 610 threading its way through homes and buildings in an easterly direction.

"Stefan?"

"Fanito?"

"Stefan!"

"Stefanito?!?"

We walked down the highway shouting their names, like Hansel and Gretel lost in the forest, except the trees were made of black people and none of them seemed interested in assisting us in our search. Totally understandable, given the situation. We'd entered an *every man for himself* reality, and walking around looking for two people—with the entire metropolis as a possible search area— appeared to be a futile effort. Death on the open road seemed very plausible, whether from thirst or manslaughter or cold-blooded murder. We needed to get off of that highway. We continued walking farther east, shouting their names. Other people walking west had reached the limits of their patience with us. Some began to yell at us to shut up and be quiet. "Ain't no Messicans out hea," and other similar comments. Maria was starting to have a real rough time. She hardly knew us. She must have felt more or less alone, she and her daughter now separated from her husband and young son. Desperately she cried out their names, and instead of her husband replying, masses of strangers were telling her to shut up and casting intimidating glares.

We did shut up, and led Maria to the far side of the road to sit on the guardrail. Her bright red face showed all the signs of advancing dehydration. She sat down and produced large, wet, sorrowful tears. The endless line of shuffling feet and grocery carts continued to flow over in the westbound lanes, undisturbed by the cries of one frantic mother.

As it turns out, this detour we were making eastbound was a blessing in disguise. We'd backtracked to the juncture with the I-10. The I-10 was the way into the heart of the City, the 610 heads west toward Jefferson Parish. That route would be much longer. To get to the Superdome, we'd have to walk down to the Canal Boulevard exit and make our way past the cemeteries and up "World Famous Canal Street" into the City and to the Dome. The distance must be double or more, more than six miles on foot. Regardless of the extra distance, we'd have never made it to the stadium using this approach. Long before we arrived at the Canal Boulevard exit, we'd have bogged down traversing City Park. The Interstate is raised up high throughout the City, but the roadway lies at ground level as it passes through the expansive park grounds. That would have meant another swim of half a mile or more.

The Canal Boulevard exit lies right in the heart of the Lakeview neighborhood. We didn't know it at the time, but Lakeview received some of the deepest flooding in the entire City, more than ten feet in places.

Our path eastward produced another unexpected stroke of good luck. The few police and police vehicles we saw on the Interstate appeared to take absolutely no notice of, and certainly showed no sympathy for, the long column of people filing out of New Orleans East. And, in turn, the mass of people ignored the cops, or displayed outright malice toward them. When a police vehicle came driving down the roadway, it wasn't uncommon for a chorus of shouts to be directed at it. Mostly things like "Where you goin'?" or "Why ain't you helpin' nobody?" "My baby is sick, why you ain't doin' nothin'?" Or just a general "Fuck you."

The officers drove on nonchalantly, as if it were any other normal summer day and not *the day of days*.

"Fanito!" Maria would shout through her hands as they were pressed like a funnel to her face.

Barreling down I-10 from the direction of the City came a blue pickup truck. As the truck got closer, we saw that it had NOPD decals on the doors. The truck passed us. In the bed, they'd tied down a small boat with a neat web of yellow rope. "¡Policia!" the women shouted, and we waved our arms to the police truck, but it kept going. Not too far ahead, at the next exit, the truck slowed, spun around in a quick U-turn, and descended the on-ramp in reverse, eventually dropping out of sight. We picked up our gear and followed the truck. Maria was determined. These men were policemen. They'd help us find the missing men in her life. By law, they'd have to, right?

Our group of six approached the truck. Two solidly built men in navy blue shirts and shorts, round hats and sunglasses were just finishing the task of untying the braided yellow ropes securing the boat. We tried to approach them in a calm, collected manner. Most everyone else we'd seen on the road acted with open disdain for the law enforcement. I wanted to make sure these guys knew we presented absolutely no threat. I said hello to one of them and he said hello back. So far, so good. The ice had been broken, and then comes Maria from out of the shadows. In hysterical, high-pitched Spanish, she says, "My husband, my son, you must help me find my son."

"Alright, slow down," said the cop on the driver's side. An African American man, his skin was medium-brown. He stood at least six feet or taller and was athletically built. The other officer stood at nearly the same height, though a little shorter and much more leanly built. His skin was deeply tanned. I thought he looked Lebanese, or Greek, maybe. They weren't wearing nametags. Inez grabbed her mother and held her, nodding at me to do the talking. I explained that we were headed to the Superdome and that some other officers in a boat pulled us out of the water, but took off with the girls' father and little brother.

The two officers listened as they hoisted the boat from the truck bed and set it down in the brown water, never once looking up from their work. The Greek-looking cop stood with one leg in the boat, balancing himself on a paddle like it was a cane. The black officer walked back to the driver's side door, opened it and, as he dug around inside, said over his shoulder, "Look." As soon as he started talking, I noticed the Greek officer drop his head, frustrated. He wanted no part of what he knew was coming. "Look for your people. We've got to take care of something. When we're done here, we're going back to the downtown precinct on Poydras, right by the Dome. If you wait, y'all can ride."

"But what about my husband?"

The officer pulled two compact black shotguns from the cab and closed the door. Handing one to the Greek cop, he said, "Maybe they're at the Superdome already. We'll be gone about half an hour. If you're still here, we'll give you a ride downtown."

He shoved the boat off and they rowed away and turned down a side street out of sight. A great decision confronted us as we stood around that navy blue truck in the gathering twilight. No one wanted to give up the search, but everyone wanted to be in the stadium by dark. Even Maria and Inez. Several mean looks were directed our way while we stood around the pickup truck with the police decals. None of them wanted to be walking, but they weren't about to *sell out* by hanging out with a bunch of cops.

We waited. Nearly a perfect half-hour later, like to the minute, we saw the little boat paddling back toward us, just the two officers, as before. I didn't hear any shots, but those shotguns weren't part of any rescue mission. They beached the boat, disembarked, and immediately went to working again with the yellow rope, totally ignoring that we were still there. I didn't know what to say, but I had the feeling everyone expected me to say something. Finally, after that awkward pause, I managed, "How far is it to the Superdome?"

The Greek cop did the talking. "We're going to the downtown precinct." And that was it. After that, another awkward silence. The cops' fingers deftly wound the rope through tie-down points along the boat and truck bed.

I asked, "Can we still get a ride?"

"Wait . . ." he replied.

Wait? Wait for what? Uncomfortably, I looked over my shoulder at everyone else. Maybe another thirty seconds passed. They tugged on their knots and tried giving the boat a shove. It didn't budge. Satisfied, the officers walked toward the front of the truck and opened the doors. As they were climbing in and seating themselves, he finally said, "You ride in the back. Hurry up and get in," then closed the door in our faces. What comes across as rude in the normal world becomes overwhelming generosity in a disaster situation. We piled into the little boat and the navy blue truck raced up the off-ramp back to the I-10 roadway, heading east again.

Several of the people walking turned their heads to angrily stare us down. I could hear their shouts as we drove past them, "Look at this shit here, hundreds of black people are out here walking across the City and the only six white people on the Interstate are getting a ride from the mutha fuckin' police. Ain't no police out here giving none a us niggas a ride, nowhere."

Emotions passed through me in quick succession. At first, I felt really uncomfortable, like we'd be torn limb from limb if, for some reason, the officers changed their minds and ordered us to get the hell out. Then I felt guilty. Like maybe it was fucked up that we were getting a ride and everyone else had to walk. And in a way it truly was. But if it was because of race, then why was an African American police officer driving the truck, indifferent to *his people's* mode of transportation? More ugly stares and ugly shouts and I decided, to hell with them and their faces. First off, I was the only person in the truck with a drop of white blood in me: a twenty-five percent contribution from my father's father, my Paw-Paw, who'd bequeathed me his guitar. The rest of me, and the rest of the people in the boat, are pure Latins. Aside from Inez and myself, the other four people on board had been born in foreign countries. They didn't think of themselves as white. White people wouldn't say they were white. But to hundreds of blacks migrating across a highway, a brown ocean underneath, we were whiter than a winter wonderland. I still can't feel too guilty for simply *asking* for a ride.

We continued much farther east than I'd expected us to, within sight of the New Orleans East High Rise. That's a bridge, not a building. The High Rise Bridge crosses the Industrial Canal, a man-made shipping channel that connects Lake Ponchartrain to the Mississippi River and the Mississippi River-Gulf Outlet

Canal.

"Aaaaahh!"

Maria started screaming at the top of her lungs.

"Waaaah!"

I had no idea what was going on. Inez and Jimena started screaming, too.

"Stop the truck, stop the truck," Jimena pounded on the back window.

The officer driving slowed some and rolled down his window. "What the hell are you doing, lady?"

"My son! My husband! Stop the truck!"

Holy cow, there they were! The two long-lost Stephens were standing in the middle of the highway looking very out of place. I'm not sure how long the family had been in the City, but Stefano wore a look like he'd been transported to Neptune; he looked so lost.

Our shouts of "FANITO" were echoed by shouts of "MAMA!" The driver popped the truck into reverse. Stefano the elder and Stefano the younger stepped out of the crowd and ran toward us. The kid was still wearing his life vest. They climbed into the boat, which was inside the truck, and into one another's arms. I even saw the dickhead Greek cop half-smile through the back window, moved by the touching reunion.

Our group was whole again, and spirits soared. There were high fives and hugs all around. The truck continued to travel east until we came to a point where the east and westbound lanes link up to form a six-lane-wide boulevard, separated by a low median. Here the driver spun the truck around and started heading west, finally, toward the City. He drove in the eastbound lanes. Honking at the *pedestrians* to clear a path. Of course, this led to more mean stares directed our way. The sun was sinking low. The time was half-past seven, with little more than an hour of daylight left. I can't tell you how happy I was to be riding and not walking. My heart went out to all of those mean-faced souls up there on the Interstate.

We were driving into the central part of the City, where homes and businesses are packed together tightly. The flooding appeared less severe in this part of town. Instead of waist-deep water like our home in the Gentilly neighborhood, houses out here in the Tremé neighborhood looked about knee-deep in water. Of course, my perception is probably dead wrong. We were way up high on the roadway and traveling at forty miles per hour. People filled the balconies of the few two-story homes in this part of town. Some were on top of roofs. Perhaps the largest building along this initial stretch, a triangular-shaped structure containing a two-story grocery, had been broken into. Dozens of people occupied the wraparound balcony on the second floor.

We were nearing Canal Street. Claiborne runs directly below the I-10 as it winds through the inner City. At the corner of Canal and Claiborne stands the old Night's Inn. I'd worked in that hotel for nearly four years. The hotel had a new name, but the building looked the exact same. From where we were, the length of Canal Street as far as the eye can see toward Harrah's Casino and the Mississippi River was an expansive sheet of brown water rippling under the fading sunlight. Hundreds of people dotted the length of the broad thoroughfare. The five-story Night's Inn has long balconies on the three middle floors facing Canal Street. Prime real estate during the Endymion Parade. The balconies were lined with men, women, and children. The building had been taken over. I'd estimate a foot and a half of water swamped the lobby floor. I had some really great times while working there: sex, drugs, and rock 'n roll. Seeing the hotel right then, as we sped along in the back of the truck, reminded me of the old times. I also realized that we were only blocks from the Superdome.

Now, we could see the massive Superdome ahead of us. It looked sad. The curving surface of the Dome's roof was normally a smooth eggshell white, but the roof was mostly gray with only patches of white. It was as if the powerful winds of Katrina had stripped the paint right off the building. Then we saw what appeared to be large holes in the roof itself. Part of the egg had cracked! *Oh my God, the storm did that! And that's the building we're going to be staying in? That's where we've been trying to get to since we decided to leave the attic this morning?* It looked as though the roof could cave in at any moment.

Katrina's destructive effects were not limited to the football stadium. We crossed Tulane Avenue, approaching Poydras Street. This is the Central Business District, the financial heart of New Orleans, the second largest port in the United States after New York City. This is where the tallest skyscrapers are congregated. On each one, scores of windows were blown out, curtains flapped ominously in the evening stillness. The worst one I saw was the Hyatt Hotel, which is oddly shaped—a thirty-story building with three curved faces. I don't think a single window remained intact on the windward face.

The truck slowed and descended an on-ramp down to Claiborne Avenue. A quick turn or two later and the truck came to a halt. I didn't recognize the building before us as a police station, but there were certainly police there now, about a dozen of them standing around talking with the first camo-clad National Guard soldiers I'd yet to see. There were more than a score of soldiers milling around beside some large Army trucks and Humvees. I thought to myself, *Now this is what I'm talking about; the heavy-hitters have arrived. I'd like to see some maniac start shooting at pigeons with these guys around. They'd call in an airstrike on his ass.*

Once the truck stopped and the two officers got out, they joined their comrades and didn't look once in our direction as we climbed down from the truck bed. The eight and a half of us just stood there for a few minutes as if in a dream, taking in the destruction to be seen in every direction. Massive skyscrapers—towers of commerce—had been blasted by the hurricane's strength. You could see broken glass glittering on the streets. The setting sun turned the sky from oppressive blue to shades of pink, orange, and purple. And mostly, there was the stillness of it all, the City's bustling financial district now a quiet ghost town. We stood in the gathering twilight and time seemed to stop. Though only a few blocks from our destination, the Louisiana Superdome, we were paralyzed with inertia.

God, I remember being thirsty. We'd finished off our gift bottles of looted sports drink, and all that remained was our gift bottle of Diet Sprite. I tried to drink some, but the bubbles burned caustically as they traveled down my throat.

A young soldier in camouflage approached us. He wore the pelican flag shoulder patch of the Louisiana National Guard. He asked us if we were going to the stadium. He spoke with a thick southern drawl, not a bayou twang. I assumed he hailed from somewhere in the northern part of the state. Wherever he came from, he was very young and friendly, and asked the right questions.

"Yes, Sir. We'd love a ride to the stadium," I said, suddenly snapping out of my daydream.

He offered to give us a ride, said we looked like we'd walked far enough. The eight and a half of us thanked him profusely. "Thank you, Sir. Thank you, Sir. Thank you, Sir."

He said, "You're welcome," and added, "but I'm not an officer."

It took me a few more interactions with the soldiers (there would be hundreds in the days to come) to learn how to properly address them. You can't just walk around calling everybody *Sir*. To them, only certain members of the camouflage club are to be addressed as *Sir*. Addressing everyone as *Sir*, well, that's just chaos. I know more than your average unemployed bartender probably knows about militaria. I've been a History buff since the fourth grade. Markings, badges, and insignia denoting rank on the arms and collars of the uniforms, for instance. I know what those symbols mean. So whenever I'd address one of the soldiers, who were still quite friendly and approachable during this early phase of the game, I'd address them by their rank. Speaking in this way triggered some kind of subconscious response mechanism in the troops. Especially the Privates, all of whom were so very young. It's like it would take them a moment to realize they were talking to a fat guy with long hair and a goatee and not one of their own. Over the next few days, I'd speak to dozens of Privates, Corporals, Lance Corporals, Staff Sergeants, Master Sergeants, Technical Sergeants, a First Sergeant, both First and Second Lieutenants, Captains, Majors, even a full bird Colonel. It was like a box of G.I. Joes come to life. And though I failed to corner a General, I did see one from afar.

The young Private with the drawl directed us into the back of a full-size military Humvee. I'd missed the chance to catch a ride in a helicopter last night on the roof, and I know a Hummer's no helicopter, but this sort of made up for it. I couldn't believe how big it was inside the open bed in the back of the truck. The eight and a half of us, plus two soldiers in full battle gear, add three guys up front, and that makes thirteen and a half of us in one truck! They drove us a few blocks slashed by the shadows of skyscrapers, the wheels crunching on broken glass below a foot of water.

In no time the Humvee arrived at the foot of the colossal stadium, though at a section of the structure I'd never been through when going to cheer on the Saints. Open rows of large bay doors at the loading dock were filled with dozens of soldiers moving around. We rolled up to an open double door at street level. I say the doors were "open" in an objective sense. They'd been ripped off of the hinges. The doors themselves were laid across crates to form an improvised ramp, or dock. The Humvee backed up to the ramp and the two soldiers in the back with us dropped the gate of the vehicle and hopped out, helping us down one by one. I thought the door-ramp was a really nice touch. I didn't even get my feet wet. Mother carried the hippo and I held the dog. We walked up the ramp and climbed up to the loading dock level. Roughly nine hours after sliding off the roof of 4899 Mandeville Street and into the arms of an angel, I'd arrived at the Louisiana Superdome.

ONLY BIPEDS MAY ENTER

The troops walked us through the loading dock to an enclosed ground-floor entrance, once again an area rarely seen by football fans. We were back outside the building, standing in what would be the first of many long lines we'd be forced to stand in over the next few days. A couple dozen people—civilians and soldiers—were hanging around by the doorway.

I saw scattered sections of police barricade set out with dogs and cats leashed to them. My heart dropped. Does this mean they aren't admitting animals? Surveying the scene, I saw that a socioeconomic cross-section of pets had been tied to the metal barricades. Big, muscular Rottweilers with spiked collars, tiny lap dogs, brindle pit-bulls, a fluffy poodle with groomed snow-white fur, a bitch mutt with long teats and battle scars, even a couple of very agitated looking felines. I noticed an older white woman laid out on a blanket in the middle of the street cradling a cat carrier. She had refused to be separated from her furry companion. My dry, empty gut seized up. The soldiers were going to force me to tether Dolja before we could enter. We'd come so far together. By sheer luck and the grace of God, we'd found the missing members of our group. We'd made it to the stadium, all of us, together. Through hell *and* high water. Now the powers that be were going to rip us apart. I spoke to some of the National Guardsmen posted outside. They all said, more or less, the same thing: "No animals will be admitted." Our dog "must be tied to one of the barricades." When asked what would become of these animals, the reply was usually a shrug of the shoulders followed by an "I don't know." Others told us that SPCA personnel were *en route* to gather up all the animals, catalog them, and transport them out of harm's way. We'd be able to find him after this was all over.

Bullshit.

Find him where? There were thousands, or tens of thousands, of people out there wandering the flooded streets. Surely, the police and soldiers had their hands full with two-legged problems. That any sort of priority would be shown to these animals just seemed ludicrous. If any Humane Society workers did show up, I don't know, maybe on hovercrafts, I could totally see them taking the only *humane* option the situation allowed: wholesale euthanization. What else were they going to do with a bunch of storm dogs?

In March 1998, a close friend had found Dolja collarless and emaciated wandering the streets. I'd taken him home and cleaned him up. This was about a month after I'd moved into the mother-in-law's apartment. I was still a senior in high school. After more than seven years, he was an important part of our family—the only member of our household that everyone got along with. And there I was, lying to my best friend as I led him over to the barricade. Mother volunteered to sit outside with him, but once we were in, I didn't know if there would be a way to come back out to bring her and the dog water or food. There seemed no point in sacrificing the both of them atop Katrina's altar. Dolja shook furiously, he would walk no farther. Dry tears in my eyes, I lifted him up and carried him over to one of the sections of barricade. Attached to it were several frightened dogs, large and small, and one really angry striped cat. The kitty had lost every trace of domestication; she was operating purely on survival instinct. She—I've always thought of this cat as a *she*, though I never checked to be sure—sat as far away from the barricade and the dogs as her tether would allow. She hissed at Dolja as I set him down on the ground. Dolja had known several cats throughout his life with us on Mandeville Street. He regarded felines as friends, not enemies. He'd attempted to get to *know* several of them in the Old Testament sense, much to our comedic delight. But this cat wasn't looking for friendship or camaraderie. Her psyche had devolved into that of a primitive jungle cat. As I began tying my end of the yellowed phone cord to the barricade, he looked at me, to the cat, and back to me, his countenance saying "Are you for real?" Knot over knot, I did my best to secure the ancient phone line. Other, bigger dogs looked him over and must have figured he'd make an easy meal or bedtime companion, whatever it is agitated dogs do to one another. Kneeling in the street, I hugged him as he trembled. He was terrified. He didn't know these dogs. He didn't understand the big picture. All he'd ever known was us, but he knew enough to know that he was being tied up; and the lamenting tone in my voice, he understood what that meant, too.

"I love you, boy. We'll be right back. It might be a couple of days, maybe a week, but when this thing blows over, I'll come for you. I will find you, boy. People are coming to take care of you, good people. And when they do, just trust them, okay? They're going to feed you and take care of you. And just as soon as I can, I'm going to come for you, my son. Trust me. I love you, boy. I love you so much. I swear to you, I will find you, no matter where they bring you."

I looked into his panicked brown eyes, stroked his fur, and kissed him on the nose. Standing up, real tears rolled down my cheeks. It was the hardest thing I've ever done in my life. I turned and walked away, certain I'd never see him again. Everything I'd said was a lie. Immediately, he began to whine and wail, the way he used to do when I first brought him home and he would sleep in the kitchen behind a baby gate, way back when he was a pup.

Awoooo-wooo-wooo-woooooooooo-woo-wooo.

My head down, chin on my chest, I kept walking. I didn't look back. I couldn't, just couldn't.

Awoooo-wooo-wooo-woooooooooo-woo-wooo.

Broken and defeated, I rejoined the group. My skin crawled. There was nothing more we could do for Dolja. For a moment, I thought it might have been better if I'd have just killed him myself, right there on the street. At least then there would have been closure. No mystery about his fate. No one could tell us how long we'd be in the stadium. No one could tell us how long it would be before the SPCA showed up. Dolja wouldn't last forever tied up under the naked sun. He was as dehydrated as the rest of us. He'd be dead in forty-eight hours, if he made it that long. But what could I do? Dozens of men with assault rifles were telling me he couldn't come in. We protested, but they still said no. Of course I couldn't strangle him to death. I've never purposely hurt an animal in my whole life, except on a fishing trip. I wasn't going to start now, in the twilight of the longest day. I'd carried him through brown water, and together we'd made it downtown to the stadium. I fell in love with the little black mutt with the brown muzzle the first time our eyes met. Loved him for seven years, and now at this moment of ultimate decision, all I could do was turn my back and walk away, leaving him to his fate. I'd never felt so filthy in my entire life. I hugged my mother. She sobbed heavily in my arms. We held each other's hands as we moved past soldiers and civilians through the doorway and entered the back of the line.

Stepping through the doorway, we could still hear his cries.

In the line before us stood twenty or thirty people filing toward a row of tables lined with soldiers. Camo-clad men and women were searching through people's bags and frisking everyone. A Sergeant stood behind the tables. He repeated the same thing over and over, as if on a loop: "Guns, knives, weapons, mace, body armor, tools, shanks, shivs, picks, or any other weapons are not allowed inside and will be confiscated."

A dozen soldiers worked the line, searching and frisking, asking questions about certain items they'd find. Surprisingly, the line moved quickly. The soldiers searched Uncle G and Jimena's backpacks and gave the plastic bag containing Klaus the hippo a squeeze, no contraband to be found.

I asked one of the young Guardsmen about some water. He said food and water were being distributed on the second-level corridor, but he didn't know for how much longer. The Sergeant rattled on ". . . tools, shanks, shivs, picks, or any other weapons . . ." I reached into the little upper-hip pocket, or fifth pocket, of my carpenter jeans and pulled out a green Dunlop .88 mm Tortex guitar pick, the only kind I ever use; I always seem to have one on me. I looked at the young Private and asked, "Is this pick okay?"

He smiled at me and said, "Yeah, man. I mean yes, Sir. You're clean. Move through that door and up the stairs."

Mother protested to one of the soldiers about Dolja outside. He told her that animals weren't being allowed and to please keep moving. After Mother made it past the row of tables, our reduced group of only eight—no half—entered the doors of a stairwell. The light was gloomy and only got darker as the stairs went up. Scores of people, people from another inspection point, filled the hallway and tramped their way higher on the seemingly endless column of steps. I took the lead, with the Cuban family behind me. Jimena, Uncle G, and Mother brought up the rear.

I realize now that over the next few minutes I was very unfair to my mother. Instead of racing up the stairs and getting frustrated at her slow pace, I should have been down there, helping her negotiate the ascent into the darkness. Remember, she has terrible eyesight, especially in low-light conditions. It used to drive me crazy, the way she'd demand that every bulb in the house be turned on. Not to mention the physical exertion factor—she didn't even walk smoothly, forget climbing flight after flight of stairs. Other than the seven steps from the patio floor to the doorway of our house, she hadn't climbed any stairs in more than a year.

Four of five turns up the staircase and the Cubans and I were well ahead of the rest. Looking over the rail as I climbed, I could see them down below, ascending slowly. They slowed a little more, and then they stopped.

"*¿Que paso?*" asked Stefano.

"What are they doing?" asked Inez in English.

I replied, "She's catching her breath, I guess."

Mother, G, and Jimena stood there talking for about a minute, and then Mother started back down the steps. "God Damnit, Cecilia," I said to myself.

The soldier said that food and water were being served, and it was well-past eight o'clock at night. I didn't want to miss the line for *dinner*, whatever that dinner might be.

"*¿Que paso?*"

"What are they doing?" Inez repeated.

"I don't fucking know."

The Cubans and I backed off the stairs and waited on one of the landings for what felt like forever, ten or fifteen minutes. Uncle G and Jimena had also gone back down; through some hand signals I told Uncle G that we'd wait where we were for them. My stomach growled and my throat burned. And I also had to calm the family I was with, reassuring them that there must be a really good reason for this, or else I'd have to kill her myself. Five more minutes, ten more minutes, the patience of the party completely drained. For every person who passed us and continued up the stairs, I thought of how much longer we'd have to wait to get some water. With clenched fists and a set jaw, I peered over the rail again, like I'd done five seconds before. There they were, the three of them, making the climb at a steady pace. I told the Cubans they were on the way up, and the five of us relaxed. The delay had me a little worked up and I was poised to vent my frustrations verbally all over my mother. They were ascending the last flight before reaching our level. I drew in a deep breath, ready to let loose. But when she came fully into view, I saw she had Dolja cradled in her arms.

"Oh my God . . ." I ran forward to help my mother, to hug her, all of the venom I'd been building up just melted away. I kissed her and the dog and hugged Jimena. Mother had done it!

She didn't give up on him. She couldn't turn her back. Turn her back like I had done. She made the soldiers believe, too. I've never appreciated her more. And, I never did ask her what she said or how she did it. I didn't need to, because

I know her. Cecilia can be very persuasive when she applies herself. Regardless of the means employed, the end result remained the same. We had the dog. We were whole again. She told me that we'd have to tie him up somewhere on the terrace outside, where other animals were. He couldn't stay inside the stadium. Whatever, outside or inside, he was in the building and not left out on the streets to die.

Interestingly, some animals had been admitted, and we and other people had been instructed to abandon ours. I assume that the animals already inside belonged to people that had been there for the past couple days, to ride out the actual storm. Now that the world had fallen apart and thousands more people were arriving, they must have felt it best that the Superdome didn't become a full-on zoo. We'd figure out what to do with Dolja soon enough. All that mattered was that we had him. First and foremost, I wanted to climb the rest of these stairs and check out this dinner situation.

Reaching the top of the stairs and passing through a set of double doors, we entered a portion of the stadium that I was quite familiar with. We'd exited one of the many sets of seemingly random and unlabeled double doors lining the exterior wall of the main concession area, right above the first bank of seats looking down on the playing field. The poorly lit hallway was full of people. Dozens, scores, hundreds of people wandered in all directions through the wide corridor. Except for the relative darkness and the sodden, crumpled appearance of everyone's clothes, it was a lot like walking into a Sunday football crowd, only there were no teams warming up on the field, no boisterous fans. But there were people. Loads and loads of them. In the corridor, in the seats, covering a portion of the playing field.

Across the field, on the opposite side of the building, I saw a ridiculously long line, fifteen people across, filling the corridor space. So, that must be the dinner line. The seemingly motionless line wrapped around the field and stands for what looked like miles. We'd get into that line soon enough. Closer to our end of the building, people who'd made it through already walked past us clutching brown bags and plastic bottles of water. I wanted that water.

Looking ahead to the end of the line, I didn't see any steam clouds or bright lights, no chefs in white coats, only camo-clad soldiers and stacks of cardboard crates. Eyeing one of the brown plastic bags of a passerby, I gathered that people were being issued MREs, or Meals Ready to Eat in military jargon. Cool, I thought. I'm such a military history dork, the first time I'd heard the term MRE was in fifth grade when my social studies class wrote letters to U.S. soldiers during the Persian Gulf War, back in 1990. A Sergeant actually responded to my letter. In response to my question: "Are there Burger Kings in Kuwait?"—I was such a burger-loving kid—he replied that he hadn't found one yet, that the soldiers often ate pre-packaged meals called MREs. About a week later, our teacher procured one and showed us the stuff inside and how it worked. I'll admit, I remember being a little embarrassed over the whole presentation our teacher made on behalf of my letter, but fifteen years later, those memories would really come in handy at the Louisiana Superdome.

The eight and a half of us agreed that even though we were thirsty, given the totally random seating arrangements and the large number of people in the dinner line, it might suit us just as well to wait a moment, catch our breath, and carve out a place for ourselves before getting into the line. It wasn't rocket science. We spotted a block of about a dozen unoccupied seats, and we set up our first residence within the stadium. It felt good, like a real accomplishment, that first time ass met seat. Twelve hours before, I was napping in my attic. And since then, we'd traveled clear across town, arrived at our destination in one piece, and gained a larger, stronger team in transit. The only thing to do was wait out the time for whatever came next. I hadn't even considered what would happen after we got to the Superdome. I'd been so focused on simply getting there that I hadn't thought that far ahead.

No sooner had we sat down than Mother started a conversation with two token white guys seated nearby. Stan, the older of the two, wore several faded tattoos on his ruddy arms. No doubt, he spent most of his days working outside. Glenn was a little shorter and fatter than me, but not by much. And though we were the same age, twenty-five, he was noticeably balding at the crown of his sweaty, white head. Glenn told us he'd moved to New Orleans a whopping seven days before from upstate New York. He'd moved to teach third grade in the Orleans Parish public school system in exchange for a free semester of graduate school at Tulane. The order to evacuate the campus sent poor, naïve Glenn to the Superdome. His foreign-sounding accent and the pastiness of his complexion combined to make Glenn the single most out of place individual I met in the Superdome. I could only marvel at the sorry bastard's bad luck.

Stan told us he'd recently been paroled after serving six years "on the farm." The farm is the common expression for Angola—Louisiana's state penitentiary— located about three hours northwest of New Orleans. It's a prison with no walls. The Mississippi River and miles of alligator-infested swamp surround the prison complex. Escape attempts are rare. Though Stan spoke easily with every black person around him, I could tell he carried a heavy racist streak. Old habits die hard. Six years of hard labor hadn't softened his prejudices. He'd found Glenn wandering the stadium like a lost puppy and taken him under his wing.

When the group was ready to get into the dinner line, Mother asked if she could stay behind with Dolja and the bags. The day's exertions had taken a lot out of her, and she said she didn't want to "fall out" in line. Stan and Glenn had already been through the dinner line and promised not to leave her until we returned. Despite Stan just telling us he was an ex-con, I felt like I could trust them to look out for Mother.

I headed back up to the concession corridor with Uncle G, Jimena, and the Cuban family. The seven of us took our place at the end of the enormous line. Ten people across at the thinnest points, the line stretched about a quarter of the way around the building. While standing in the concession corridor, we passed one of the bathrooms. The smell emanating from inside was enough to knock you down. From what I could see, there were no lights either. No wonder it smelled so bad, no one really knew if they were hitting the toilet. The line crept onward, past one of the concession vending kiosks. The place had apparently been broken into—napkins, ketchup, crushed tortilla chips, and other trash lay scattered everywhere. One guy climbed over the counter carrying a box of Coca-Cola syrup. A box of syrup. What can you do with that? Another walked off with three big bags of nacho cheese sauce. I suppose that's more useful than Coke syrup, but that's a whole damn lot of cheese.

Every step forward brought us closer to water and food. And, with every step, I had to watch that I didn't kick anyone. Several people had chosen to set up camp in the corridors, whole families spread out on blankets and cardboard mattresses lined the walls. They preferred to be horizontal, rather than confined to a stadium seat, despite the foot traffic and the foul stench coming from the bathrooms. We continued inching our way forward. I noticed that behind us in line were only about fifty or sixty people, as opposed to the hundreds that were in front of us when we'd started. We were some of the last people in the stadium to get fed that night. I hoped they still had some left.

After about an hour, we'd inched our way to the front. Ahead, several folding tables formed a corner in the oval-shaped corridor. Behind the tables were several soldiers unloading freight pallets stacked with brown cardboard boxes. Other pallets were stacked with crates of water bottles in plastic wrapping.

Over to the side I heard a soldier telling somebody, "I told you already, no seconds. We've got to make sure there's enough for everyone." The man continued to protest.

"No, come back at breakfast. You're not getting anything else tonight. Move along now, please."

The people ahead of me moved aside and I stepped forward; it was my turn to get served. "Excuse me, Sir." I still hadn't gotten used to the military hierarchy. "My mother is disabled, she couldn't make it through this long line. In fact, she is missing several prescription medicines and . . ."

The young soldier cut me off. "If she's not in line, we are to assume that she is provided for and does not require assistance."

"Yeah, but . . ."

He said, "Everyone in line gets two water bottles and one MRE." As two other soldiers handed me these items, he continued, "If a person is not in line, they are assumed to be provided for . . ." and so on and so forth.

Each member of our group pled for additional water, recalling tales of our recent adventure. Each in turn received the same speech, two bottles and an MRE. Nothing more, nothing less. I realized that I'd learned something as we walked back toward Mother and Dolja. The military personnel I'd dealt with had responded in a manner devoid of emotion and an almost complete lack of individual thought. Only the mission mattered, and the entire team thought as one. A finely tuned human machine under the direct mental control of an officer behind the scenes, one man doing all the thinking and decision-making for dozens or hundreds of pumping arms and legs—a very efficient system for accomplishing a task. I'd never seen the military functioning up-close before.

By the time we got back to our seats, Mother, Stan, and Glenn were warm friends. Mother does have that way with people. We cracked open some warm water and examined the thick, rubbery brown pouches they'd given us and called food. The outside packaging of mine was labeled "Chicken & Rice." Jimena had "Cheese Tortellini" and Uncle G got "Beef Stew." Uncle G joined the Marine Corps in 1978, a few years after completing high school, when he was twenty years old. In those days, the Marines were still eating C-Rations and K-Rations (packaged meals—predating the MRE—which fed U.S. soldiers throughout World War II, Korea, and Vietnam). The MRE concept had yet to see the light of day. The brown plastic pouch was as foreign to him as it was to the rest of the group. The Cubans had received a like assortment of cafeteria-sounding meals. When Fanito tore open his pouch, I think he expected to find a bag full of "Jambalaya." Instead, he had bags full of other bags. An MRE is an entire meal kit, not just chicken and rice, but also peanut butter, chips, crackers, jelly, bread, and squeezable cheese dip. Gather a few MREs and you could fill a whole snack tray. Jimena even scored a pouch of, honest to God, Peanut M&Ms in hers. In a separate pouch were instant coffee, sugar, matches, a moist towelette, a square wad of what they'd labeled toilet paper, and a tiny bottle of Tabasco sauce. Being from south Louisiana, I felt proud that our service men and women across the globe were enjoying what I'd always considered a local condiment.

Most mysterious of all was a clear, green plastic bag with another pouch inside. As we walked through the corridor I'd seen several of these green bags discarded intact. A couple of the Cubans were about to do the same when I stopped them. "Wait, you need those!" I shouted.

Much more recently than fifth grade, I'd seen the old "Gunny" himself, R. Lee Ermey, on television demonstrating how to heat an MRE. You poured a little water in that green pouch and it started a chemical reaction with the other thing, or something like that, and you dropped the pouch of food, Chicken & Rice in this instance, into the bag. It would be surrounded by chemically heated water, thus warming the food.

I poured a couple of sips from my water bottle into the green pouch and to everyone's amazement the thing started to steam up and, in about a minute, began to noticeably warm the water. Eureka! Ten minutes after that, I was eating a hot pouch of Army food off the end of a long, brown spoon. After helping our group get their meals warmed up, I assisted several of the people sitting around us to get some water in the pouch and warm their rations. By the time I finished my Chicken & Rice with a few drops of added Tabasco sauce, I swelled with pride knowing I'd assisted maybe thirty people—men, women, and kids—put a hot meal in their stomachs.

Like true-blue hispanics, Jimena and Mother rejoiced upon discovering instant coffee and sugar in our MRE kits. Between the four of us, we had six bottles of water to split since Mother hadn't received her issue of a ration. Six bottles, four of us, we each claimed one. I chugged most of mine as soon as I'd opened it. After watering Dolja from my cupped hand and heating our MRE pouches, we were down to 750 ml of water, a bottle and a half, to last four people and a dog until whenever breakfast was going to be served. And now they were making coffee, further draining our water supply. The instructions on the packet said to combine with six ounces of hot water. After carefully measuring what we estimated to be six ounces into two of our empty bottles, they tried to heat the water using their spent MRE pouches. In the end, they wound up drinking room temperature water with freeze dried coffee mixed in it.

A couple hours passed, the time had to be somewhere around midnight. By then I was thoroughly bored with the whole situation. Maybe I should have grabbed that H.G. Wells novel when I had the chance. I should have done a lot of things while I still had the chance. All of that seemed like it had happened a thousand years before. A lifetime ago.

The crowd in the stadium had quieted, but never did collectively go to bed. Several thousand bored individuals, with none of that instilled Army discipline, weren't conforming to a schedule. I'd napped for only a handful of hours during the past three days. Add to that the unconventional nature of the day I'd had so far, and there was no argument: I needed a solid night's sleep. Unfortunately, that wasn't going to happen. Not for me, at least. I looked over at Mother. She'd zonked out as soon as we finished sharing our MRE, despite having just drunk a bottle of overly caffeinated coffee water. Mother can fall asleep anywhere, and she had. She'd fall asleep in the car on the way to the store, blocks away from the house. I've always wished that I could do that. Instead, I have great difficulty falling asleep, even in my own bed. I always have. A precise set of factors must be in place to achieve a comfort level, both physical and mental, before the lights shut down, and I'm out. Otherwise, I just stare at the walls or watch the fan spin while my mind races.

Sitting there under the spotlights (the playing field and seating area were the only well-lit parts of the building) and wiggling around in an upright, narrow stadium chair wasn't my ideal level of comfort. These seats get uncomfortable when watching a three-hour football game. I'd been in the chair for more than three hours; no one had won the game, because there was no freakin' game. There was only the one massive organism: the Dome itself. The Superdome had become the exoskeleton, which contained several thousand individual cells, or people: no heart, no spleen, and definitely no central nervous system controlling things. No two cells were alike or acted the same way. And the organism could never quite switch off and hibernate. Too many free radicals moving around. And that's what I'd become. A tired, shifting cell in an uncomfortable seat. This first night at the stadium would prove to be, far and away, the quietest night of our experience. With numb legs and a numb ass, sore feet and altogether too many appendages to get properly comfortable in my seat, the time passed painfully slowly. When the breakfast line would begin to form, I had no idea, but it wasn't forming soon enough.

A handful of times, I'd nod off, catch a couple seconds or minutes of actual unconscious sleep, but then wake again to a burst of boisterous talking nearby or the sound of my own snoring. I looked at Dolja curled up on the seat next to me. He was the perfect size for life in a stadium seat. As a five-foot ten-inch, two-hundred-pound insomniac, I was having a rough time of it.

And so ended August 30th, 2005—*The Longest Day, or The Day of Days*, in my universe. Morning started with me wrapped in hospital gowns up on my roof back at 4899 Mandeville Street, and ended with me sitting in a prime seat on the forty-yard line, fifteen rows up from the playing field of the Louisiana Superdome. The day had been a trial from the start, and would end with my third sleepless night in a row. At least on the roof I'd been able to lie down and stretch out, and the air was cool and fresh.

Frustrated, I twisted in my chair while the rest of my group dozed. And after what felt like decades, the black voids in the roof—much larger than they seemed in the dark of night—began to change color. The sky began to lighten from deep-charcoal to pink and orange through the giant holes Katrina had made in the roof of the Superdome. A new day dawned on the flooded City of New Orleans, our first full day in the stadium. Wednesday, August 31st, 2005. The day things fell apart.

WEDNESDAY
AUGUST 31ST, 2005

MORNING

Two for Five

At seven o'clock in the morning, the line for food began taking shape. Thousands of people from all parts of the stadium were filing into the concession corridor. Jimena and Uncle G decided they'd hang back with the dog and the Cubans while Stan, a very groggy Cecilia, and I stood in line, but not before using the last of our liquid to make more coffee-flavored water. I declined the coffee. I've never been a big coffee drinker.

In the interest of dental hygiene, I chewed the two pieces of white gum from the previous night's MRE. Months or years later, when talking to friends who'd served in the military, they told me that the gum in the MRE was purposefully designed to have a laxative effect. Whether that's true or not I don't know, but I do know that the flip side of what they said was true. The meals themselves would block up your normal daily processes. Eating MREs constipated me for days to come.

Glenn had left our place in the seats late the night before, maybe around three o'clock in the morning. Upon our arrival, the National Guard had set up a defensive perimeter across the 30-yard line. The area before them lay open to colonization, behind them, government territory. In the middle of the night the Guard had pulled back to the opposite 30-yard line at the far end of the field, opening up forty additional yards of living space. As more people moved down from the stands, Glenn decided to carve out a spot for himself.

Stan and I were sitting and talking while the others slept. Stan spotted Glenn down on the field, a solitary, chubby, young white adult alone on his blanket, surrounded on all sides by hundreds of black families piled on blankets. Stan pointed to where Glenn sat and said, "He's going to get himself into trouble; fuck, he'll get himself killed down there. I don't know what the niggas are like in Albany, but he's in New Orleans now. He already got cursed out for talking to someone's kid. I don't think he's a pervert. I don't know. If he is, I'll fuck him up, but they'll get to him first, and they'll kill him. You can't try to be silly and make these kids laugh, not in the middle of this shithole."

Stan's prediction proved true. Shortly after Glenn spread out his blanket, a shouting woman caught my attention. She shouted something to the effect of "What da fuck you thank you doin'? Keep yo' eyes off my fuckin' baby."

After that, Glenn rolled over on his side, covered his head with his arms, and went to sleep. The Superdome was no melting pot of good feelings. For some time afterward, the little boy on the next blanket gazed over at Glenn, wondering why his new friend with the funny faces didn't want to play anymore.

The sun had come up, and long shafts of light poured through the square holes in the high-domed roof. A strong Christianity-based fanaticism could be heard throughout the stadium. Rapture, Revelation, Noah, and the gang. Mostly,

I paid these prophets little attention, but I heard more than a couple of people say they saw a cross floating in the beams of light. Mother said she saw it. Maybe it was like one of those computer generated 3-D pictures that were popular in the 90s. Some people had trouble discerning the hidden images; I know I did. Or maybe I simply wasn't holy enough. Either way, I didn't see any cross.

The entire organism had come back to life, all cells awake and moving. At the far end of the building, soldiers were stirring and people migrated from their seats and the field up to the concession corridor to stand in line for breakfast.

Unfortunately, on our way to the line, I felt the need to use the bathroom again, so I found the nearest one—a large, rectangular room done in white tile, its rear wall a long, continuous urinal. The shorter walls were each lined with a dozen black-doored stalls. It is very hard for me to describe the conditions. They'd become so foul. Feces and urine overflowed every toilet bowl and covered the floor so that the entire floor space became one continuous puddle of human waste in various states of decomposition, from the very fresh to the several days old. The shafts of daylight pouring through the roof marginally increased the visible light in the otherwise pitch-black bathrooms. In the gloomy darkness, I couldn't distinguish colors. I flicked my cigarette lighter and all of the colors came to life for an instant. The wall and ceiling tiles were white with back grouting. The walls of the stalls were black, and everywhere else was brown and yellow. Worse than that were pools of red blood. I don't want to know how they got there. Clumps of sodden toilet paper polka-dotted the floor.

At the center of the room was a large, round communal sink. There was a bar that you step on and hundreds of small water jets spray all around the sink, three-hundred sixty degrees, enabling several people to wash their hands simultaneously. But that was during normal times. In Katrina times, the great hand sink, the size of a small Jacuzzi, had become a community toilet. A nightmare cauldron of rotting shit stew. A black boy around four years old stood knee deep in the muck splashing around with his hands. The smell alone was more than enough to make you vomit, but the sight of that kid started me retching. I ran toward the light of the hallway as pee spilled down the inside of my jeans. I hadn't quite finished my task but I had to get out of there.

The muscles down my sides hurt from the involuntary heaving, but after about an hour of standing in line for breakfast, the pain subsided. Mother was with us this go-round, so we each received a ration: one liter of water and an MRE. As soon as we returned to our seats they started making coffee again. I found some kind of fruit punch flavored electrolyte drink mix in mine. I mixed it up with some water and enjoyed a warm bottle of Army Kool-Aid. No one used their heating packs to warm their meals this time. From here on, the mysterious green bags would only be used for making coffee. This early in the morning, maybe eight-thirty, the temperature inside the stadium must have been no less than eighty-five degrees, and would only increase as the day wore on. The last thing in the world I wanted to drink right then—well, it would have been the brown stew up there in the bathroom sink, but second would be a hot cup of bad coffee. But they drank the stuff up, and then wished they had more. For Mother, the little packs of dried Folger's Crystals became this panacea: able to cure every ailment, somehow the caffeine compensated for the lack of her other medications. She could never get enough coffee packets.

I fed Dolja some crushed-up crackers moistened with fruit punch on a green plastic heating bag at my feet. After eating more Army food and drinking the sugary drink mix, I really wished I'd gone and looted a toothbrush out of the busted drugstore we'd passed on Elysian Fields. Over forty-eight hours had passed since last brushing my teeth. All I could do was chew my two white squares of peppermint flavored laxative Army gum.

After spending what seemed an endless night in our seats and having a chance to stretch a bit walking through the line, returning to those seats brought back all of that ache. By the time the Cubans returned from their trip through the line, my gang and I decided we'd migrate down to the field and see if Glenn minded a little company. With a full belly, lying down flat sounded very appealing. The Cubans decided they would stay in the seats. We'd be able to see one another and communicate, if needed. So, for the time being, our posse would be split in half. I'd been the only one of us awake to see that lady yelling at Glenn the night before. I kept it to myself. I'd become so eager to stretch out my legs I didn't want to frighten anybody out of making the transition from the stands to the field. Besides, with the coming of daylight and another ration of food and water, the mood of the crowd seemed to have improved. Some teenagers were throwing a football around on open bits of turf downfield from Glenn's blanket. Kids were squealing and babies were crying; life filled the air.

Glenn looked like a different man, a defeated man. His eyes were red, as if he'd been crying. He welcomed us to make ourselves comfortable on his blanket. Somewhere in those puffy eyes I saw him smile a little, glad to not be alone down on the field any longer. After that, he rolled onto his side and didn't move for most of the rest of the day. He hadn't gotten up to go through the meal line. I suppose he was just waiting for the time to pass, hoping he'd get back home soon. At least he had an intact, dry home to dream about going back to. I had no idea what to call home anymore.

It felt so good to recline, take off my slippers, and run my stinky toes through the artificial grass on the field. I rubbed the aches out of my knees and hamstrings. I also opened up the black garbage bag with Klaus the hippo inside. I hadn't checked on him since we'd climbed out of the attic. Mother carried him over her head as we walked through the high water on Elysian Fields, but as the water rose to swallow her head, I saw the bag dip in more than once. Sure enough, my hippo felt moist in spots and had begun to acquire that mildew smell. The black bag would only serve to act as a greenhouse for further mildew growth, but I acknowledged there was nothing I could do about it right then. At my first opportunity I'd get him cleaned up, but until then, Klaus would have to remain in the bag. The bag with the hippo inside served as an amazing pillow. Finally laid out flat, I soon fell asleep—some of the best sleep I would get throughout the entire experience. When I woke, Uncle G said I'd been out for nearly four hours. Despite not getting a full night's worth of recuperative rest, I woke up feeling amazing. Prior to that, I'd slept less than four hours total in three days. Four hours in one uninterrupted stretch had me feeling like a million bucks.

Except for a stomachache, that is. I could only grit my teeth as my insides writhed and twisted. Several times, I farted noxious clouds of gas. I ran up to the shit-filled bathroom and tried to have a shit of my own. With my shirt over my face, I fought to hold my breath, fought for every breath I *didn't* take. Fought to not breathe in the incredible smell of filth. And, at the same time, tried to move my aching bowels, but to no avail. I couldn't understand, when I'd flick my cigarette lighter, giant logs covered the ground piled atop one another, but I couldn't go. After maybe a minute, or ninety seconds tops, I ran out of there gasping for fresher air. There was nothing I could do. The Army food had turned my large intestine into an impassable barrier, solid as concrete.

When I got back down to the field, Mother asked me if I'd walk her up to do the same thing at which I'd just failed. She said she couldn't stand going into the chamber of filth. We found her a dark spot in the concession corridor one level up. She backed up against a big steel vertical support beam. I did my best to stand in front of her and ward off prying eyes, with mixed results. This was how low we'd sunk. My mother crapping in the hallway while I stood guard against the only thing lower—the literally dozens of men walking past us who tried their best to peer around me to catch a glimpse. She finished the deed and cleaned up with a wad of MRE toilet paper. I covered the spot with a hunk of cardboard. She certainly wasn't the first person to give up on the horrid bathrooms and instead relieve themselves in a more common area. And she definitely wouldn't be the last. The entire stadium was quickly becoming an open sewer.

On our way back from the bathroom I noticed the soldiers had set up a nurse's station near the food distribution tables. After sitting back down on the field, I felt swallowed by boredom once again. I decided to take a walk and talk to these nurses. With nothing else to do, I thought maybe I could convince these people that Mother was sick enough to get us out of here. She looked better than she had yesterday, but I was still worried about the heat and the total lack of her prescription medicines. Once we'd gotten back on the field, she'd kind of switched off and became spacey and childish, a sign of a coming episode.

The line to see the nurse proved refreshingly short for a change, only about twenty people in front of me. It moved quickly. Like me, most people were in line to ask questions on behalf of another person. I received what I imagined to be the same reply as everyone else. Behind a desk sat a tired looking early middle-aged white woman wearing scrubs and a lab coat. On a normal day she probably looked quite attractive without much effort, a naturally pretty face; but not this morning. Her face looked weighed down with a ton of suffering; her professional training hadn't prepared her for a day like this. Behind her a couple of soldiers cast shadows against a row of curtains serving as a makeshift clinic.

"Good morning, Nurse."

"Morning. So, what's the problem, Sir?"

"I'm fine, other than my current surroundings." She nodded at this. "It's my mother. We did a lot of walking and swimming yesterday, and she's not used to the heat. We had to leave all of her medications at the house when we left. She's starting to show symptoms like she's going to have one of her seizures."

"What medications does she take?"

I ran off a laundry list of the pills I'd last seen on the end of the table in the mother-in-law's apartment.

"We have some of those. She'll have to go without the specialized medications for now."

"Which ones do you have and how many can you give me?"

"None."

"None?"

"Correct, she'll have to do her best without those pills."

"But you said you had some of them."

"Not enough to just hand out to everyone. We're set up to only handle the most critical life-threatening cases."

"So, if she has a seizure down on the field, someone can come and get her so she can be treated, right?"

"If she has a seizure on the field, she'll have to get herself up here to be seen by a nurse, and then possibly receive some meds."

I could see I'd lost the chance to be evacuated on medical grounds. Now I was just interested to hear what she'd say to: "And what if she starts, like, dying down on the field?"

"If she starts having trouble, bring her up here and she can see a nurse. There's an emergency triage if she's in real danger."

I spoke to her directly now, not to the scrubs or the lab coat. "There really isn't anything you could do, is there?"

"No one knew how to prepare for this, and it's only getting worse. We're so overwhelmed, and not just in here, but across the whole City. No one is helping. The National Guard is getting worried about the safety of their people."

"Before the safety of us, is what you're saying . . ."

"Son, honestly, if you're mother gets sick, this first aid station may not be here. They'll probably be pulling us out of the stadium."

Nervously, I asked her, "Are the Army guys going to leave entirely?"

"I don't think so, but I don't know for sure."

"Wow . . . " Her words sunk in like dull blades. I made a quick gesture as if looking at my surroundings and said, "I hope they stay."

The woman spoke to me now like a parent, rather than a patient. "Don't worry, your mother will be fine. Go take good care of her. Stay together and you'll both be fine."

"Thank you, I will. Ma'am, I'm sorry that you're in here in this mess."

"Thanks, but I'm sorrier for you."

And with that, I walked away and back to the field, working over the things she'd said. If the Army abandoned the stadium, nothing could stop total hell on Earth. Meal time, water, food. If those things disappeared, I didn't want to imagine what came next. On my way back down I noticed that the soldiers had pulled back from their position at the thirty-yard line and departed from the playing field entirely. More people were on their way down to fill in the open space.

Upon returning to the group, Uncle G asked, "What did they say?"

"They can't help. They don't have anything to help us with. They don't know shit. I just hope they keep giving us water and food."

"If they don't, it's going to be a riot."

"A riot would be bad."

"Riot is coming," Jimena stuck the period at the end of our conversation.

Mother had nodded off while I was away. It made me smile to see her breathing rhythmically. She needed the rest if she was going to fight off her ailments. She had one arm around Klaus the hippo, her face hidden from the light by the other. Shortly after my return from the nurse's station, the boredom crept back. Again, I wished I had a book, or a newspaper, or anything at all to read. In a hotel at least they usually provide a Bible. And even though I'd read that book from cover to cover, I would happily have picked one up and started *In the beginning*. I wound up reading all of the ingredient labels on our MREs. I could not believe how much sodium they packed into those things. The entire contents of the package contained between three and four times the recommended daily allowance for that one mineral. No wonder the food dried me up and made me terribly thirsty. Even the pouch of fruit punch I drank contained high amounts of sodium. At least with the drink mix they could call it electrolytes. All of that salt may be harmless to young adults in the physical prime of their lives, people like, I don't know, soldiers, but most of these people were anything but soldiers, and anything but fit. For a man or woman on a special diet, perhaps with a heart condition, this food was as good as poison. So far, I'd enjoyed exploring the packages and tasting the variety of items therein, but from then on I'd be more careful about monitoring my salt intake. Mother's, too. With my full ration of two half-liter bottles of water, I still felt sluggish and bloated. The food seemed a likely culprit.

Uncle G had also nodded off. Jimena sat warming a half-bottle of water to make yet more coffee. I laid there with the little speakers pressed against my ears, trying to listen to some *Houses of the Holy* to pass the time, but with all of the ambient sound around me, I could hardly hear the music with the volume on full blast. I'd taken off my shoes and the artificial grass of the football field felt soft and damp under my feet. I wiggled my toes in it, dug them in deep. After playing around, the bottoms of my feet came up black. I inspected closer and found, to my amazement, artificial dirt in the artificial grass. Packed down under the close-cropped plastic grass were millions of tiny rubber pellets, nice cushioning for tackle football players. I collected about ten of the pellets—they were difficult to dig out of the grass—and rubbed them in my fingers. After letting them fall back to the turf, I noticed my fingertips had become gray. With nowhere to properly wash my hands, they stayed gray for the next couple of days.

Mother and Uncle G awoke. Jimena served up some coffee and said something to Mother in Spanish, to which Mother replied, "Oh my God, girl. Me, too."

"What did she say?" I asked.

"She said she wishes she had a cigarette to go with the coffee."

"Jimmy, do you have any money? I've seen a couple people selling cigarettes," I said.

"Ree-lee?" she replied with a smile. "Dee full box or one at a time?"

"I'll go find out." She handed me a five, a ten, and a one dollar bill. She said to get whatever I could, but to not let anyone rip me off. Simple enough instructions. I placed each of the bills in a separate pocket, so when it came time to negotiate, the seller wouldn't see the total sum I'd come to parlay with and try to haggle me for more. Sometimes you gotta be a gangsta, ya know?

I didn't have to walk far. Seated a couple blankets away, I spied a black woman about thirty years old, with intricately done-up hair and long, fake fingernails. She puffed on a cigarette, with two packs sitting between her bare feet. Next to her, two young children wearing bathing suits slept soundly. She seemed approachable enough, so I broke the ice.

"Hey, how's it goin'?"

"It's goin'."

"Word, I . . . I just wanted to ask if you maybe had any extra cigarettes you might want to sell."

"No, deez mine. But Shirl got some. Whoa! Shirl!" she shouted to another woman on a blanket nearby.

"Yeah, girl."

"Dis man lookin fo' some cigrettes."

Shirl sized me up and said, "C'mon nen."

I thanked my contact lady and walked over to negotiate with Shirl, a very thin woman with large eyes. Her tube top shirt revealed several faded tattoos, and she was missing one of her lower canines.

"You can sit down."

I sat. In a large plastic shopping bag covered by a blanket, Shirl had five cartons of a brand of cigarettes I'd never heard of and one carton of KOOLs. Shirl and the first lady I'd met were both smoking KOOLs, so I figured those were off limits. The other cartons were also green, so I asked, "All of those are menthol?"

"MmmHmm, how you wine up hea? You a hansome Spanish boy dat talk good. Why you in hea wit all us niggas?"

"Didn't leave when I was sposed to, ya' know?"

"Yes, in-fuckin'-deed, I woulda been out dis bitch! God damn, I woulda been out dis bitch!" her volume rising with each new exclamation.

"Right on, you, me, and everyone else. Look, I got five bucks. Will you sell me a pack of those cigarettes for five?"

"Hell no, da cigaress is mine."

A look of confusion must have crossed my face. She smiled, revealing that missing lower canine. "Da cigaress is mine, dem cigaws."

Nicotine withdrawal can only be countered by a ready source of nicotine, so I said, "Then, can I buy a pack of those cigars?"

"Fi' dollas?"

I slipped the bill from its assigned pocket. "Fi' dollas."

She had the pack in her hands, looked at it, and appeared to fight back a mute dry heave. "Baby, you can take two a dem fuh fi' dollas. Dey nasty as a mothafucka."

I dropped the bill in front of her while she opened one of the cartons and dug out two packs.

"Killer, thanks Shirl."

"MmmHmm, you welcome."

This was by far the best deal we'd get during our stay at the Dome. As our stay lengthened and supplies decreased, the price of a dollar per cigarette would become the common black market rate. None of that mattered just yet. Walking back to my family on the blanket, I examined my purchase. The box had a black top hat on it. In fact, they were called Top Hats. Top Hat Menthol 100s, to be precise. Returning to the blanket, I produced the two packs and eleven bucks. Uncle G returned the unspent money to his backpack.

Jimena inspected the boxes and said, "Is not Marlboro?"

"Gene, tell her we ain't at a motha fuckin' convenience store. Good work, baby. Two for five," Mother replied.

Obviously let down, Jimena tapped the top end of the box against the heel of her hand and tore open the cellophane. Inside were twenty long cigarillos in brown paper with yellow filters on the end. Though claiming to be menthol, they didn't smell the least bit minty. I touched the flame from my lighter and breathed in. Cough cough.

"This shit is awful." Ugh huch kuh Ahem, by the third drag the things became tolerable enough to puff on, but the smoke was so harsh that inhaling it was impossible. Despite the vile flavor, the Top Hats were doing the job. Halfway through and we were done. With the nicotine receptors in my brain sated, I stamped out the butt under the sole of my shoe. Thankfully, the artificial turf didn't burst into flames upon contact with the red embers.

Walking in the Grass

There were still a few hours until dinner. It was maybe a little after three o'clock. Everyone in the stadium was wide awake. I told my people that I felt like going for a walk. Despite being in my mid-twenties, my always overprotective mother pleaded with me to stay on the field and within sight.

"Okay, Mama."

It felt good to take long strides. The muscles in my legs were still tight from the uncomfortable night in the seats. The broad, white out-of-bounds stripes on the sidelines were almost universally clear of people and made a nice walking path. Upon reaching the end zone, I decided to make a left and walk across the back of the end zone, and then turn left again and go marching up the opposite sideline. By the time I returned to my starting point, I'd walked a three-hundred-plus-yard rectangle around the playing field. Deciding I was in no big hurry to be bored again on the blanket, I continued walking. By the third lap, I did return to the blanket to drop off my shoes, and continued walking my laps barefoot on the fake grass.

On my stroll, I saw there was a football game in progress. Like a real game, almost. Several younger guys, older teens and younger twenty-somethings had control of a twenty-yard section of the field with an end zone in front of them to score in. Nine-on-nine, they were playing full-tackle football, barefoot without pads. People on the field and in the stands would cheer and boo, depending on the action, and for about an hour and a half, a few hundred of them held their focus on a common interest. I realized then that one of the greatest problems facing the residents of the Superdome, myself included, was the overwhelming boredom. Thousands of people had been placed together with absolutely nothing to do. They say that idle hands are the devil's playground. Well, what about twenty thousand plus idle hands? Keep the football game going, organize a tournament, power on the P/A and give the mic to a pastor, a dizzy bat race. Anything would have been better than nothing. But nothing was what we had. Watching those guys play, I wanted so badly to run out there and ask if I could throw a pass to someone and participate in this one spark of community entertainment. But instead I saw myself as I surely must have appeared: a chubby hispanic guy with eyeglasses and a ponytail. On that field, my ass would have been slammed so hard into the turf I'd still be picking tiny rubber dirt pellets out of my teeth. Instead, I kept on walking my laps.

Then came maybe the most powerful thing I saw throughout the ordeal. The first couple hundred people to arrive at the Superdome walked into a moderately organized and decent set-up. They even had cots lined up for them. It's worth mentioning that by this phase of the adventure, I'd totally forgotten there'd been some big blob of bad weather named Hurricane Katrina, the lightning and booming thunder, the ghostly winds. That stuff happened to someone else. My life started yesterday around lunchtime when I slid off my roof. Since then it'd been a short life of brown water and brown MREs. This may sound silly, but I ask you, what's more terrifying? A whole bunch of thunder bursting while hunkered down in a hallway, or 20,000 turds on the ground?

A couple hundred people became tens of thousands overnight. Those cots were a prized item in the post-Apocalypse/*Mad Max* sort of reality we experienced. Army cots denoted seniority and prestige and comfort. Believe me, I wanted a cot.

Lined up against the padded wall that surrounds the playing field, down in the red zone where the seats press in close to the action, were two cots lined up end-to-end long ways against the padded wall. From one end of the double-length cot to the other, maybe fourteen feet of canvas, sat thirteen little black babies in a row, all pudgy and wearing only diapers. The oldest about two years, the youngest maybe nine months, old enough to sit up. Each baby looked overheated and uncomfortable, like they should be bawling and screaming their little baby heads off. But they were quiet. Not a single one of them cried. The whole row of them, all thirteen, they just sat in a row like little baby blobs.

Before them stood a black man in his thirties wearing a do-rag and an oversized, brightly colored Polo shirt. He stood there waving a piece of cardboard from a box that once held MREs.

Flap Flap Flap Flap.

The man kept a constant breeze blowing on the row of babies. Sweat poured down his face and into his eyes, his brightly colored shirt darkened with perspiration at the chest, back, and armpits.

Flap Flap Flap.

As long as I walked, he flapped that piece of cardboard, like a slave cooling a Sultan in the *Arabian Nights*.

Flap Flap Flap Flap.

Tireless, he continued for hours, fanning the row of unhappy babies. Never once did I see him stop, not to stretch his sore arms, not for a sip of water.

Flap Flap Flap.

I admire that man, then and now. His visage should be added to Mount Rushmore, as far as I'm concerned. He's a hero. He was saving infants' lives. And though his efforts likely have been forgotten, I remember. Sir, on behalf of those babies and of all mankind, I say, "Thank you." His perseverance has given me hope in my life that I could do the same, if the situation demanded it of me. Doing the right thing because it's what needs to be done, or dropping dead in the effort.

On and on, I walked around and around the field in giant rectangles. Every lap increased my stamina. I felt like I could walk around the field forever. My legs never felt stronger, blood pumped freely throughout my body. Perhaps it was the Army food, but I had strength I'd never had before. Lap after lap.

I passed this one old lady sitting on a cot pressed against another padded wall, right in front of the small flat section reserved for disabled fans to park their wheelchairs. Disabled or not, these parking spaces for mobile seats were closer to the actual playing field than any others in the stadium. Like ultimate seats. And before them, on the cot, the lady sat. An old white lady, her hair a deep, dark gray. She wore a long, plaid dress that must have been nearly as old as she was. The impression I got from her is that the only reason she was still living was because she just hadn't been fortunate enough to die yet, that she'd been ready and waiting since the water rose.

A handful of shopping bags were stacked on either side of her on the cot, protected from theft by her thin, feeble arms. An enormous pile of trash separated her from most of the other people on the field like a barricade. On her side of the pile, several adult diapers lay wadded up among the refuse. From what I could see, she had neither food nor water. To acquire those items, she was required to pass through the line. Otherwise, the Army would assume she was provided for. Walking through the line would mean leaving the cot. While in line, someone would surely make off with her cot. I saw people stealing each other's cots while they simply had their backs turned. Fistfights would break out over cots. She held onto the long crossbar under her knees with a white-knuckled grip, glaring at anyone who came close. Anyone who really wanted it could have easily just pushed her over and taken the cot, but she let everyone see that she would fight for her greatest possession in this world. Wherever she'd lived before, whatever the hurricane had taken from her, she wasn't going to leave this life lying on the ground in a pile of trash. She would fight for the dignity of dying while lying on a simple Army cot.

After many decades of living, this is what her life had become. As time passed, the pile of trash grew ever larger, and her place in this world shrunk. Despite her stern-set jaw and cold eyes, she didn't wipe the tears that streamed down her cheeks. By the time we were leaving the Superdome, days later, that pile of trash grew so large that it swallowed the entire section of wall she'd been sitting against, five or six feet high. The base of the pile occupied dozens of square yards. I wondered if she lay buried under all that mess, or if she'd evacuated her prized cot before the end.

In no way was this an isolated trash pile of great size or breadth. Multiple trash mountains dotted the field and corridors, large enough to consume many old ladies. What had been freestanding cans, these trash receptacles had overflowed into great, wide heaps of stinking garbage. To walk around the base of some took me twenty yards off course. The only trash we were creating was composed of cigar butts, water bottles, and MRE pouches. We hadn't had a chance to bring many personal items. A lot of people showed up with much less than two bags and a hippo. Other people brought everything they could carry from their homes, mostly clothes, odd pillows, cushions, bedding, and loads of baby gear. Day by day, more of these items were discarded along with large amounts of water bottles and MRE plastic and cardboard.

In hindsight, the trash piles were enormous tinder boxes waiting to go up. One arsonist could have burned down the whole stadium with the flick of a lighter and killed thousands of people. The Army was in no way prepared to fight a fire of that magnitude. If fire had come to the Superdome, I wouldn't be writing this now. Blankets with people on them and the surrounding mounds of trash covered so much of the field you could hardly tell it was green anymore. I thank God in Heaven that no fire broke out. Hundreds of people were smoking on the field, myself included. Yet nothing burned but tobacco and lung tissue.

Hours passed as I walked. The shafts of radiant white light beaming through the holes in the roof traveled across the playing field and high up into the stands. Very few people were sitting in the uppermost nosebleed level, but just like at every Saints game, a couple guys sat in the very last row at the top. The mid-level, the smallest section as far as number of seats, held many more people than the larger uppermost. The majority of people present occupied the lowest level of seats and the playing field.

Looking high above me as I walked, long banners inscribed with the iconic names Pete Maravich and Archie Manning were hung from the ceiling. Pistol Pete—the only reason a person might remember that the New Orleans Jazz NBA franchise ever existed. Archie Manning, "The New Orleans Saint," a hero to everyone, King of The Crescent City. Also, Dave Dixon, the original owner of the Saints. Another banner displays their division titles won in 1991 and 2000, respectively. As long as I can remember, the Saints have been part of my life. Deep in my childhood are embedded songs like "Bless You Boys" and "Who Dat" and "I Believe," names like Swilling, Johnson, Jackson, and Mills, better known as the Dome Patrol and that first appearance in a playoff wild card game in '87 and the crushing 44–0 loss to the Minnesota Vikings in that game. I was seven years old.

Also looming way up high on the stadium walls are mounted two Mitsubishi Diamond Vision screens. Installed in the early 90s, these two-story-tall LCD screens were the razor's edge of technology decades before nearly every home contained a flat screen television. Those Diamond Vision screens must have cost several hundred thousand dollars when new, if not millions. I walked my way up the field—the ten, the twenty, the twenty-five—*He's got some daylight, folks*—the *thirty-five, the forty—he's crossing mid-field, he could go all the way!*

I chuckled upon remembering a Saints game I attended with my dad and some of my uncles back on Christmas Eve in 2000. Sunday Night Football week seventeen action, the Rams were the enemy back then in the geographically absurd NFC West, before the NFL restructured the divisions in 2002. I coerced my beautiful Abuelita into sewing me a black and gold Santa costume for the prime-time broadcast: the red portion of Santa's suit done up in black, Santa's white trim in gold. She also made half a dozen extra Santa hats for the rest of the gang. We did some pre-game partying down in the New Orleans Centre building, just across the wide, brick walk path from the Superdome. I was totally wasted drunk before we even got into the stadium. A man in a gold blazer with a Saints emblem embroidered on the breast approached us to tell me my costume was fantastic. He asked us for our seat numbers. Costumes this good get put on television. Totally stoked about being on television, I jumped around and danced the entire first half. A couple minutes into the third quarter, my steam ran out. I sat down in my chair and passed out for fifteen minutes. That's what they showed on ESPN, that's what my Papi saw that night as he watched the game on television: a drunken, black and gold Santa snoring like an animal. I was twenty years old.

Thinking about Saints games, Tulane games, and the lame-ass Super Fairs they'd do every year, those were all good memories, great memories. I loved the Superdome and, in a lot of ways, I'd grown up in this building. Going to the Superdome, for whatever reason, was a special thing. Commuters pass the building every day. The structure is an integral piece of the New Orleans skyline. Passing a monolith of a building every day is one thing, but it's another when you get to actually go in there. Cheering and screaming for my team, tens of thousands of people all having fun for the same reason, that's what happens in the Superdome.

The things I saw while I walked, to me, felt all the more depressing because of *where* we were. Sick babies, sick elderly people, sick people of all ages. This building wasn't constructed to contain so much suffering. In all, I walked between twenty-five and thirty rectangles. I traversed that field six ways from Sunday.

Afternoon gave way to evening, and before too long it would be time to get in line for our evening rations. The sun was setting on the City of New Orleans, a city in great pain, a stadium in the throes of despair. The next time the sun's light kissed the Superdome, it would be shining on a different place. Tonight would alter everyone's plans, would change everything. Tonight, blood would be spilled.

July 25th, 2005: Klaus celebrated his third birthday just a month before the hurricane. Here he is being held, nice and dry, by his proud grandmother. Author's image.

Monday, August 29th, 9:50 am: The last drop of rain had fallen over an hour before on a "dry" street. This amount of water took an hour to collect. Remember the green van. Author's image.

Monday, August 29th, 4:40 pm: Roughly six hours from the previous shot, the water has risen from inches to feet. See the green van? Taken from my roof. Author's image.

Monday, August 29th, 7:25 pm: Just as the sun is disappearing, this image shows my truck and Uncle Gene's van flooded out on our sloped lawn. The last sliver of the green van's roof is visible. Author's image.

Wednesday, August 31st, Afternoon: Team 4899 Mandeville Street resting on Glenn's blanket. That's the face you get when you say, "Hey Mom" to a delirious Cecilia. Dolja and his phone cord leash and the snout of a musty hippo are also visible. Author's image.

Wednesday, August 31st, Afternoon: This picture shows the broad pathway between the Superdome and the New Orleans Centre building. Thousands of people would pack themselves into this space like sardines. This would become the path to freedom. Image courtesy J. Sterrett.

Thursday, September 1st, Morning: A corkboard mounted near one of the entrances to the Superdome. A last-ditch effort for people to leave some info for missing loved ones. Image courtesy J. Sterrett.

Thursday, September 1st: Yes, it's hard to look at. Can you imagine the smell? This is just one of dozens of stalls in one of dozens of bathrooms located throughout the Superdome. Image courtesy J. Sterrett.

Thursday, September 1st, Afternoon: Superdome campsites and the path to freedom. How many thousands of souls are jammed into the walk path, inching their way toward the rest of their lives one busload at a time? Image courtesy J. Sterrett.

Thursday, September 1st, Afternoon: Days after landfall, families are still making their way to the stadium. Image courtesy J. Sterrett.

Thursday, September 1st, Afternoon: National Guard troops arriving from neighboring states dressed in full battle kit and loaded for bear. Makes me wonder what they were really thinking they were walking into as they entered the stadium. Image courtesy J. Sterrett.

Friday, September 2nd, Afternoon: Via the rumor mill, word had spread that the President would be taking a helicopter tour of the city today. Eventually, this would read, "HELP BUSH GET US OUT OF HERE." What really gets me—then and now—is where did this woman get the chalk? I didn't find any chalk in my MREs. Author's image.

Friday, September 2nd, Afternoon: The smoke is coming from the fires we saw reflected off the skyscrapers the night before. This picture also shows the shady overhang between the stadium and the terrace—prime real estate. Arrow points to a "water buffalo" (military jargon), a five-hundred-gallon potable water container. The Superdome residents drained it in about fifteen minutes. Author's image.

Friday, September 2nd, Afternoon: Your author, loosened up after a cup of grog, proudly donning Jeanine's canvas bag for a cap and a handkerchief around my neck. Notice the discarded jug of Kahlua to my right. Author's image.

Friday, September 2nd, Afternoon: I took this picture not for what it shows, but for the memory I get from it. Directly below where I am standing on the stadium terrace is the body of a dead girl who floated her way to the base of the stadium. The same girl the bastards with the glass bottles were using for target practice. Author's image.

Friday, September 2nd, Evening: Food, water, pillows, cushions, blankets, and a cot—all Superdome acquisitions. As the number of people decreased, our comfort level increased. Who these items belonged to, we'll never know. Except, that is, for the food, water, and cot. Those belonged to Uncle Sam. Author's image.

Sunday, September 4th, 2:30 am: This is our Air Force plane unloading us at Fort Chaffee AFB in northwest Arkansas. In moments, we would re-board the plane and fly to Little Rock AFB in Jacksonville, Arkansas. Image courtesy J. Sterrett.

Mid-October 2005: Six weeks after sliding off of the roof, I returned to 4899 Mandeville Street to see what could be salvaged. The whole city reeked of mold and decay, and despite the hazmat suit and mask, the smell upon entering almost knocked me down. The wristwatch was set to go off every twenty minutes to remind me that I should not linger too long inside our beloved family home. Author's image.

WEDNESDAY
AUGUST 31ST, 2005

AFTERNOON

Ascent into Hell

The dinner line proved uneventful, just more of the same crowd and the same awful smells. It's interesting how quickly people can get used to something. Even when that something is as sad and gross as our surroundings were. The conditions in the concession corridor deteriorated by the hour. It reminded me of some kind of tropical cave, humid and sultry, pungent and poorly lit. Drops of condensation fell from pools of moisture on the low corridor ceiling overhead.

I'd spent most of the day hopped up on Army food, walking in circles. I sat on Glenn's blanket, hungry for more. They'd issued each of us three bottles of water this go-round. I took this as a good omen. I figured more water was a preliminary indication of better things to come, like an easing of the logistical strain beginning to show itself. A random guy on a nearby blanket said he thought the extra water meant that the Army would only feed us once a day from then on. I considered what he said, hoping he was wrong.

Not that going hungry concerned me. We'd saved the odds and ends from our previous MREs and certainly wouldn't starve. In my blissful naiveté, I still enjoyed tasting the different flavors of the meals. So far, the pork rib in BBQ sauce item definitely held the number one spot. I yearned to find more of the cafeteria-style, McRib-esque pork patties with the dumb black lines on them, as if this culinary abomination had ever seen an open-flame grill. Think what you will, I liked the filthy things. Dolja did, too. I used the sauce to get him to eat bread, even a little applesauce with crackers crushed in it. He'd eat anything with a little ketchup or barbecue sauce on it.

While the rest of the gang prepared coffee and chatted, I stretched out my legs and drank a bottle of grape flavored, powdered drink mix. Each MRE had some kind of drink mix inside, laden with caffeine and sodium: Kool Aid-type stuff in different flavors, tea, apple cider, or lemonade. The coffee came standard in all of the pouches. The fruit punch I'd gotten on the first night was my favorite, but I continually opened my meal bags to find another pouch of grape powder.

The radio still played nothing but static, so I tried to listen to some Led Zeppelin. Again I wished for something, anything, to read. Hours passed and evening eventually became night. I slipped away to find a place to pee. The bathrooms had become so foul that even passing near one of them started me to retching. There were plenty of shady spots around for a guy to relieve himself. I know how gross this sounds, but sanitation had totally given way to survival, and anything that brought a person into contact with those bathrooms ran totally contrary to any definition of the word survival. And, believe me, everywhere I went, someone else had gone there first. I started walking back to the group.

Stan and some new people were talking to Mother and the rest of the gang. I'd lost track of Stan. Remembering what he'd said earlier, I was surprised to see him down on the field. A balding, black man in his mid-fifties introduced himself as Angel. I'd met several angels out there on the high seas, and before me stood another, in more than just name. Angel struck me as a rock-solid guy, and he lived up to this premonition. He wore his hair—graying along the back and sides—pulled into a tiny button of a ponytail. He and Stan seemed to already be acquainted and talked like old friends. I wondered if Angel had been *on the farm* with Stan, but after a couple minutes of conversation I began to doubt that. Angel seemed like a real stand-up guy. He talked about coaching baseball, always referring to his team as "his kids." He hauled around scrap metal as a hobby and gave the money to his church, and he loved to fish. Also with him were a lovely café au lait-colored Creole woman named Becky and her son Isaac. The boy was about thirteen and had a very light complexion, many shades lighter than me. And though closely cropped, I could see the hair on his head was a deep shade of auburn. African American people with complexions this fair are not unheard of in New Orleans. The City has a long history of interracial love affairs. If you want to learn something interesting about New Orleans, enter the word *plaçage* into your search engine.

Becky, the mom, was very personable, and she and Mother got on like long-lost friends in no time at all. Stan brought this group to us with a purpose—more like an offer, actually. Stan and Angel were recruiting me for an expedition. They'd both returned from a journey through the upper levels of the stadium. I'd stepped only briefly onto the second level, but they said they'd been all the way to the top. And the farther they went, the weirder things got. Becky felt that her son needed to see what was really going on in the stadium. The situation, the whole mess of it, God willing, was a once-in-a-lifetime experience. The things happening here would never occur again in human history. Becky thought that Isaac, her only child now growing into a young man, would benefit from the exposure in the long run. Upon hearing her request, Stan said he thought about me right away. Even at the time, I knew I would want to write it into a book one day. I'd shared these thoughts with Stan up in the seats the night before.

"You won't believe the shit people are doing up there, man." Totally intrigued, I declared that I was in. Uncle G and Glenn declined. Jimena wasn't going anywhere potentially scarier than where we already were. Mother and Becky were talking each other's ears off. Mother told me that she'd like to go see some crazy shit with us, but didn't care for a long march with so many stairs.

"Tell me about it and be safe, baby," she said to me and returned to her conversation with Becky. I grabbed two Top Hats from our dwindling supply and joined my companions already climbing the stadium steps leading up to the concession corridor where we received our meals. From there we walked down a stalled escalator and into the main fan corridor, which wrapped around the exterior of arena space on the terrace level. Thousands of sweaty people filled the space from wall to wall. Several would shout above the crowd at random, exclaiming their frustrations to everyone, and no one at all. The National Guard received the lion's share of scorn over the state of affairs. The entire mass of people all seemed to be moving in no particular direction. No one stood still.

Angel led the way, followed by Isaac and me. Stan brought up the rear. Angel led us into one of what I've always felt to be the strangest features of the Superdome. I always called them the worm-ways or worm tubes; they're sloping tunnels that wind through the stadium in place of never-ending banks of escalators and stairs. To be sure, the stadium contains many stairwells and escalators, but the worm tubes provide a convenient alternative. The path, as wide as a small apartment, was definitely wide enough to drive a pickup truck or van through. The coolest thing about them is that they are completely carpeted, floor, wall, and ceiling. As kids, my cousins and I would play in the tunnels, tuck in our arms, and roll down the carpeted slope like Jacks and Jills. The carpet all around changed color and pattern the higher you went. Some orange and red, others blue and purple. Remember, the Superdome was built in the mid-70s, so the patterns of the carpet were funky, to say the least. Any truck or other vehicle attempting to drive through the worm-ways at this time would crush many dozens of people beneath its tires. The tunnels were filled with people who'd made their Superdome home here. Every time I moved my feet, I kicked someone else's foot, or had to step over an arm.

The air in the tunnels was heavy and impossibly still. The carpeted tunnels smelled nearly as bad as the bathrooms down below. The light around us faded to an oppressive gloom before we made it to the first turn. The tunnels were so ghastly dark it made walking through the lounging residents terribly hazardous. Instead of taking steps I shuffled my camo slippers across the carpet and waddled like a duck. Luckily, Angel had a small flashlight in his pocket. It cast a dim, yellow light as we advanced, its intensity similar to a single fluorescent glow stick. The yellowish light played with the shadows of the scores of mole-people living in the tunnel.

Many of the people we saw looked aged to the point of downright ancient. One old woman lay on a mat like a kindergartner might use for naptime. With every breath, her entire being wracked with heaving coughs. Two old men lay side by side on the carpeted floor. I couldn't tell whether they were breathing at all. Just past them, two small children napped on a beach towel at their mother's feet.

The smell of rotten urine all but overpowered me as we continued our climb. I wouldn't have long to wait before finding the source of the smell. At our next turn, in a flat spot, I felt the carpet soaking wet beneath my slipper-shod feet, and our dim light played on the surface of puddles that had formed and submerged the carpet. We'd discovered the bathroom of this worm tube. Mixed with toilet paper and feces, I saw an enormous puddle of the yellow nacho cheese sauce leaking from a torn plastic bag. White maggots crawled among the whole mess. I dry heaved and continued following Angel's light.

The true darkness closed in the higher we went. I pulled out my cigarette lighter and gave it a flick every so often to supplement the dim glow of Angel's light. The bright flash of white sparks created when I'd flick my Bic appeared all the more brilliant in the blackness of the tunnels. To the mole-people residing in the worm-ways, this proved totally unacceptable. Shouts of "Quit that shit" were followed by "What the Hell ya'll doin' in hea anyways?" "Flick dat lighter again and you liable to get fucked up." Quickly, the lighter found its way back into my pocket.

Farther on, I heard some grunting, moans, and labored breathing emanating from the blackness ahead. Muh uuh mmh uuuh. Moments later, we came upon an incredibly fat man squatting down, taking a shit right on the carpet. It sounded like he, too, was having trouble passing his Army food. Mere feet away, two people were having sex on the ground, modestly covered by a white bedsheet. I couldn't tell from which party the grunting originated, maybe a little of both.

The entire scene there in the worm tubes, to me, felt like walking through a black and white piece of World War II refugee camp footage. The misery here was real, palpable. The oppressive darkness of the tunnels only reinforced this image. Life in the worm tubes made our spot down on the field seem posh by comparison. I have to believe that many of the people sitting in those dark tunnels had been, or would be, there for days. A walk through the worm tubes truly felt like a glimpse of the end of the world. We continued on through the tunnel. I wondered if it would ever end. Much to my relief, there was light ahead, real light coming from the second-level concession corridor. Upon exiting the worm tube, Isaac and I began sucking in the fresher air, much to Stan's amusement.

"Enjoy that? We're just getting started."

After the prolonged sensory deprivation/olfactorily overwhelming journey through the miserable tunnels, I couldn't imagine what could possibly be worse, but Stan seemed very sure of himself. Stan never struck me as a man to embellish in tall tales. Isaac and I caught our breath and continued on the tour. The mid-level concession corridor is much narrower than the main one below, but the conditions were much the same, if not worse. People were lying in the hallway at random, and the bathrooms were just as wretchedly foul. I noticed more people were arguing with one another up here. The tension was much stronger. On the lower level where we hung out, in both the concession corridor and the larger main entry corridor, armed soldiers walked among the crowd in twos, threes, and fours. No soldiers patrolled this level. I held little faith that the next level up would be any better. After walking around the corridor for a few minutes, we resumed our climb. Angel led us to a stairwell, which we ascended for a flight or two. He pushed open a door, and we stepped into a part of the stadium I'd never been in before. I soon realized why.

We'd entered a white hallway lined with red doors. It looked more like an office building or a hotel than part of a football stadium. The only light came from the glow of red EXIT signs above some of the doors. The air in the hallway reeked of tobacco, marijuana, and crack cocaine. Yes, I know what crack smells like. I'm from New Orleans, after all. Crack and coke are like another tourist attraction, right up there with *beignets* and *crawfish étouffée*. Along with the strong smell of drugs were the more familiar smells of feces and urine.

A guy staggered past me and into the stairwell clutching a nearly full bottle of whiskey. Another guy, to my right leaning against the wall, sipped from a bottle of gin—a full liter, and not cheap stuff either. Crushed beer cans littered the floor. I'd seen a few people passing bottles out in the second-level concession corridor. As we passed an open red door, I dared to look inside. Carpet, couches, and glass chandeliers. I couldn't believe my eyes. The next door revealed the same thing. This room looked empty, so we walked inside. Sure enough, these were the luxury suites. For the first time in my life, I stood in one of the coveted skyboxes. This one had been ransacked early on, from the look of it. The tiny one-person-at-a-time bathroom had shit pouring out far into the room. More crap lay piled behind the wet bar. Broken glass and the broken television set told me that any alcohol in this room had been removed long ago. Lots more crap in the living room. This suite had become some kind of community toilet.

"Come look at this," Stan said. He'd found a guy curled up like a baby, asleep on the cushionless couch.

Back into the red light of the hallway a couple doors down, we came across two younger guys, late teens or early twenties, taking turns kicking the door of a still-sealed virgin room. Clump Bump Clump Bump. They both looked worn out for the effort, but alas, the door remained tightly shut. As I lit my first Top Hat, Stan said, "Dumb Fucks, you're workin' too hard."

The two guys stopped kicking and looked at him like they meant to kill whoever had cursed at them so casually. Stan stood at least five inches taller than either, and weighed as much as both of them combined, solid muscle. They took a step back. One found the balls—or brains—to ask, "Wha chu talkin' bout, man? Tha do' wone fuckin' open."

"If you can't go through the door, look . . ." Stan jumped up and tapped the corner of a square tile in the low-hanging ceiling. It moved. "Go over it."

They both nodded. One guy boosted the other up and over. Within seconds, the door opened from the inside. The two guys closed the door in our faces. We turned to leave. I'll never forget young, pale as can be, little mulatto Isaac looking at Angel and saying, "Just like some niggas. Didn't even say 'thank you.'" Angel paused to nod and smile at the boy in the dim, red glow of the EXIT signs. Every dozen steps brought us to another opened suite. Along with beer cans and broken glass, there were a handful of syringes on the ground. When we entered the stadium, I know that our bags were searched and I got frisked thoroughly. I assumed that the drugs being consumed had entered the building via one body cavity or another.

Proceeding around another curve of the hallway brought us face-to-face with two tall, muscular black guys. One wore sunglasses. They stood blocking the last four or five doors before the dead-end of the hall. The doors beyond the two sentries were open wide. About a dozen men and women passed bottles, cigarettes, and pipes in the hall. A cacophony of voices boomed out from the open doors. I think we'd found Party Central; the *raphe nuclei*, the pleasure center of the great organism's brain. The guy with the sunglasses displayed a hard, cold countenance. The other guy looked younger and was one of those people whose big teeth make it look like they're always smiling. He smiled us over from head to toe and said, "Get outta here, y'all. Dis ain't fo you."

"You cool, man; we cool. We just movin' through," Angel said. "I don't give no shit about what you young punks do."

"The fuck he say?" Finally the mute with the sunglasses spoke.

"He said that we're leaving. Calm down, dog," Stan said, straightening himself up, showing the two fellas how little he was intimidated by either one of them.

Personally, I didn't want to get stabbed or beaten to death in the scariest hallway on the planet. Things here were worse than the Carter Apartments in *New Jack City*. Way worse. This was no time for a brawl. The hoard of junkies was stirring. They'd caught wind of the exchange. The odds looked grim. Three men and a boy versus a hallway full of crack-heads.

Stan and the sunglasses guy stood about a foot apart. You couldn't cut their stares with a knife. Shit was tense. I looked over at Isaac. His eyes were huge; he looked petrified by fear. I put my hand on his shoulder; he flinched. Squeezing a little tighter, he turned his face. There were streaks of tears on his cheeks. He didn't want to die either. I moved him over and he took a step toward me. I positioned myself between him and whatever was going to happen next under the red lights in this narrow hallway.

"Nigga, that man ain't done nothing to you," the smiling guy said to his companion.

"I just wanna bring this boy back to his mother in one piece," Angel said. "I know you bad, bruh, but you know you got a mama out dea' somewhere."

Still staring at Stan through his glasses, the guy said, "Old man, get this kid and this white mothafucka outta hea before I kill somebody."

"Yeah, get this lil nigga outta hea. Dis ain't fo you, lil nigga," chimed in the smiling guy.

Stan took a step back, and then another. The four of us stepped into the next EXIT door, opened it, and went inside. That was close. I felt myself shiver as the rush of adrenaline swam through me. Angel pulled out his light. It was dark as hell. The stairs in the Superdome were mostly concrete. This high up, all the stairs were metal grating. The clang of our footsteps on the metal in the near-empty stairwell echoed off the close walls, creating an eerie sound. I could hear other footsteps from above and below, but couldn't see the people. Up and down, I saw only black nothingness. Ahead of us, the faint, red glow of another EXIT sign. Rather than ascend or descend, we chose door number three. Pushing our way in, we found ourselves in another hallway of luxury suites. Angel said if we moved through, we'd get to a different set of frozen escalators that would take us back to the worm tubes. Isaac said he was done with worm tubes. I had to agree with him on that sentiment.

"Alright, we go to the seats. Go that way instead," Stan said to Angel.

"Still gotta fine nem escatalas to get off dis chea' level dough," Angel retorted. "We gonna juz walk tru. Stan, don't be stoppin' ta talk ta nobody."

A guy sitting in the hall asked if I had another cigarette. I did have one more, but told him, "No." Instead, I offered him the last inch or so of the Top Hat I'd been nursing. He looked at the brown paper and long yellow filter and asked, "Dis weed?"

"Naw, man. Just a little cigar." I replied.

"Hmpf," he snorted. "Sho look like weed."

He took a deep drag on the filter and his eyes got real big as he inhaled. Immediately, he started coughing like he was going to die. I watched him coughing and had to smile.

"What da fuck you smoke, man? That shit nasty," he said in between gasps for air.

"Yeah, you right. Throw it away if you don't want it," I told him.

"Nuh, nuh, nuh. I ain't gonna tro' it away. Na." He hit it again and started another round of coughing.

We left him there with his Top Hat to asphyxiate and made our way through the white corridor with more red doors. More people were lying on the ground in this hallway, but there was less broken glass. The takeover here had been less savage. We found the dead escalator, but Stan and Angel were conversing and continued down the corridor. Isaac and I had no choice but to follow. Ahead in the corridor, where it would dead-end like in the other hallway, someone had busted the last EXIT sign over the fire escape stairs. The end of the hallway was shrouded in near-total blackness. Faint light emanated from the open doorway—flickering candles, I assumed. Angel stopped walking. "Jus wait hea, na." Isaac and I stopped, too. Stan moved on ahead into the shadows.

After a moment, Isaac turned to Angel and asked, "What's he doin' now? He gonna get us killed."

"Naw, we been tru hea bafoe. Dem pimps. Dey done took ova dis whole haw-way."

Isaac's eyes grew wide, "For real Unk? They pimpin' hoes in tha' Superdome!"

Under our breath, we all laughed at that one.

Stan came back a moment later. "You were right, Jelly, price went down."

Angel slapped his knee and gave a hoot, "I tole you, nigga! C'mon na, tell me. How much?"

"Forty dollas to fuck," Stan replied matter-of-factly.

"Yes indeed. Hooo-woo fowty dollas, yes in-fuckin-deed. You ready? Go 'head on young man, my treat."

His knees buckled under him, and for a moment I thought Isaac was going to faint right where he stood.

"Maybe next time, Jel," Stan said with a smile. "Unless Bruce here has some money he wants to spend."

"Naw, yeah, yeah Stan. I'm straight. Maybe next time."

"Alright man," Stan said, slapping me on the shoulder.

"Come on wit it na," Angel said to Isaac, snapping him out of the trance he'd sunk into.

Unbelievable, I thought. In the red glow of an EXIT sign, we'd found the *red light district* of the Superdome. We turned back in the hall, made our way back up the escalator, and then ducked into another staircase. Stan led us farther upwards, toward the nosebleed seats.

The uppermost concession corridor had never seen, and would never see, a patrol of police or soldiers. People on this level would have to travel down many stairs or dead escalators to get their food and water ration. The use of any stairs in the stadium was a total ordeal in itself. The stairwells were roads, and the corridors they connected teemed 24/7—like an old black-and-white newsreel showing a busy train station in the 20s. A trip from up here down to the main corridor where we received our food, plus standing in line for that food, could easily take more than three hours. Definitely a rough place to set up a residence in the Dome.

It didn't take me long to realize that the people up here had climbed this high in order to put as much distance as possible between themselves and any semblance of authority. No boots treaded here. This was the Wild West. If there were a lot of people doing drugs down by the luxury suites, then this uppermost level served as the repository for all the straight-up junkies. People just sat in the corridor smoking their glass crack pipes so casually, I really had to do a double-take.

Since we were up so high and the climate control for the building was out of service, it was noticeably hotter up here. The rising hot air created a sauna on this level. Most men were shirtless, many women wore only their bras on top. Everybody I saw looked miserably hot and in desperate need of a shower. Don't get me wrong, I needed a shower, too. This was Wednesday night, and I had last washed myself Saturday afternoon. I felt gross, but these people just exuded body funk from every pore. I tasted a bit of that funk with every breath I took.

Stan led us through the corridor and out toward the seating area. This high up and this far out, the seats could only be reached by crossing one of several catwalks that spanned a great chasm below. The Superdome is as tall as a thirty-story skyscraper. The fall from one of these catwalks was a straight drop of over sixty feet to a behind-the-scenes service corridor wide enough for two big pickup trucks to pass each other.

Most areas in the stadium were terribly dark, but the service corridor down below was lit up like Times Square. Except for the playing field, these behind-the-scenes areas received the lion's share of the available electricity.

Looking down at the gray concrete floor many stories below, I saw that someone had taken the plunge. Whether this person, this man, had been pushed or jumped on his own, I'll never know. However he got down there didn't make him any less dead. The man's body lay mangled and twisted, a streak of red blood pooled by his head. This was the first corpse I saw in the stadium. It wouldn't be the last.

I ignited the last Top Hat I had on me and took a deep drag of the putrid smoke. I'd never seen a dead person outside the proper confines of a funeral home. I could only empathize with the person. If ever there was a setting conducive to suicide, the Superdome was it. All I could do was keep smoking and move on.

Past the catwalk, we stepped out into the nosebleed seats and took in a bird's-eye view of the stadium. Isaac and I spotted our respective mothers down on the field and tried waving to them, but they were engrossed in conversation and took no notice of what was happening high above their heads. We found a row of empty seats and sat down while Angel and I shared the little brown cigar. Stan closed his eyes as if he were about to take a nap. Twenty or thirty minutes later, we got back on our feet and went back more or less the way we'd come. We crossed the great canyon on a different catwalk. Down below, I could still see the body of the jumper, but someone had draped a white sheet over his body. The area of the sheet closer to his head was already saturated in red blood. It struck me that someone, one of the soldiers I presumed, had taken the time to cover the corpse and not just move it out of sight. But the whole City had been destroyed, they couldn't just load him up in a van and take him over to the coroner. And so the body stayed there on display for all to see.

The catwalk we crossed was crowded with people. The one we used on the way up had a person or two lounging on the open-grated path, but this one held many more. I'll never forget the go-to-hell look a woman with short gray hair gave me as we passed her on the catwalk. She saw me watching her as she hit her crack pipe. She looked up from what she was doing, and for a moment her cloudy, yellow eyes met my own. If looks could kill, that would have been a shot straight through the heart.

Back down the central escalators we went, all the way down. Finally, the four of us arrived back on our own level, but instead of walking straight to the field and over to our people, Stan and Angel had one last stop for us on our grand tour of the organism and its many organ systems. They led us through the main exterior corridor, where we'd started hours ago, through the turnstiles and glass doors, out into the night.

The scene outside was unlike anything I'd ever seen before. Worse than anything I'd ever seen on television or in movies. Passing through those glass doors, and out onto the brick terrace that surrounds the exterior of the Dome, I walked into another world, another reality, another America. I can think of nothing in my knowledge of History to compare it to. Perhaps a mixture of a 19th century bread riot, a heavy metal mosh pit, and roughly ten to fifteen percent of the Old Testament. You know, the good parts.

Imagine blinding light and absolute darkness, inhumanity layered atop a canvas of violent boredom. The terrace around the stadium as wide as any four-lane highway, including the shoulders. The four-lane highway circling the exterior of the building like Saturn's rings. About a lane's width overhung by the Dome's superstructure, the rest exposed to sun and sky. A night that is cloudless and dark as pitch. The entire City as dark as pitch beneath a thin, waning moon—not much more than a fingernail.

The soldiers had erected a tower of scaffolding at the far end of the terrace, width-wise, across from the doors we'd walked through. The tower commanded a line of barricades, manned by soldiers, all fully armed. Beyond the battle line is the wide walk path that connects the Superdome to the New Orleans Centre Building. The multi-level open atrium of the New Orleans Centre is where I'd pre-gamed with my dad and uncles while dressed as black and gold Santa Claus. The wide path was empty. The soldiers had attached two floodlights to the tower, as powerful as they were massive. These were real U.S. Military search lights bolted up there. The tower stood about twenty-five feet tall. From where I stood, just outside of the entrance to the stadium itself, the tower loomed large across the terrace, more than fifty feet away. At this distance I could see the full throw of the lights as they spread across the crowd on the terrace. The space in between me and the tower was jam-packed full of people, mostly shirtless black men. Their skin, slick and shiny with sweat, would catch patches of the bright white light on a shoulder, a neck, a raised arm, the white of an eyeball, or a set of teeth. Initially, I thought of a rock concert, but in reverse—the light shining on the crowd, rather than on the band. Soldiers moved in shadow along the tower, the stage. From their vantage point, the crowd was illuminated.

Hundreds, if not thousands, of people gathered before the barricade, bathed in the light from the tower. Much like the people inside the building, no one appeared capable of standing still for even a split second. The way the light played on the naked skin of so many people gave the entire mass a writhing, almost monstrous, appearance. Like a million eels trapped in a kiddie pool.

Many, if not most, of the people out here were fighting one another. Not at all like the big rumble at the end of *The Outsiders*, but in pairs: one-on-one. I studied the crowd and decided that there was absolutely no method to the fighting. No ugly words or anything like that. One guy would just take a swing at the guy next to him, and then it was on. The crowd cheered and screamed at every punch. Granted, these weren't fights to the death, just an exchange of blows until one guy fell. By that time another fight had broken out, and the bystanders' attention would immediately draw to them. And on and on and on it went.

No single champion emerged from the masses. There would be no title bout. The combatants took their licks and moved on to the next battle. The crowd was revolting out there beneath the Army's floodlights. I didn't feel like hitting anybody, but you better believe I was on my guard. At any moment, I expected someone to take an arbitrary swing at me. The fights would start so randomly that it felt like nowhere was safe. And though we stood well away from the epicenter of the brawling, I worried that the crowd would just suck me in and start beating me. Even back by the doors, far away from the rays of the Army lights, an occasional swing started an outright duel.

Members of the fairer sex were not uninvolved in the mayhem. Some of the most vicious fights I saw took place between women. When the guys would throw down, lack of space to brawl kept the fights short and violent. The half-dozen fights that included women caught the attention of everyone nearby. People made room and cheered on the amazons as they kicked, scratched, and pulled one another's hair. One girl ripped off another's hair weave. For this, the hair puller got jumped by three lithe, lean, hood rat chicks. The trio of them stomped the girl so hard that some men from the crowd actually broke it up, the only such instance I witnessed of people intervening to end a fight.

Poor little Isaac could only stare, mortified by the spectacle before him. He'd positioned himself snugly between Stan and Angel. I simply couldn't believe what I was seeing. Stan seemed highly amused as we watched brawl after brawl begin and end. In the short time I'd known the man, I hadn't seen him smile this big before. Angel had started talking to some of the other bystanders. They said this madness started as soon as the sun went down, that the fights had been going on for hours.

And you may be asking yourself, "A thousand-man fistfight directly in front of Army soldiers? Why didn't they go and break up the fighting?" It's the freakin' United States Army, *Be All You Can Be* and stuff. They all wear polished boots and matching outfits. They're armed to the teeth. Why not step in and stop the madness? I'll tell you why. Because they were scared. I mean no disrespect to our nation's military; I'm not talking about courage. I'm talking about the scale of the situation. Think about it militarily. They're outnumbered three thousand to one, if you consider everybody in the stadium. A high percentage of the population is overtly verbally hostile toward their presence, even though they are issuing them food and water. I looked at one of them, probably a nineteen-year-old kid, clutching an assault rifle, surrounded by people who are supposed to be red-blooded Americans like himself. He'd been sent to keep them safe, and the masses are blaming HIM for all their present woes. Right before his eyes and the eyes of his comrades, these people, these fellow Americans, are beating the snot out of one another.

The soldiers remained behind their barricade. They never stepped in: they just let the crowd of people beat each other—fighting for no other reason than that the person standing next to them was just as frustrated as the next person in the crowd. Hell, it was Army spotlights that gave the crowd enough light to fight by. In my estimation, the soldiers were anticipating a full-scale code red or code blue, whatever they call a big-ass RIOT. Fear emanated from that silent tower. The soldiers carried M-16 style rifles. To my knowledge, there's no non-lethal way to shoot somebody with one of those. If anything, the bullet would probably pass through the intended target person and maybe five more before flesh and bones stopped the bullet's flight. The crowd was so densely packed with angry humans. If the three-dozen soldiers behind the wall opened fire, hundreds of people would go down, possibly including me. I do believe they would have started throwing lead if the crowd's hostility toward them became more than verbal out there on the terrace that night. The Army's presence was now merely a sideshow. They had lost control of the Superdome. The soldiers held their collective breath with the safety on. They'd lost the stadium momentarily, but they weren't going to allow themselves to get beaten into the ground by a mob of New Orleanians.

What started three days before as a weather event had devolved into a peacekeeping mission, like Mogadishu with flooded streets.

Time itself ticked differently out on the terrace. We'd been out there for at least half an hour, but with the excitement and pumping adrenaline, my senses told me I'd only been out there for a few minutes. Our entire journey thus far through the stadium felt like a half-hour in duration, but the watch on Stan's wrist told us we'd been pioneering for nearly three hours. The four of us re-entered the building. The melee showed no indication of stopping anytime soon, better that we leave it to the professional fighters.

Once back inside the larger outer corridor, I began to notice the physical effects the grand brawl outside was having on the populace. Every direction I looked, I spotted someone bruised or bleeding. Swollen eyes and busted lips were most common. A couple of people walked around with large gashes to their heads, blood running down their faces and staining the collars of their shirts, if they wore shirts at all. One guy with a large cut on his forehead had stuck several squares of MRE toilet paper to his head in order to suppress the bleeding. He looked pretty comical, despite obviously being in a lot of pain. What a biological nightmare this place had become. Pee and shit puddled everywhere, and now dozens of untreated open wounds, blood dripping on the ground wherever these individuals happened to go. The risk of contracting an infection in these conditions must be insanely high, a nasty pathogen's dream come true.

Along with the bruises, lacerations, and the other wounds so many displayed, I noticed some people were carrying items even more alarming. Remember the exclusive and sought after Army cots? The single most prized item issued by the United States military to the people of the Superdome? Now the people of the Superdome were dismantling the cots, tossing the canvas aside and arming themselves with crude clubs fashioned from the aluminum legs and support bars. Most of these club wielders moved through the corridor solo. Some of the clubs had already been proven in battle, red blood drying on their ends. One gang of about eight guys passed in front of us, all clutching their blunt objects.

A swing from any one of them would probably be enough to kill someone, or at least put them in an extended coma.

The walking wounded with their improvised bandages and aluminum clubs: those are the images I've taken from that walk through the corridor. The night of a thousand fights, no love or respect for one's neighbor, and the Army on its heels. Those are the images I took from the battlefield on the terrace, coupled with the drugs and sex on the upper floors, and all within a stadium containing tens of thousands of people. The stadium was no longer an organism or refugee camp. It had become a powder keg just waiting for a spark to set it off. And every bottle of spirits that made its way out of the luxury suites and down the throats of the frustrated, club-wielding residents brought the match and the fuse closer to ignition. We wouldn't have much longer to wait. The spark was on its way.

In hindsight, I am enormously thankful that my companions and I made it back from this sojourn in one piece. Maybe a little foot-sore, but intact and breathing, without a contusion between us. Stan and Angel, our guardians throughout the expedition, had made good on their pledges to Becky and Cecilia, and returned Isaac and me safely to our respective mothers. I sat on Glenn's blanket, kicked off my shoes, and asked Jimena for two Top Hats, lit one, and gave the other to Angel. He smoked and laughed as he told Becky how Isaac's jaw dropped when he told him he would be next at the brothel. Becky smiled as he spoke, watching her son out of the corner of her eye. Mother smiled, too, but the raucous vibe of the ladies' conversation upon our departure seemed very much subdued compared to before. If something was up, and I felt there certainly was, I'd hear about it soon enough. After the story had been retold, Angel and Stan bid us farewell and left the playing field to return to the seats.

Little did I know, that would be the last time I'd see my buddy Stan. By simply being there, he'd made a strong impact on my group and me. He didn't exactly do anything special, but I would never have gone on that journey without him, and our group wouldn't have adapted to the life in the stadium so easily after our arrival the previous evening. Stan, wherever you are, thanks.

WEDNESDAY
AUGUST 31ST, 2005

NIGHT

A Thousand Throat Scream

Reclining on Glenn's blanket, I laid Dolja across my stomach and scratched behind his big radar-dish ears, reclined my head on the bag containing Klaus the hippo, and smoked my cigarillo. The pickup game farther down the field had ended, the open space had filled with more people and their belongings. Midnight wasn't far away, and most of the crowd had begun to settle down for another night in the Superdome. For many others, the night had just begun.

"Glenn, if you don't mind, show Bruce that thing you did with the dog," Mother asked. "That shit is too funny."

Judging from the way Jimena rolled her eyes, I knew this had to be good.

"No, Cessy. Is disgusting," Jimena protested. But by then it was too late.

All Glenn did was extend his left arm, his hand closed in a fist. Immediately, Dolja jumped off my lap, mounted Glenn's arm, and started humping. The dog was tearing that arm up! Uncle G and Mother cracked up laughing. I laughed, too. Jimena could only scowl.

"Oh no, he's at it again," chuckled Becky as she stroked Isaac's hair. The boy had laid his head down in her lap and fallen asleep almost as soon as we'd returned from our exploration. The kid had seen a lot that night. I think he'd overloaded some of his circuitry. I felt myself let out a couple of yawns. Other than the power nap I'd taken earlier that morning, I remained far from officially caught up on sleep.

After a minute or so, Dolja lost interest in Glenn's arm and curled himself up by Mother's feet.

"Aww, he's worn out. B, you shoulda seen the load he shot earlier," said Glenn.

"Oh my . . ."

Glenn smiled, "It's a good thing they have those handi-wipes in the MREs."

"Y'all are so crazy. C'mon baby, wake up," Becky roused Isaac from his sleep. "C'mon, we're going back up to the seats for the night. There's too much room down here for these people to act crazy. Anyway, we're getting out of here tomorrow, so let's try to get some rest."

Intrigued, I asked, "You're leaving tomorrow?"

"Hope so. First person I see with the Bureau, me and my son are gone."

"Ummm . . . What?"

"Becky works at that big building on the Lakefront," Mother said.

I knew the FBI building on Lake Ponchartrain. It's less than a mile from the University of New Orleans, where I'd gone to college for the preceding five years.

"Yeah, I know the FBI building. Are you in some, like, deep cover-type shit? Because I knew you were too smart to be in here."

"So are you, and no. But let's say Danny Smith and the Bureau owe me one."

"Holy shit. You're for real, too."

"I'm for real."

"She's for real," Isaac said, rubbing his eyes as he sat up.

"Wow."

"Bruce, she's going to call Mommy and Papi in Florida to let them know where we are," Mother said, taking my hands in hers.

"Someone will call them. I got the number," Becky said and tapped her purse for reassurance.

I couldn't pass up the chance, I had to ask, "Okay, so . . . you're going to get evacuated tomorrow. We'd really like to get out, ya know. Maybe we could tag along?"

Mother frowned and shook her head.

Becky said, "Baby, I wish I could. Shit, I don't even really know if the Bureau is gonna help us. But I tell you this, I'm gonna make 'em."

"She's a good woman. She wants to help us, Brucey."

Mother's eyes welled up in tears at the thought of my grandparents in Florida, a thousand miles away and worried to death about what must surely be on a television station somewhere. No doubt they were watching. Anyone with a grandmother, especially an Abuelita, knows how desperately emotional they're prone to becoming during times of crisis. Mine is no exception. In my mind's eye I saw her beautiful brown face twisted in pain, big alligator tears and the endless mantra of lamentations, pet names, and prayers. I squinched my eyes and felt the tingle in my sinuses. Blinking away the rush of the moment, I looked around at the piles of trash surrounding me, thought of the junkies in the worm tubes, and decided: fuck that. I'm glad Grandma's crying on Aunt Helen's couch in Florida and Papi is there with her. They don't need to be here. My God! I'd rather spend the rest of my life in here than to have my incredible and awe-inspiring grandmother look at this place once with her waking eyes. Not for a split millisecond. But if they got word that we were okay, or that we were alive at least, that knowledge might help alleviate some stress.

"Son, you and your family need to stay together, and someone'll get y'all out of here and back to your family. Just stay together. I'm going to get my family out of here if I can. You're gonna need each other. C'mon now, let's go find us a seat."

Both Mother and I stood up and gave her a hug goodbye. Isaac and I shook hands like men. "Look after your mom, man," I said.

"Like she would let that happen. Peace out."

And with that, they were gone.

With them and Stan and Angel gone, the only thing to do was wait out another night and get in line for breakfast. However, before my gang could rest, they wanted more coffee. They regretted that they'd already drunk up all of the packets we'd been issued. And here, Glenn spoke up and saved the day. He said he couldn't stand the instant coffee, but he'd been collecting them like souvenirs to do God knows what with at a later date. He surrendered his collection to us, nine little red packets of freeze-dried coffee. He'd eaten the accompanying sugar straight from the tiny brown packs. No problem there. Hard-core hispanic coffee people don't need no stinkin' sugar. My mother leaned over and kissed him on his unwashed, sour-smelling cheek. Coffee to go around. The world was safe again. I stretched out my tired legs and stared up at the ceiling.

The sounds of the crowd, the calls and loud talking over distances, the squeals of children, squeals of joy and pain, the hum of thousands of conversations and shuffling feet. I closed my eyes and listened to the heartbeat. Nuzzling the dog, eyes closed, I let my mind project a slideshow for me. Pictures. Memories. I hadn't taken the time to consider everyone else. Papi and Abuelita were safe in Florida. I knew that much, and that was fantastic. I'd spoken to most of my friends before they'd evacuated. They'd all scattered to points across the state, most to nearby Hammond and Baton Rouge. I wondered if Baton Rouge was under water, too. My dad and his crew were definitely out of the City, but not that far away. I thought of Simone, holed up in a police station somewhere worried to death, wondering if her daughter was safe. But there were so many other family members and extended family members and friends I hadn't spoken to and didn't know about.

My eyes snapped open. The stadium was still there and I was still in it. The holes in the roof were still there, and I was still beneath them wearing the same clothes I'd put on Sunday morning, sitting on a dingy comforter that wasn't mine, sitting on the twenty-five-yard line of the mother fuckin' Superdome! All those guys and girls were probably in hotels with air conditioning and clinking ice cubes around in their drinks, or at the homes of friends and relatives.

I'd seen a camera crew walking through earlier. They didn't stay long, but the thump thump thump of helicopter blades could occasionally be heard through the holes in the roof. Then the realization hit me. This whole mess was probably being televised. My friends and family were watching, wondering where I was, or if I was even alive. We tried to use Jimena's cell phone several times, but couldn't get a signal. Neither could anyone else in the stadium who we spoke to. A non-resident reading this a decade later might be saying "Duh! No shit it's being televised." The networks didn't show anything else for days, but we were so cut off from any kind of media, I had no way of knowing that hourly updates were being furnished by the likes of Anderson Cooper and Geraldo Rivera. In our contemporary wi-fi based society, being totally cut off from the outside world sounds like madness. To hell with satellite communication. If I couldn't see it in front of my face, it didn't exist.

The offers I'd been presented to join this person or that friend to evacuate came flooding back; a warm smile spread across my face. I didn't have to be here, but I was. Maybe I was supposed to be here, whatever that means in the metaphysical sense. Regardless, here I was. Let everyone watch, let the nation and the world sit and watch. I had grape flavored drink powder, and my family had instant coffee. Sure, this whole thing sucked ass. The bathrooms were psycho-gross and I was bored to tears. The house, a wreck. The City, a wreck. But I was alive. I could feel the change in the air as sure as I felt the goose bumps rising on my skin. Things would get better and the Army, Navy, police, the fucking FBI, they'd get us out of here. And somehow everything would be okay, eventually. This place was horrible beyond belief, but these were just people. I'd been through the worm tubes and back, and I'd come out alright. I wasn't afraid. Besides, I'd be able to tell this story for the rest of my life, and people would buy me drinks to keep on telling it. Now that's a powerful incentive to persevere.

I enjoyed the revelry for I don't know how long, ten minutes, maybe half an hour. Except for the dull buzz of small talk, the entire crowd had lost its voice. Quiet ruled. Then, some loud shouting from far away started attracting people's attention. Most of the stadium took notice. So loud and desperate were these unintelligible exclamations. Folks down on the field and up in the seats had begun migrating toward the far end zone. After the next round of shouts, I determined the origin of the faraway disturbance: high up in the stands. Rubbing my eyes, I noticed people inching toward the main concession corridor where we got fed. Another round of shouts, most of the population on the field had crossed the fifty-yard line. The far end of the field was packed with rubbernecking onlookers. Anything that happened in the building was a welcome relief from the oppressive boredom. The crowd had gathered, all eyes pointed upward to the unseen source of the shouting.

Way back at the twenty-five-yard line I was on my feet, staring downfield.

"What's going on, Bruce Juan?" Uncle G asked.

The anticipation was fierce. I might have been holding my breath. Uncle G was on his feet, too.

"Crazy people shouting, I don't know . . ."

Up in the seats, hordes of people were moving toward the end zone hoping to catch a glimpse of what there might be to see. And then it happened, another volley of shouts. Unlike the previous ones, these weren't muffled words, but a single, soul-tearing, shrill scream immediately followed by POW! . . . POW! POW!

Three shots rang out. Three shots fired in quick succession. Big shots, from one of the assault rifles the soldiers carried. Three shots, and anything resembling peace and order vanished into thick, humid air. The three shots heard 'round the Dome.

Over my shoulder, I heard Jimena scream. Her voice instantaneously became lost, as many thousands of other voices screamed as one. Panic swept through the crowd. Sheer terror filled everyone's eyes. Horror escaped from their throats, and hundreds of screams filled the air. People in the stands threw themselves down rows of seats and stairs. They crushed one another trying to put some distance between themselves and the blasts of gunfire. Everything seemed to slow to an impossible rate of action as the panic consumed the crowd on the field. The mass of them, hundreds and hundreds of people, turned upfield and ran for their lives. The far end zone had been filled with nosy onlookers, from the back wall of the playing field out to about the ten or fifteen was a single solid mass, dozens of rows deep and as wide as the sidelines would allow. The space between us on the opposite twenty-five-yard line—I mean right on the lower left non-existent number twenty-five if you're looking at the fleur de lis on the field—had cleared substantially. Trash piles, blankets, scattered people, and scattered trash still littered the field. Very little green turf showed through, but individual camps had cleared as the people moved downfield to investigate the loud shouts.

POW! . . . POW! POW!

They turned away from the shots, and, as one mass of humanity, they fled. People went DOWN and were trampled by dozens of others. Someone faster than the one ahead would shove that person to the right or left and they'd go down. People straight-up leaped over groups on their blankets. Some didn't jump far enough, and crashed onto the families below. Children, old people, and anyone else in the path of the panic were simply consumed by the charge.

I'd never witnessed anything so magnificently primal. How do you describe a tidal wave of human beings? More than a thousand bare feet pounding the ground for all it's worth, rumbling like thunder. Hundreds of souls crying out at once, the crushed and the runners alike. I couldn't take my eyes off it.

A teenage girl wearing a pair of fuzzy pink flip-flops tripped on someone's leg. As she fell flat on her face and the crowd ran her over, she cried "Mama!"

The crowd parted to negotiate the giant trash heaps, creating even larger human pile-ups. A couple of more athletic runners leaped over the trash piles like spawning salmon. The volume of the runners and the urgency of the moment, ridiculously fueled by panic, pushed them onward. The less agile crashed straight into the trash heaps, the scattered debris would trip up more people, and more people would fall.

Tick Tock Tick Tock Tick Tock. The wave moved upfield. I could only stare in awe. The human tsunami, the yells and screams, on they surged. The thirty-five, the forty, the forty-five, crossing mid-field, they could go all the way.

The wave pressed forward. Uncle G asked a question, which tore me from the paralysis I'd entered. "Bruce, what do we do?"

The forty, the thirty-five!

"Get down and cover your heads!"

Glenn from New York, Jimena, Uncle G, Mother, and I balled ourselves into a tight knot. Dolja sat protected in the center of our formation. In the final seconds, we inched ourselves closer together to tighten the seal. Before I could breathe twice, they were on us.

Knees, elbows, and heads: people crunched across us as the wave broke upon our bodies, like a solitary rock being slammed by the incoming tide. The wave broke over our huddled mass. Adrenaline I'd never known before pumped through my veins. Some of the runners did complete the full hundred-yard dash, but the charge lost its impetus after passing over us. Several long seconds passed before we agreed it would be safe to lift our heads and look around. People were shouting and crying. Others were helping people who'd been trampled get back on their feet. Though many sported new cuts and bruises, aside from the terror, no one seemed to have sustained any permanent injuries. The field looked more a wreck than ever before. Trash was strewn around even more haphazardly than before the charge. The people dusted themselves off and tried their best to locate their former campsites. Maybe thirty seconds had passed since the three shots tore the night to pieces.

Apart from a few thumps, the five and a half of us who'd huddled down together on the blanket were no worse for the wear. Jimena lit the last Top Hat from the first box and tossed me the second to open. One of the runners had kneed me in the thigh, so I stood up to stretch my leg. To my amazement, several people were starting to make their way back to the far end zone, heads tilted upward. They'd run from the shots, but their curiosity about what was happening above was so strong that they walked right back into harm's way. Unbelievable. The curiosity must have been contagious. Scores of people followed and, within minutes, hundreds had made their way back downfield.

"Can you believe these fuckers?" said Mother through a cloud of gray cigar smoke. "They run away like a herd of zebras in the jungle, and now they're right back down where they . . ."

POW! POW! POW! POW!

Four quick shots and another thousand-throat scream swallowed her words. There was no time to think, only act. Another stampede had begun. Only minutes after the first charge subsided, the panic was on again. Down we went, protecting ourselves and each other. People ran, jumped, and scrambled over us, but from the start, this charge lacked the force and fury of the first. Just like a wave crashing on the beach, which hits the sand and withdraws back until the next washes onshore, the crowd of runners started their way back to the far end zone and closer to the shooting. Up in the corridor I could see and hear a squad of soldiers moving toward the scene. I warned everyone to be ready for another charge, the troops were going in.

"Go get them bitches!" Mother shouted, kneeling with the dog between her legs.

"How long can they keep this up?" Glenn asked rhetorically.

POW! POW!

Another charge started, but never really took shape. Some ran past us, but the majority simply ducked their heads for a moment, ran ten yards, and resumed spectating. The shouts continued, the shooting continued, and, to an extent, the stampedes continued. None of the subsequent charges could compare to the desperate fear of the first. A total of six times, the crowd surged forth, and each time the people went right back to the far end zone, hoping to catch a glimpse of the unfolding violence.

In the stands and on the field, everyone was on their feet. The shots had attracted all attention. The corridors and the worm tubes emptied, crowding the seating areas with onlookers. Twenty-thousand people experiencing the same adrenaline rush. I could feel the collective tension standing there on the twenty-five yard line. Blood pounded against my eardrums, and the hair all over my body stood on end. My eyes scanned the turbulent crowd and were met by apprehension, fear, and anger. *So this is how the riot begins, I thought to myself. And when this conflagration finally ends, they'll need bulldozers to remove piles of battered corpses.* I clenched my fists.

"You gotta let us outta here."

"The Army is killing us, y'all."

"We wanna leave!"

"They ain't lettin' nobody leave."

Then the individual shouts became one great uproar. I stood there as motionless as a tree, rooted in artificial turf. The whole vibe had changed. There would be no more football games on the field. This was dog-eat-dog, every man for himself, fuck thy neighbor. The entire stadium seethed. The organism metastasized rapidly. This was war.

"We're getting out of here in the morning, Bruce. We'll find an exit. We'll find a way. If we stay, we'll get killed 'cause we're not black," Uncle G was hyperventilating and his pupils were tiny black points. One-hundred percent adrenaline-induced survival mode. "In the morning, we'll be ready."

Shaking my head, I said, "They're not letting people out."

"And where the fuck you gonna go?" Mother added. "Back to the house, Gene? The whole City's flooded, asshole. There's nowhere to go."

"Bruce, tell her to stop. She can stay here and die in a pile of shit if she wants, but we're leaving, and both of you should come with us."

"What are you tryin' to say, bitch?" Mother said to Uncle G.

"I'm saying that we need to get the FUCK out of here. Is she deaf?"

"G, she's saying that if we leave, we have nowhere to go. If it's this bad in here, how bad is it going to be out there? There ain't no Army out there, it's the Wild West, ya' dig? At least we have water and food, and a roof with big-ass holes, but it's a roof, right?"

"Bruce, you and your maw are going to get killed. Jimena and I are going to get killed. You think Grandma wants that?"

"No, she would want us to stay together."

"Then come with us when we leave. You two stay here with the stuff, I'm going to go talk to Stefano and see if they want to come."

Uncle G got up, and the conversation ended there. Stefano and his family had remained in the same seats they sat in when we arrived yesterday.

Mother was adamantly opposed to the idea of trying to find a way to escape. When morning came a few hours later, it was well past two a.m. "He thinks he's the only motherfucker in here planning to try and get out? All of these crazy bitches in here are gonna be running around trying to get out, Bruce. They're not letting people out. What does he think he's doing?"

A little while later, Uncle G and Jimena returned. "The Cubans are in. We'll meet up with them first thing in the morning."

"What about breakfast, Uncle G? We don't have much water."

"Bruce, we need to leave. We need to get out of here as quick and as early as we can."

Nothing I could say would lessen his determination.

"I'm staying here, and any of you can stay with me," offered Glenn.

I said, "Look, everyone get some rest. It sounds like we're going to have another big day tomorrow, but if these fuckers start running around like a bunch of crazy antelopes again, we need to protect ourselves. I'll keep watch. If I get too tired, I'll wake one of you up, okay?"

Of course, there was some protest, but they were all exhausted and emotionally drained. One by one, they curled up and fell asleep. My adrenaline high had worn off. I was exhausted, too, but this was war. I needed to protect my crew. It had to be me. I lit up a Top Hat and started pacing tiny rectangles around our blanket. The sun will be up soon, I told myself. Then I'll wake one of them up and we'll get out of here. And we'll just have to wait and see what comes next. It was as good a plan as any other, and, at the same time, it wasn't a plan at all. Where *would* we end up? We would end up wherever we were when the sun set tomorrow. No more, no less. It was really not a plan at all.

THE RUMOR MILL

So far in this narrative, I have purposefully avoided writing about what I call the rumor mill. The rumor mill—the convective sharing of misinformation throughout the Louisiana Superdome—was an ever-present, practically tangible thing. Unless you were totally deaf and mute, the rumor mill couldn't be avoided, and everyone participated at some point. If we were all cells in a great, repulsive organism, then the rumors fed the organism.

So, what were they saying? The same things you probably heard on television. The more terrible, the more quickly it would spread. Things like the abduction and rape of children, the rape of elderly people, the rape of anything weak and vulnerable. It's very possible, but I didn't see it. And even though some of the people I saw were criminals beyond any shred of doubt, the overwhelming majority of the people in the Superdome were just normal folks: men and women, mothers and fathers, grandparents, kids. They were just trying to ride this thing out, like my family. Aside from locking oneself up in one of those luxury suites, absolutely no privacy was to be had by anyone, anywhere. I find it hard to imagine that if I or anyone else in the stadium were walking through a corridor and saw a guy raping a child that they wouldn't at least tap him on the shoulder and be like, "Look, buddy, that's not cool." But the Dome is a very big place. And in reality, I saw very little of it. With so many people, a determined offender could probably have succeeded in harming a vulnerable resident. Rumors of murdered children also passed through the mill.

Mother was groped by a guy as we stood in the dinner line, which infuriates her to this day, and I did meet one rape victim in the flesh. A young black woman with a pretty face, around twenty years old. She might have been five foot two. She wore nurse's scrubs and a pair of tan Army boots. The jackals had ruined her other garments. The soldiers found her lying naked as the day she was born. The girl I was introduced to at what would be our last camp in the stadium didn't say much and stared at the ground more often than not, but if the talk around the group was humorous and people were laughing, she'd smile. Those three monsters had hurt her, but she didn't seem broken.

Other rumors were more far-fetched. One of the most popular, then and now, is that the U.S. Government, or whoever, deployed highly trained demolition crews to destroy the levees that flooded the Ninth Ward. Now there is something to this claim. During the Great Mississippi River Flood of 1927, some levees on the east side of town were charged with dynamite and exploded in order to "save the City." The blown levees flooded many of the "blackest" parts of town, including the Ninth Ward. If the same levees were dynamited during Katrina, with the same sinister intention, then this deplorable act achieved roughly the same result as during the Great Flood on the Mississippi: it failed. Just like during the Roaring Twenties, in 2005 several levees broke, not just the one, and most of the City flooded anyway. To blow apart a chunk of earth as large as our levees, it would, well . . . look like an explosion had gone off, right? The Ninth Ward levee breach looked an awful lot like the London Avenue Canal breach, which looked an awful lot like the Seventeenth Street Canal breach. And, folks, I am fully conscious of the fact that we do not live in a utopian society of racial harmony. Far from it. But, seriously, much change has occurred since 1927 in this country. In my most conspiratorial mindset, I just can't picture George Bush Junior saying, "Blow the wall and flood out the niggers," even if he is the spawn of the actual devil.

Another rumor that I found amusing in a terrible sort of way has to do with the jumper we saw on the upper level, the one the soldiers covered with a white sheet. The story goes that his gay lover had dumped him for another man shortly after everything went to hell. They arrived at the stadium together, and then he found himself on his own. Jump. Or, here's the short version I heard several times: "He a punk. He ain't a punk no mo."

Later on, there would be a great buzz concerning the death of another man in the stadium. Once again, I didn't personally witness this going down, but the story has been corroborated by many different sources. It goes something like this: A mother and her young daughter—the age of the child fluctuates between four and ten, depending on the storyteller—are walking up one of the escalators holding hands. Like a demon from a nightmare, a man rushes past them down the steps. Gravity and speed are on his side, and he grabs the girl and keeps running. Her mother loses her grip. Pandemonium breaks out. Both mother and child scream for help. The man is stopped by some other men walking nearby. The child is safely returned. This guy had already raped and murdered two, three, eight children—again, depending on the source. They present this piece of shit to a couple of soldiers and explain what had just happened, adding that this guy has been hurting children since his arrival. The soldier explains he would like to help, but there's nowhere they can take this guy, and no one to watch him. There was no "jail" at the Superdome. Hearing this, the pedophile guy started taunting his captors "Y'all can't do shit to me," or something to that effect. The soldier interrupts him, "Not so quick, pal." Again, the soldier tells the would-be vigilantes that there's nothing he can do, "So I'm going to walk away now, and you men do what you feel needs to be done with him. I'm turning my back." The man's smile evaporates like so much brown water. The group of men beat him to death with their fists and feet, then toss his body on a pile of trash in the outer corridor. Years later, I heard this story again from a man in Arkansas who told me he'd heard it from one of the guys who did the actual beating. Why would the man confess to a total stranger if he wasn't really trying to get this act off his chest? And when this non-Superdome resident told me this story nine years after the incident, he had no idea that I knew what, more or less, his every next word would be.

I've made this wide digression into legend and rumor because I want to end it with the rumors I heard about the shots that Wednesday night—the shots that started the stampede. I'll share this tale, and turn my back on the rumor mill forever, and leave it for the historians to sort out. Some loud shouts drew everyone's attention, and then BANG BANG BANG, the charge was on.

The tale goes like this. Two guys were fighting up in the concession corridor. Unlike most of the fights I saw outside that were for deranged sport, these guys were out to really hurt each other. This caused the initial round of shouting that got everyone's attention. One guy had gotten the upper hand on his opponent, and he continued to beat the shit out of the guy after his opponent had stopped fighting back. A simple round of fisticuffs was about to become a murder. Two soldiers, a male and a female, arrived on the scene and tried to break it up. The aggressor's blood was up, his adrenaline pumping, and something the soldiers said to him pushed him over the edge. "You talkin' to a Nuwallin's nigga now." He cocked back his fist and punched the male soldier so hard the soldier crumpled into a pile on the ground, his facial bones shattered. He proceeded to disarm the soldier before his wide-eyed female partner could raise her weapon in response.

POW! POW! POW! Shot the woman twice in the leg. He fled into one of the stank, rank, dark, filthy bathrooms clutching the rifle. The following shots, which prompted the next stampedes, were from the guy resisting the efforts of the soldiers to flush him out.

By the time most people stopped running from the shots—there would be some runners with every burst, but no wholesale charge—the soldiers had gotten organized.

Pa-KOOM!

POW! POW! Pa-da-da-da-da-Dow! POW! POW!

The soldiers tossed a flash-bang grenade into the bathroom. Pa-KOOM! And then rushed in there blasting. The man's corpse was dragged out in a black body bag, or so sayeth the rumor mill.

THURSDAY
SEPTEMBER 1ST, 2005

MORNING

Life, Death, and Instant Crystals

Looking up into the rafters, I saw the sky fade from black to light purple. Dawn was imminent. The holes in the roof were good for that much, at least. I'd stayed awake the whole night, improvising brain games to pass the time. Most recently I'd been humming riffs and mouthing the words to songs I'd written with my first musical venture, a three-piece thrash band we called MooseKnuckle. We'd play in the tiny second bedroom of the mother-in-law's apartment. When I say tiny, I mean I've eaten at tables larger than this room. Good thing there were only three members. I played bass and supplied the vocals. My buddy Jay, the bartender at Lorenzo's, was on guitar, and my main man, Chief Jugando, was on drums. I could barely play the thing, but holding an instrument really fanned my creative fire. I wrote a lot of songs for us to jam on. They weren't very good, but it sure was fun. In my effort to come up with new material, I transcribed my telephone number into a riff using the digits like tablature. I have to admit, it kind of rocked, and eventually made it into the line-up. Post-Katrina, we re-formed under a new name with an additional member and played that song with my old phone number live on stage a dozen times.

I waded a ways into a trash pile near the padded walls and relieved myself. Time to wake everyone up. I gave them all a nudge, except for Glenn, and sat down. I rolled over on the hippo and closed my eyes. They were so heavy. It was very early, so they decided to make some coffee before we set out, no real surprise there. At least I'd have time for a catnap. I must have nodded off. The next thing I remember is Mother giving me a nudge.

"Mwuh! Yeah?"

"B, they're ready."

"Okay…okay."

Uncle G and Jimena were already on their feet with backpacks on. I stood up and grabbed the hippo. Mother led the dog. The Cuban family was ready, too. Stefanito had his life vest on again. They were ready to get out of the stadium and back into the water. They gathered up their things, and together we ascended the stairs to the concession corridor. By this time, the smell of the bathrooms consumed the entire corridor. Brown footprints covered the ground and a steady puddle of urine the size of a school bus had formed in the hallway. Some people just stood in the hallway and peed in the puddle.

We pushed our way through the crowd and got the hell out of there, through some double doors and into the exterior corridor. Mother was right, we weren't the only people with escape on our minds. The corridor swarmed with activity. Individuals and families running in all directions. Total madness. In the distance to my left, several people were screaming and fighting on the escalators, the whole mob around them pushing and shoving.

Uncle G and Stefano were leading us across the corridor and out to the terrace. This made me really nervous. I'd been the only one to witness *the night of a thousand fights*. The terrace scared me; they didn't know that. Through the glass doors we went, out into the seven o'clock sunshine.

More madness. People running in every direction, a horde of a couple hundred pressed against the soldiers' barricade shouting at them for relief. A woman raised her tiny child over her head and shouted "She can't eat the shit you give us! I need some formula for my baby!"

We didn't try pressing our way through to the barricade. Clearly, no one was being allowed through. Soldiers with slung machine guns stared blankly from the tower down at the crowd below. Looking straight at the New Orleans Centre building, we first turned right, weaving our way through. One of the large, sloping ramps leading down to the street level lay ahead. Our group traveled through the tumult and hit another clot before the ramp. The Army barred the way with big camouflage-painted trucks, sections of barricade, and about thirty armed soldiers. The thronging mass of people chanted "Let-us-out! Let-us-out!" All around, people were shoving one another and small fights were breaking out. The Cubans were terrified. Jimena was about to explode. They hadn't seen this side of the fury. We tried moving around the edge of the large crowd gathered in front of the ramp. It's a big, round stadium. There would be another ramp farther ahead.

The crowd was so dense, we couldn't find a way around. We'd have to bulldoze through. Instead, we slithered back into the hall corridor and regrouped. Mother was breathing hard, the Cuban family clenched in one big bear hug, Jimena was in tears, and Uncle G was back in the animalistic survival mode I'd seen the night before. He talked fast and low like a quarterback in the huddle.

"There's an open door to a stairwell over there. Let's see if we can get through that way."

As we moved toward the door, someone running through the corridor gave Mother a shove, and she went down hard on one knee. Grimacing, she held my arm, pulled herself up, and got back on her feet. She limped a little with each step. I know she'd hit that knee hard, but she didn't drop Dolja. Clenching her teeth, she nodded her head to me and we continued on.

Except for the dull light flickering through the doorway, the stairwell was totally blacked out. I pushed in ahead of the group to the rail, looking down to the base of dozens of banks of stairs. Bright sunlight poured in through open doors. After a couple of adjusting blinks, I could discern the smooth-shaven faces of several soldiers looking up at me.

I turned to my group, "Dead end. The Army is blocking the stairs. Go back!"

"Gene, no! What are you going to do? We are trapped in here with these animals. Why won't they let us leave?" said Jimena in borderline hysterics.

"We'll find a way, baby. Don't worry."

"We go back around and try the other side. They can't block every set of stairs," added Stefano.

"Are y'all for real? It's the Army. They can do whatever they want. We're wasting our time," replied Mother.

"Ces, stop upsetting everyone. We're going to find a way out," Uncle G said.

"They AREN'T letting people OUT!" she screamed at the top of her lungs. Veins were visible all over her forehead. Her eyes were wide, and her hands were shaky. Another outburst like that and she'd surely short circuit. This was not the time or the place for one of her seizures.

I tried to intervene. "Let's calm down and try and regroup here. They want to check the stairwells on the other side. Instead of fighting through these hallways, let's walk across the field."

"It is too far, not in the way," said Jimena.

"And we might miss our set of stairs to get us out of here," added Uncle G.

"There aren't any stairs to get out of here, Eugene. No stairs, no doors, no . . ."

"This way!" shouted Stefano, cutting Mother off. Our group had no choice but to follow.

In a matter of moments, we hit another solid mass of people and could go no farther. Mother made her stand. She was through with the game. "If y'all want to run around this fucking place for hours, go ahead. This is stupid. You're stupid. Go 'head on. I'm going back to the field."

"Mom, wait!"

"Naw, fuck that. I'm done with this running around shit. I'll take the dog. We'll be fine. To hell with this."

"But, Mom, we can't split up."

"You heard her, Bruce. She wants to stay here and crawl around in shit till she gets killed. If you want to live, c'mon with us."

And so this was the fork in the road. The Cubans had already moved on. Jimena shouted at them to wait. Uncle G asked me again, "Are you staying with her or are you coming with us?"

"I'm not leaving her alone."

"Bruce, we don't want to die in here . . ."

With the screaming, fighting, closely packed crowd all around us, I could appreciate the fear I saw in my uncle's eyes. The residents had revolted, the stadium defiled. And more than that, our home and our lives were defiled, just three days before. Only two days had passed since we'd swum down Elysian Fields Avenue. Now we stood face to face amongst the maelstrom. Catastrophe wears no clothes. Fear burns like fire. And the fear of death burns brightest. The screaming crowds, the fighting, it was all just so much manifest fear. As silly as it may sound, the fear calmed me and helped me focus. The fear wasn't going to make me be afraid. Mother wasn't afraid. This Thursday morning, fear controlled the Superdome, but I didn't have to let it control me. I knew this wasn't "goodbye."

"We'll be on the field. Look for us on the field."

"Take care of your mom."

"She'll be fine. Dolja, Klaus, and I, we'll be fine. If you make it out, that means we will, too. Just maybe not today. We'll be on the field if you don't."

"I need to get Jimmy out of here. We need to go."

"Then go. We'll be alright. I love you."

"I love you, Bruce Juan."

We embraced there in the swarming corridor, and then they were gone. Rushing away to find an exit, a way back to the brown water. In here, there was only chaos, but outside, the brown water controlled everything. Chaos, by its very nature, allows for some freedom of movement. The water restricted any movements. At least in here it was dry and we could move. Right now, we needed to move out of this crazy hallway.

Mother and I shoved our way through the corridor and back into the concession corridor. The seats and the playing field spread out panoramically before us.

"I need to sit down, baby. Just a minute, so Mama can catch her breath."

"Okay, let's find some empty seats."

Though not the most comfortable, the Superdome doesn't lack for places to sit down. I spied a patch of empty seats about halfway down the steps, right on the aisle. I asked Mother if she could make it down about a dozen rows. She smiled and told me that going down was the easy way. We walked past several small groups of people sleeping and talking to get to the rows of open seats. Dolja sat on the ground at our feet, Klaus resting on the seat between us. Mother asked if we had a cigar left. We didn't. We didn't have anything but the half-empty bottle of water crumpled up in my pocket. The section of the stadium we were sitting in was on the complete opposite side of the building from the previous seats we'd occupied. Instead of looking at the base of the *fleur de lis* on the field from around seven o'clock, I was looking at the top-point of the black and gold emblem from somewhere around one o'clock.

The field and the stands were so calm at that moment—a very different vibe from the bedlam taking place out on the terrace. Mother used her hand to cover her tightly shut eyes.

"My head hurts so bad, B. It hurts so bad . . ."

"I know, Mama. I'm sorry."

"Why, God? Why is he so stubborn and stupid?" She was working herself up even more.

"He's . . . so . . . stupid. There's no one . . . at home. . . ." She bit down on her words, leaned forward, and started convulsing her shoulders, her arms crossed tightly across her chest. She threw her head forward, back, then forward again. "Nuh, nuh, nuh, nuh, nuh, nuh. B . . ." She pulled her knees up to her chest, then

his odor production. He'd lost everything. I wondered if anyone knew his name. This really was no place to die, but the expression on his face was so pleasant. He made me smile. And, as sick as it may sound, the smell didn't bother me that much. The piled-high bathrooms smelled much worse than this friendly looking gray-haired man with the smiling face, waxy skin, and eyes that would never open again on their own. Don't get me wrong, the smell in my nose was pungent, broken, and gross. Like rancid butter and rotting vegetables and meat. But mixed in there amid the horror was a definite underlying sweetness to the smell. Like an over-ripe orange that has split in the sun. Notes of pine, maybe. The fact that a dead person's corpse rotting a dozen feet away from me didn't bother me all that much, not nearly as much as you'd think it would; instead, it's the fact of it not bothering me that still upsets me to this day. The entire Superdome experience could easily be described as one long olfactory nightmare. Why should smelling rotting human carrion locate itself in my memory banks as one of the less offensive experiences of the week? I don't know, maybe I'm a monster. Maybe I'm sick. Maybe I need help, but compared to 20,000 turds lying around, I'll smell dead people all day, any day.

With the living and the dead cohabitating, the entire scene had taken an enormous metaphysical step forward—or backward, I'm not quite sure. I watched a group of young men ascending the steps. They were loud and raucous. That's what initially drew my attention to them. Walking past the gray old man with the gray beard, one leaned in, clapped his hands in the old man's face, and shouted, "Wake up!" Much to the amusement of himself and his companions, the man didn't wake up. He just kept on smiling.

Another bit of commotion on the next level of seats above us caught our attention, and the attention of everyone else on our end of the building. The piercing, shrill scream of a woman in grave pain cut through the regular hum of a thousand conversations. My first thought was that someone was murdering the poor girl. Anxiously, our collective gaze sought the source of the scream. From where we were sitting, I couldn't see much, but I did spy a whole bunch of people hunched over something. Many more stood on their seats around the spot, attempting to catch a glimpse. We sat in suspended animation. Another scream. No one breathed. A minute later, a tall black man with a shaved head stood on a chair at the very epicenter of the concentration, raised his arms high, and exclaimed, "It's a girl!" A thousand throats and a thousand hearts raised a cheer. Mother and I were two of those throats, two of those hearts. It was a powerful, splendid moment to be a part of. The organism had lost a cell. The old man with the gray beard, he wouldn't be waking up. But just like our bodies regenerate new cells, the organism had produced a new baby girl. A precious new baby born into a brown-water world that none of the grown people around her asked for or understood. That child should be entering middle school soon. I hope that she is happy and healthy. Her birthday is Thursday, September 1st, 2005. God bless that girl, and every child forced to participate in this mess.

A couple of rows away, Mother and I saw a man holding his infant son in his hands. The baby was all smiles and gurgles. The man would bounce the baby and say, "Dea' he is. Dat's my nigga. Dat's my lil nigga."

Mother said to him, "Your baby is beautiful. He looks happy. Keep up the good work."

He replied, "Yes indeed, I love my lil nigga, ain't dat right." And he continued bouncing the smiling baby.

The breakfast line was starting to form up in the corridor behind us. Even after our planned escape attempt, Mother's seizure, talking with Tutu, and the birth of the baby, we hadn't yet hit nine a.m. I asked Mother if she felt strong enough to do the line. She said that she wasn't hungry now, but definitely would be later on. She would make it through the line to get coffee regardless. We had no food and no water. She said we needed to get some supplies, or we'd be in for a really long day. Sounded like a plan to me. We asked Tutu if she'd like to join us in line. She declined. Unlike us, she'd arrived at the Superdome well prepared. She brought food and water and soft drinks and cigarettes to last her for several days. She said she tried the Army food, but preferred what she had in her stash. Another goodbye followed, and another round of hugs.

You know, this lady Tutu, she didn't know me or my mother, but she was there for us in possibly our darkest hour of the entire experience. To her, we were just a pair of nobodies, and she could have easily just sat there and watched Mother shake. Like the men in the fishing boat who saved us from our attic, who could have just left us in there until we wasted away into so much human beef jerky. But they didn't. They helped. They needed to know that the people around them in trouble had a hand, and a hope, and a chance to get themselves out of that trouble.

Mother and I made it through the food line fairly quickly. Most people had given up on the interior of the stadium, and instead chose to seek a way out and join the madness outside. Uncle G and Jimena were out there. I hoped that they'd found a way to get out and were well on their way to God knows where.

The soldiers who gave us our food looked like they were worn down. Their once-crisp camouflage uniforms hung limp and wrinkled from their drooping shoulders, but they weren't taking any chances. Not after last night. For every soldier handing out food and water, two stood behind them with rifles in their hands.

We received our rations and decided that going back to eat in the stands by Tutu and the dead man just wasn't the best place for us to enjoy our breakfast. I led us down to the field for what would be the last time. The expansive lawn of fake grass had the appearance of a yard sale that'd been hit by a tornado. Clothing and trash lay strewn about in every direction, but many of the people were missing. Among them was Glenn. I looked for him at the spot we'd left him a couple hours before, the place he said he'd be if we came back. Both he and his blanket were gone.

Nearly seventy thousand seats surround the playing field of the Louisiana Superdome, but the only permanent pieces of "furniture" down on the field are the two long aluminum bleacher benches on the sidelines, where the players sit. The real deal. No one was sitting on a ten-foot section at one end of the roughly sixty-foot bench.

Mother and I, Klaus, and Dolja sat ourselves down, our butts resting on the opposing team's bench above the *fleur de lis* on the field. Across the vast expanse of trash were the home team benches. The benches of the powerhouse Saints. Even if this was the visiting team's side of the field, Super Bowl champions have sat on this bench. The Superdome has hosted more Super Bowls than any other building, and suddenly Dolja was peeing on Walter Payton's footprints. If you don't know, Walter Payton is arguably the best NFL running back of the 1980s. He won his ring in this building. Joe Montana, Brett Favre, and Tony Dorsett won rings in this building, too.

Mother and I ripped open our MREs and ate our morning meal while shafts of brilliant light beamed through the ceiling over our heads. Maybe it was the angle, or the back support—I'd never sat on bleachers with a back bar—but that had to be the most comfortable set of bleachers I'd ever sat on. Much nicer than the rigid, narrow-assed stadium chairs with their useless padding. With the piece of flat metal behind me, I was able to press my back against something solid, and I worked out some of the knots from my stiff shoulders. Mother and I shared a bottle of grape flavored Army Kool-Aid more or less in silence. I could tell she enjoyed the back rest on the bleachers as much as I did.

Just then, Dolja, who'd been sitting quietly since relieving himself, leapt to his feet and barked fiercely at a man walking past. He pulled his phone cord leash taut. Luckily, I'd tied the other end around one of my belt loops. But he was pulling. He was angry. I tried to reel him back in, but the cord snapped! For a split-second he ran free, chasing the man, before I scooped him up.

Ruff! Ruff! Ruff!

Mother and I tried to calm him down, but he was having none of it. He'd been righteously calm throughout our stay, so far, but something about that one guy, out of tens of thousands, set him off. And that was his breaking point.

Ruff! Ruff! Arooof!

The dog was inconsolable. I started to get worried. If people were walking around beating each other up, and disarming and shooting soldiers, what would stop someone from straight-up kicking the little mutt for three points clear through the uprights? To hell with that.

Mother held him while I tied the remaining bit of the phone cord to his collar. His leash was short to begin with, now it was a comical two-foot strand, barely enough for him to stand while I stood holding the other end. I lay down on the turf and Mother handed him to me. I tied the end of the line to the base of the bench and stroked his ears and smoothed the fur on his back. I told him it was okay if he needed to freak out a little, everyone in here was entitled to lose themselves for a moment, and many people had and had not come back. "But you can't go running off, boy. We need you here with us."

He seemed to calm down a little bit, but when the right person would walk past, he'd rise up again on his paws, growling and barking.

I dug around in our MRE pouches, and between the two of them we'd scored some peanut butter, a tube of strawberry jelly, and a "slice" of Army bread— singlehandedly, the strangest excuse for bread I've ever come across. A cross between a communion host and a large, soft saltine cracker, the square piece of bread was incredibly dense and required plenty of saliva to get down. After tearing the bread into strips and coating them with peanut butter and jelly, I fed them to the dog a morsel at a time with my right hand, while always holding a small puddle of water for him to lap from my left.

Bit by bit, he and I shared this open-face sandwich and washed it down with a bottle of water. I let him drink all he wanted. He wasn't barking or growling now, just licking the sticky jelly from my fingers. This is, and will always be, the most memorable breakfast I've eaten in my entire life, there in the shade of the opposing team's benches, while sunlight poured through the roof of the Louisiana Superdome. Just me and my dog. In a funny way, I wish that moment could have lasted just a little bit longer. Very few times have I ever felt so content and beautiful.

Though the day was still quite young, we were both exhausted. Mother had run around the stadium, climbed mountains of stairs, had a seizure, and stood in line for breakfast. I was working on my, count 'em, fourth straight night without sleep. A personal record. The drowsiness weighed on me, sure as the peanut butter sinking in my belly. I needed a nap.

Mother lay down on her side on the aluminum bench, and I stretched out with Dolja down on the turf. Moments later, I was out.

Voices . . . familiar voices . . .

When I opened my eyes, I found myself looking straight at Uncle G sitting next to me in the fake grass. Mother and Jimena sat next to each another on the bench sipping coffee water.

"Bruce Juan."

I was a little shaken, but more than that, I was really happy to see him. That mess back there happened in the inferno of the moment. No use beating it to death.

"Hey, what time is it?"

"Almost noon, no, three after," Uncle G said, looking at his wristwatch for absolute confirmation.

Add two hours to my meager sleep total, still less than ten hours out of the previous eighty. Wiping the crust from my eyes, I asked, "What did you find?"

"Nothing."

"That good?"

"Well, we found you two. We didn't see Glenn, and we started to get worried. Jimmy thought she saw your maw on the bench; she saw your silly shoes, and then we saw the dog."

"Word, where're the Cubans?"

"Up in the seats, I think. Bruce, this place has fallen apart. The people are crazy, but what can we do? They won't let us out. There's nowhere to go. There's nowhere that's safe."

I let his words roll around in my mind for a moment before imagining a possible slice of the bigger picture. *Nowhere's safe.* Not in this building. It certainly appeared that way, but, then again, we never tried looking. We never thought to ask.

"We don't know that."

"We can't stay in here another night. We can't stay here on the field. Where do we go?"

"I don't know. Let's go ask the Army."

"But, they have this place locked down."

"That's what I'm trying to say. We go find where the soldiers are, and we stay close to them."

"That's a good idea, but all the soldiers are outside now. They've completely left the building."

"Then we go outside."

The girls had been listening to what we were saying. Jimena added, "*Le gente afuera estan loco.*" (The people are crazy outside.)

"I know that, but it's worth a try. The Army's outside, so that's where we need to be," I said.

Mother said, "He's right, my baby's right, I tell ya. Let's go."

And with that, our reunited family group, four and a half strong plus a hippo, ascended the stairs and departed the field. Never again would I run my toes through the cool fake grass of the New Orleans Saints playing field.

Throw Me Somethin' Mister

Outside, an announcement: "Ladies and Gentlemen, we know you have been through a lot. We understand your frustration. We understand that you are ready to get out of here, and that's what we're going to do: get you people onto buses and out of the City."

An older black Sergeant who reminded me of Danny Glover addressed the teeming crowd before him from atop the tower through a megaphone. Each statement met with a volley of derisive cat calls and outright booing, except for the last bit. That was met by thunderous applause. He continued, "We will begin loading the buses, dozens of buses, hundreds of buses. We will begin loading very soon. We won't be able to evacuate everyone today, so we're asking you to remain patient for just a little bit longer, and we'll all get out of here together."

Hundreds of people shouted at the man, "When?"

"Where will they take us?"

Or things like, "My brothers are in Mississippi."

Or "My mama's up in Memphis."

The man with the bullhorn let all of these statements wash over him like so much brown water.

"People, I can't guarantee that everyone will be sent to their city of first choice, but we're going to get everyone out of New Orleans, and that much I will guarantee."

Again "When?"

That seemed to be the word of the day, *when.* This crowd's store of patience had evaporated long ago.

"When?"

"People, we're going to ask you to form an orderly line here in front of these barricades, then we'll move you across this walkway to the buses lined up on the street behind me. Ladies and Gentlemen, you've never seen so many buses. We know that this has been tough, and we will no longer force you to stay. You can leave if you choose, but know you will NOT, I repeat, will not be allowed back inside if you leave, and will not be allowed on a bus. You will be on your own. We recommend you try to be patient and wait for a bus. The line will form at the barricades to my right and left. Thank you."

The wide brick terrace between the Superdome and the New Orleans Centre building laid wide open and virgin. Except for some combat boots, no one had yet to use this portion of terrace.

Looking at the tower, we stood a ways to the left, directly before the barricade. At the far end of the terrace, soldiers were setting up another line of barricades in front of the huge glass doors leading into the New Orleans Centre.

"Guys, we're in the perfect spot. This is where he said the line would start. We'll be the first ones out of here, come stand by me," I advised my gang. Dutifully, they stood with me at the barricade. A few minutes later, when the soldiers moved the sections of barricade from in front of the crowd, we stood in place, as per the instructions of the Danny Glover Sergeant.

Unfortunately, we must have been the only ones to have heard this. A human wave at least a thousand strong charged across the walk path down to the hastily erected line of barricades at the far end. All the while, the soldiers yelled at them to come back and wait where we stood, but it was too late. Instead of first in line, we stood in position to board maybe the sixtieth bus. And, big surprise, people were pushing, shoving, and outright fighting to get closer to the front.

We decided to scrap our dreams of immediate evacuation and let everyone else kill each other. We could wait a little longer. So we reverted back to the original plan.

There were soldiers all around. I homed in on the one with the most stuff on his collar. I could tell he was a Sergeant, but didn't exactly know to what degree. The pattern of his stripes was familiar enough, but I didn't know what to make of the peculiar diamond in the center of his rank insignia. Now I know that the tiny diamond resting on its side denotes the rank of First Sergeant—the highest rank attainable by a soldier in the U.S. Army before becoming an officer. First Sergeants are responsible for many administrative tasks, as well as morale and team building for every soldier in their unit. A man who needs to be everywhere all the time. It's a lot of responsibility, and a great honor.

And along comes long-haired, scruffy goatee-wearing me, "Excuse me, Sergeant."

"What do you need, son?" he replied with a sly smile. Addressing the soldiers by rank was a fantastic method for breaking the ice. The majority of the crowd more likely would have said something like "Hey, motherfucker," rather than "Excuse me, Sergeant."

The man had a warm feel about him that I could detect through the rigid, soldierly way in which he stood. That's why I'd selected him as the man to approach. That, and his apparent seniority. In my experience thus far living with the Army, Privates weren't the best at answering questions. Their decisions are made for them. After deciding it would be okay to be a little more casual, I said, "Sarge . . ." His face twisted into something stony and unspeakably military. Swallowing hard, I continued, "Umm, Sergeant, my family and I, we'd like to get out of here as much as anyone else, but, you know, we're willing to wait our turn. We're willing to be the last people out of here if we just had somewhere we felt safe . . . to wait it out."

"You and me both," that soothing grin returning to his square-jawed face.

"Yeah, well, sir, is there a spot around here where your guys are set up, a spot that we could park right in front of and wait until our bus gets here?"

"Son, don't call me *sir*."

"I'm sorry, Sergeant Rogers." Spotting rank was one thing, but every soldier wears their last name embroidered on their chest.

"There's a barricade set up around to my right. Look for the stalled truck. Other people have set up there. You and your family go join them. It's quiet over there. My guys aren't going anywhere. They're not going to leave the truck."

I pointed away, "To your right?"

"Just be patient. We've got a whole lot of people to move. I like your dog."

"Thank you, sir. Aww shit, I mean thank you, Sergeant Rogers. You're a life saver."

"Good little rat-killing dog."

True to his word, just around the curve in the terrace, we saw a broken-down Army truck with a solid group of soldiers hanging around. This was the first time I'd really been out on the terrace during daylight and not running around like a crazy person. Though I could smell the stagnant water all around, the air felt cleaner than indoors. The late summer sun felt good on my skin. And though there were people and trash everywhere, it just seemed less oppressive and less sad than inside the stadium. There was absolutely no breeze, but that didn't matter. We were outside, and we weren't afraid. I stepped around an enormous pile of crap just sitting there roasting on the hot bricks in the hot sun, but that was okay, too. At least with the sun there was light enough to see where we were going and what we were stepping in, or trying not to step in.

Surrounding the truck were about seventy-five people of mixed races: Blacks, Whites, and hispanics, all seeking the Army's protection from the rest of the crowd. Now that I think about it, I don't remember seeing any Asians, Indians, or Arabs at the Superdome. These groups must have had good enough sense to leave town at the proper time.

As previously mentioned, a portion of the super structure of the Superdome covers about a fifth of the width of the terrace. This shady spot had been claimed by people, and there proved no available real estate underneath. We'd be making camp under the broiling sun and cool stars.

Leaning against the camouflage-painted truck, a silver-haired soldier wearing sunglasses stood out amongst all of the baby-faced others. I approached him from across the barricade, and, spotting his rank before I spoke, said, "Excuse me, Major."

A Major. A man with hundreds of underlings. Except for slightly raising an eyebrow, not a muscle twitched throughout his whole body. He didn't even turn his head from whatever he was looking at away to his right, off into a dimension I couldn't see.

"And what can I help *you* with today?"

He really stressed the "you." It unnerved me. Maybe I'd jumped too high and should've looked for another Sergeant. Maybe he couldn't remember the last time someone spoke to him without saluting first. I don't know. Honestly,

I was still relatively enamored by the whole military presence, the G.I. Joe collector's twist on this crazy adventure. The Army, as I'd come to understand it, functions as a well-greased machine, or tries to. Nothing about the Superdome was well-greased except for the corridors tracked slick with urine and poo. I figured, so what if this one man holds the rank of Major in the Army? Rank and protocol aside, I'm not, nor have I ever been, in the Army. Talking man to man and not officer to grunt seemed like a reasonable enough way to approach the conversation.

Undaunted, I said, "Sir, a Sergeant Rogers back there told my family and me that this would be a safe place to camp."

"He did, did he?" the Major replied, turning to look at me for the first time.

"Uh, yes, Sir."

"Well, help yourself. My people aren't going anywhere, and from the look of that line of people trying to get on the buses, you're not going anywhere either anytime soon."

"It does look that way. Thank you, Sir."

"You'll be fine. Move on, son. I've got a lot of work to do here." He turned his head back to whatever he'd been staring at before I walked up, and that's where our conversation ended.

My gang and I found an open spot and sat ourselves down. The day was definitely warm, but thankfully not broiling hot. We had no shade, no cover, not even a baseball cap between us. From our new spot, we could see the City from a new perspective. The brown water surrounded the stadium, and, judging from the flooded cars all around, was around three feet deep—enough to swallow the headlights on most cars, but barely enough to wet the front bumper of the big Army trucks. Three of them were cruising down the street toward the stadium, moving at a good clip, a Humvee in the lead, pushing their wake throughout the CBD in all directions. The trucks continued up a large ramp not far from us. The contingent of soldiers blocking the ramp parted to allow the Humvee through. The three trucks stopped where they were. The Hummer turned onto the terrace, and I could see that several soldiers were tossing MREs from the back to the crowd gathering on either side. It reminded me of a Mardi Gras parade, and I surely wasn't the only one. Remember, this is New Orleans, a recently destroyed New Orleans, but New Orleans all the same. Old habits die hard. Several people shouted "Throw me somethin' Mister!" to the troops tossing brown packaged meals instead of plastic beads. In case you're unfamiliar with the vernacular, you're much more likely to hear "Throw me something, Mister" than "Show your tits" during carnival season.

They'd toss a box full of meals and drop the empty cardboard box over the side, adding it to the trash pile in which we'd grown accustomed to living. This haphazard method of distributing food, though festive, wasn't very thorough. Uncle G caught a meal, but none of the rest of us did. As the Hummer moved on, most of the people walked away without receiving an MRE.

With the excitement past us, we sat back down at our place in the sun. I hoped a water truck would pass by soon. Once again, we were dreadfully short of water. Inside the stadium, this wasn't as much of a problem, but out in the afternoon sun, dehydration could be a real issue.

More and more people were pressing themselves onto the wide walk path and into the bus line, several thousand by then must have been compressed in that one space. These were your pushers, your shovers, your fighters, and no-goodniks. Those of us out on the terrace, away from the line, enjoyed a bit more elbow room, and a more subdued, community-type feel began to surface. Don't get me wrong, thousands of severely stressed people still filled the terrace, the field, and worm tubes, but the most violent and disturbing elements seemed to have disappeared when the line filled. And with them, the fear and unpredictability they brought to the party. Now, this would be solely a test of human endurance, and the ability to wait and cope. Things were far from perfect, but they'd definitely improved. The finish line was in sight, it was real.

Across a sea of thousands of angry people stood a barricade, and past that barricade, freedom. Past that barricade was the rest of our lives, our families, our futures, our hopes, and dreams. We simply had to wait our turn. The sun slowly crossed the sky and hid itself behind the tall buildings with the shattered windows. This was the evening of Thursday, September 1st, 2005, one of the most surreal nights of my entire life, and the night which most often appears in my dreams. In fact, this night seemed so apart from reality, I still sometimes find it hard to believe that it wasn't a dream.

Thursday
September 1st, 2005

Evening

FLAMES IN THE NIGHT

The sun sank, and afternoon became twilight. A new set of enormous floodlights had just been illuminated at the barricade in front of the New Orleans Centre entrance, joining the ones on the tower. A swath of people, wide and deep, winced in unison when the brilliant spotlights flicked on. They blasted the same sterile emergency room shade of white light that the tower lights produced.

The skyscrapers all around bore the scars of Katrina's wrath. I'd seen the windward sides of most of these buildings on our trip to the Superdome, with nearly every window blown out, some with curtains waving like white flags in the breeze. From this vantage point, most windows were intact, maybe one in eight busted out. The cloudless, orange sky shone on those glass windows. We were far enough from the line on the walk path that I could hear the quiet, the wings of flies buzzing, the brown water lapping all around. The flies, surprisingly, didn't become a huge problem in our stadium full of trash, but they were there. Other than the murmur of nearby voices, the whole experience had become forest-campsite quiet, kind of eerie, in fact. Countryside, outdoor silence, no cars, no traffic, just the mirror windows of skyscrapers reflecting the orange and purple sunset. No streetlights or neon signs, just four distant Army floodlights and the setting sun. Only things missing were weenies and s'mores.

Among this new group, I met several interesting people. People from all over creation. The men who'd come the farthest to live in the Feces-dome were two guys from Austria staying at the India House, an infamous-in-a-good-way hostel in the City. I've heard there's another India House in Memphis. Hans was skinny and had brown hair, and he only spoke German. His buddy Klaus did all the talking and translating. Hans was okay, but Klaus really sticks out in my mind, not least of all because of his name. When I pointed at a black garbage bag and said my hippo named Klaus was in there, I don't think he really understood what I was getting at. Klaus had a big belly and really terrible teeth, all black around the gums, and he spoke English like Kermit the Frog speaking in a German accent.

I met a guy named Steve wearing a leather motorcycle jacket that looked like it had been repeatedly run over by a train and left in the sun and rain for a year. He was never without it. If he took it off, he'd tie the sleeves around his waist. Steve was okay, he talked fast and often, and a young black woman in blue scrubs and tan Army boots followed him like a shadow. This is the girl I mentioned earlier, who'd been sexually assaulted and left for dead until found by a group of soldiers. She went by Jo. I conjured the image of Steve in his leather jacket swearing to protect her like a knight at Medieval Times. They never separated, not for a moment.

A woman named Jeanine had a full head of curly, gray and white hair, though only in her mid-thirties. She wore thick eyeglasses, and upon first glance, I assumed she must be a school teacher. My assumption proved correct, but not in the way I'd initially imagined. My guess was that she taught pre-Kindergarten, possibly third grade, little kids. In fact, Jeanine taught graduate school courses and had traveled across the globe doing research. Her specialty: traditions and mysteries of the Jewish religion. She tried to describe some of the finer points of Hassidic study and beliefs, modern and ancient. I had no idea this topic went so deep, but, then again, the Jewish people have been accumulating beliefs and traditions for more than five thousand years, so I can see how there'd be an abundance to be learned. Jeanine herself wasn't Jewish, but raised Lutheran. She'd left Michigan and come to New Orleans for college a decade and a half before and never left.

Another woman I met and talked to for quite a long time was named Cathy. She and her seventeen-year-old son Jason had crawled into a passing boat from the second-story window of their home in Lakeview. They'd hitched a ride up Canal Street on top of a Police S.W.A.T. team riot tank sort of thing. Cathy seemed to be in a state of motor functioning shellshock.

Cathy introduced me to her son, Jason, while he was deep in conversation with man named Tom, a white guy wearing Roy Orbison glasses. Tom was in his mid-forties, a native of Indiana. He rented half of a duplex in the "Bywater" section of the Ninth Ward. The Bywater is a tiny sliver of a mixed neighborhood in an overwhelmingly black section of the City. Tom stood well over six feet tall, weighed about two-hundred and fifty pounds, and spoke with a rich *basso profundo*. Tom would become the welcome fifth member of our group over the next couple of days. He grew very close to Mother and me, and helped us enormously both during and after the whole Superdome experience. Tom had been in the stadium longer than anyone else I met, being among the very first people admitted when the doors opened the previous Friday night, while Simone and I were watching busboys vomit milk at Lorenzo's. Tom enjoys experimental rock from the 70s and fantasy novels, and he immediately showed a great interest in Mother, but in a very genuine and gentlemanly way that I admired. He was a good guy.

Of course, there were many, many other people around our new camp, and each one displayed their patience and charms. It was an easy spot to settle into, even after the Army left us and their broken down truck. About two hours after my talk with the Major, in which he assured me he and his soldiers weren't going anywhere, he and his soldiers did leave their position, and set up a new barricade about forty yards down the terrace. Shortly after, a group of people made themselves a spot underneath the trunk, so as to be in the shade. None of that really mattered, the Army troops were still within eyesight. And, more than that, we'd found our place in the organism. Our organ system. The respiratory system, if allowed to pick. I could breathe easier out here. We'd found this little corner of the terrace and were determined that this was where we belonged. I wish we had found it sooner, but better late than never.

As the sun disappeared, the glass on the buildings ceased reflecting all of that brilliant pink and orange light. It was the stars' turn to shine. Like when I was out on my roof, the stars shone brighter and more plentifully than I ever thought possible in a City of over half a million people.

In the wink of an eye, the glass windows lit up like the sun had returned from the nighttime darkness. I don't remember hearing a big boom, but I certainly remember the flames. The word around the stadium was that some kind of a chemical storage facility across the river had exploded; why, I don't know, and I actually never saw the towering flames, just their reflection on the glass windows of the skyscrapers. Brilliant fire and flames danced the night away, as if projected upon dozens of fifty-story movie screens. The pyrotechnics show all around us contrasted sharply with the darkness, the stars and the sterile white light of the Army spotlights. Every once in a while, low rumbling explosions could be heard over the water-lapping quiet. Surreal is the word I most often use to describe that effect of light and dark, of blackness and fire, silence and sound. The fires burned hot all through the night, and, in a terrible sense, they kept me warm. The bouncing flames, reflected off of a thousand windows, were a cathartic display of just how destroyed my City truly was and how much work there would be to do if she were ever going to thrive again. To me, she looked like a goner. I had no sure way of knowing that the fires were only burning on the west bank. Reflected on the buildings, the flames seemed enormous and close. For all I knew, the French Quarter was burning and the fire was spreading, creeping closer to the Superdome with every moment that passed. If that had been the case, nothing could have saved the City, or us, from total annihilation. Try to imagine ten thousand souls running through a flooded metropolis engulfed in flames. That is what I saw reflected on all of that towering glass down in the Central Business District on September 1st. In those orange flames reflected on the cold silver glass, I saw a glimpse of the end. Those flames were going to erase New Orleans from the map for eternity; turn off the lights and watch it burn. It was the closest to the apocalypse I ever hope to get.

And yet, everyone around me was so calm, like they were sleepwalking. I felt like I was sleepwalking, I'd missed so many hours of sleep over the preceding days. I think I was starting to crash, which undoubtedly added to the unreal dreaminess of the skyscrapers and flames.

Somnambulist or not, five days before I'd wound my chest-length hair into an elastic ponytail holder until my dark, brown naps formed a neat little button just above the nape of my neck. My hair had been up in this bunch for five days. I didn't have hair anymore; I had a single, giant knot. I couldn't even remove the band holding it all together.

Cathy told me that crocheting and weaving numbered among her varied hobbies, which also included gardening and playing piano. She said she wished she had some yarn to work, that it would help clear her mind and pass the time. I offered her my knot of oily hair, and she accepted. I laid my body down on a flattened cardboard MRE box and laid my head on the soft, heavenly, comfortable thigh of this woman I'd just met earlier that afternoon while flames blasted the glass windows like fireworks on New Year's Eve. The kind of comfort that comes from seeing the hand of the Grim Reaper outstretched before you and looking into his hollow orbits: the peace of knowing that you're already dead. I laid on my right side, head in her lap, while she worked her fingers through my knotted hair for at least three hours, maybe double. It's hard to count time at night when sunset truly means "lights out."

Cathy talked and talked to the side of my head as she worked her fingers through every strand. She talked about her life, her son, the man who used to be her husband. More than anything, she talked about God and how powerful He is. Not in some hyper-Book of Revelation, fire-eating sense, but how God is in control of everything we were witnessing. How God made New Orleans with its topographical challenges possible, but that life in this beautiful City came with an ultimatum, that He might want this gift back one day; and that if He did, all He had to do was send a flood and He'd take it back overnight. She confessed that for her entire adult life she'd tried to cheat God and only lived in two-story homes. On the ground level she maintained a very bare living space; only her beloved piano, which couldn't be brought upstairs, would be vulnerable. However, she and her son, whom I heard laughing with Steve and Tom, stored all their memories, their lives, up on the second level. She said that the first floor of her home she'd given to God long ago, but the upper level belonged to her and her Jason. When she climbed out of her bedroom window and into a boat, she began to wonder if her lifelong plan had really been enough. The brown water lapped at the first-floor ceiling when they escaped; how high was it now? Only God knew.

There with the blazing glass all around, sitting on a terrace high above the new urban shoreline of the Gulf of Mexico, I have to say, Cathy made a whole lot of sense. I never did fall asleep on her, despite my exhaustion. She ensured this, or counteracted it, by repeatedly yanking on my tangle as she attempted to unravel my five-day dread. Cathy was a talker, for sure, but I listened quietly to her revolving rant for hours until she dropped my hair lump, threw up her hands, and said, "I can't do anything with this."

I'd thought all of those busy fingers back there yanking and tugging were actually doing some good work. I patiently listened to her go off about her entire life for hours, though I did enjoy it. When she finally threw up her hands and quit, she hadn't even freed the band holding the entire mess together. She did move the knot down about two inches and well over to the right, creating a lopsided furry meatball about the length of George Washington's ponytail. Right then I accepted the inevitable truth. The hair had to go. At my first opportunity it would be snip-snip, goodbye hair. I contemplated asking one of those soldiers if they had a pair of scissors.

I twisted my lump back into the band as best I could as Cathy began talking to someone else. I stood up to stretch my legs. The thick line over on the walkway didn't seem to be moving at all. I couldn't tell if anyone had made it onto a bus. They just seemed to be standing still. All the while, the flames danced on the buildings and hundreds of people shuffled along in the shadows around us. I told the gang that I needed to go take a pee. I asked Uncle G to dig my flashlight out of his bag. I'd last used it up on the roof to flash at helicopters. I moved away to our right, farther down the terrace toward where the Major and his soldiers had set up their new barricade. With so many of the people crowded in the line, it really wasn't hard to find a quiet spot in the pitch darkness to take a piss over the side of the railing onto the City street beneath.

I heard some shouts, concerted shouts, not the usual cacophony of the crowd. Looking down toward the barricade, I saw a body of soldiers standing in line, rifles across their chests. An Army truck with its high-beam headlights illuminated the squad. I went in closer to investigate. They put on quite a show. One man would shout some unintelligible phrase, and the remainder of them would respond some other gibberish in cadence. They split into a two-rank skirmish formation, each man about a yard from the next one to the right, to the left, and behind. The other soldiers shouted at the people around to back up, and the soldiers moved pieces of the barricade. The line of soldiers moved forward through the barricade and into the Wild West, followed by the truck.

The way they stood and stepped, the cleanliness and crispness of their uniforms, these guys were new to the party, no doubt. Many of the Privates I'd seen working around the stadium looked terribly young, pimply, and, I'll say it, kind of goofy in their uniforms: like a high school ROTC carrying real assault rifles and trapped in an unspeakable human hell. These fresh guys, they were tall and bulky with muscles. As they got a little closer, I noticed they carried bad-ass looking shotguns in place of M-16s. The patches on their shoulders weren't the Pelican State flags of the Louisiana National Guard. They looked more like diamond shapes patterned from individual stars.

What the hell, I figured they wouldn't shoot me for asking, "Where're you boys from?"

"Arkansas. Move aside."

The line of them passed me toward the bend in the terrace, which led to the tower and the congested walk path, and the flaming skyscrapers. As the truck passed me, I saw that there were several soldiers behind the vehicle distributing items being tossed down to them from other troops standing in the back of the truck. One fella, built like an NFL tight-end, medicine ball-tossed me a package of twenty-four shrink-wrapped water bottles, Nestle Pure, and moved on.

I ran back to the gang to show off my prize. Twenty-four bottles of water just handed to me like it was nothing. We'd been waiting in line for hours to get two! I offered them up to my neighbors and handed out about half of them. "Check

it out, y'all. Army dudes from Arkansas. The fucking cavalry HAS arrived!"
A handful of our team, Mother among them, walked forward to greet, thank,
and even cheer the soldiers as they passed. Marching forward, most of them
remained stone-faced, others did smile. Steve, in his leather jacket, scored a case
of water, too. Steve and a couple others returned the bottles I'd just given them,
though I said that this was unnecessary.

After re-collecting most of what I'd handed out, Tom reached over and said,
"Here, trade ya."

He tossed me a pack of Kools with eleven whole cigarettes inside. In return,
he grabbed three more water bottles. I can't stress enough how huge this was.
The majority of the people I saw in the stadium were smoking cigarettes; after a
couple days in here, cigarettes were worth more than Kuwaiti crude.

"Dude. Tom."

"I wouldn't give them to you if I didn't have more. Don't worry about that.
Besides, I'm thirsty," he replied in his low, sub-woofer voice.

I tried to hand one each to Mother and Jimena, but Tom had already supplied
them with a box that had six in it while I'd walked off to relieve myself. Tom was
a good dude like that.

I noticed Jeanine and Cathy talking to each other. I walked over and sat down.

"We're leaving," Cathy said.

"You're going to get into the line right now?" I asked.

"As soon as we're ready," replied Jeanine. "It'll be daylight in a couple hours.
The line looks like it's moving quickly enough. And now that more soldiers are
here, hopefully the line will move that much quicker."

"Word, wait, what time is it?"

"After three in the morning."

"Shit, well good luck guys. I think we're down to wait until a bus rolls up on
us, to hell with that line. Here, take some water."

Very quickly, Jeanine replied, "No, we have everything we need."

Cathy walked off to go check on Jason and his level of preparedness. Jeanine
adjusted the eyeglasses on her face and looked into my soul with her warm,
brown eyes.

"Look, we are out of here. I've got everything I need. I've got stuff that I won't
need anymore. Is there anything that you need? Anything that would help you
out?"

I'd arrived at the stadium with a dog and a hippo, and the clothes on my back.
Aside from water and Army food, I didn't have any possessions. I thought for
a moment about what I wished I had the most, something that would help the
achingly slow time pass more smoothly. "Do you have anything to read that you
could leave me?"

"Umm, let me think," she said, as she dug around in her large shoulder bag
that could probably hold more junk than a suitcase. "Most of what I brought

with me are hard to find one-of-a-kinds, really technical volumes . . . oh, here you go! I have another one of these where I'm going. Here, you might like this one."

First, how did she know where she was going? These buses evacuating people weren't taxi cabs to other cities, but I supposed when you got to wherever the bus let you off, you'd be able to go to a place of your own choosing. America is a big nation, not all of it was flooded and burning. It's interesting, until that moment, I hadn't thought that far ahead. I didn't have the slightest idea of where I was trying to get to, I just knew that I needed to get somewhere other than where I was.

Jeanine handed me a thick paperback book, much larger than a trade paperback in length and width. On both sides, the cover was all black. The title in tiny white letters I read aloud with a blast from my flashlight, *Interpretations of the Meklita*?

"Yeah, it's a must have for a history guy like you. Hold on, I've got some other stuff you might be able to use."

I held my flashlight for her while she dug around in her bag. I flipped my new book open to a random page just to see if I could figure out what a Meklita was. The answer wasn't on that page, but I figured out what the "Interpretations" portion of the title meant. The left-hand pages of the book were written in Hebrew, the facing page in English, with lots of footnotes. I tried a paragraph from the English side of the page. It read like computer code. When I asked for something to read, I hadn't figured she'd hand me a tome of ancient Hebrew law. I've probably got this all wrong, but from what I understand, the Meklita, named after the Rabbi who wrote it, is a two-thousand-year-old school of thought concerning the laws written in the five-thousand-year-old book of Exodus.

"I can't wait to see how it ends," I joked.

Jeanine laughed and said, "Here, I've made a little kit for you."

In a blue and white striped travel case for toiletries, she'd packed a clean handkerchief, a travel size tube of toothpaste, and this tiny plastic box with a Renaissance-era portrait of a lady and a unicorn posing together on the cover. Inside the box were three cotton swabs and a Band-Aid. "I put those in the case so they'd stay dry."

"Thanks."

"And here," she snatched the book and the striped bag from me and stuffed them into a little canvas library book bag. "Now you can carry all of your stuff." She beamed with selfless satisfaction. Cathy returned with Jason. "We're ready to go," said Jason.

"So am I, just saying goodbye," Jeanine returned.

"Good luck. I know you'll be fine, but good luck and thanks again for the book," I said.

"You just might pick up on some Hebrew." We gave each other a big hug, then she said, "I want you to have this, too." She handed me a folded-up twenty dollar bill.

"Hey, I'm not taking your money. Some Q-tips is one thing, but . . ."

"No, I want you to take this. You don't have any money. I know that. You might want to buy yourself something one day. Let me do this for you."

I hugged her again, and hugged Cathy and Jason, too. Jeanine plopped an absurd gray hat with an enormous pink bow on top of her curly gray-haired head, the kind of hat ladies might wear to a fancy country club for tea. With her hat in place, the three of them walked off toward the beams of light on the soldier's tower. I slid the twenty dollar bill into the fifth pocket of my jeans, next to my green Tortex guitar pick. I wouldn't spend it for a couple months, but eventually I did.

I laid myself down next to Mother on a piece of cardboard, slid Klaus the hippo under my head and watched the flames for a little while longer, puffing on one of Tom's cigarettes. I touched the twenty in my pocket and thought of how lucky I was to have met such kind and generous people here in this great pile of trash and poo.

All things considered, we'd had pretty good luck from the start. As I closed my eyes, I hoped that our luck would hold out for just a little bit longer and we would get on a bus together and leave in one piece. Maybe then we could start thinking about where we would go next.

FRIDAY
SEPTEMBER 2ND, 2005

Cocktails on the Veranda

The next thing I remember was hearing Mother's voice. I opened my eyes to a purple sky quickly turning blue—the dawning of another day. The flames on the windows had disappeared, their reflections victim to the increasing sunlight. I stood up, stretched, and cracked open a bottle of water. The Army floodlights clicked off one by one.

Mother, Jimena, and Uncle G were up early. They'd slept while Cathy tugged on my hair all night. The remaining crowd stirred, so there was nothing to do but join them. There was no way I'd be able to get back to sleep with the sun and thousands of shuffling feet. Grape flavored Army drink or coffee water and Kool 100s completed the breakfast menu. We'd definitely slowed our Army food consumption rate. I can't speak for the rest of my crew, but I hadn't truly moved my bowels since arriving at the stadium. The previous time was Tuesday morning, into a grocery bag, up on my roof. Three days and several MREs later, my gut felt like a piece of lead. Three days and thousands of calories, and I didn't have the slightest urge to go. I thought maybe I just needed more time to digest it all, but that was bullshit. I'd seen at least twenty thousand turds with my own eyes, and smelled countless others. Everyone else seemed to have no trouble at all processing the soldier chow. But, ugh! I felt so dense, and yet somehow blissfully unaware of my epic constipation. I could have eaten an entire ration for breakfast and not batted an eye. But, no, that would only add more concrete to the immovable foundation I'd already laid. Just grape drink and water for breakfast, I'd figure out what to do about lunch later on.

Looking toward the giant line of people, I spotted Jeanine's floppy gray hat with the help of the enormous pink flower on top. They'd progressed about a quarter of the way across the walk path, but now that the hot sun was rising higher, I knew their time in line wouldn't be quite as comfortable as it had been during the overnight hours. After watering Dolja, I knew it was once again time to water the City. I walked back around the terrace, closer to the line of soldiers, and right past them altogether, walking farther around the terrace than I'd yet ventured. The soldiers had abandoned their line across the terrace and were gathered around one of the giant ramps leading down to street level. The farther I walked, the fewer people there were, reminding me more of what Woodstock looked like after everyone had left the muddy fields strewn with clothing and garbage. Standing over one of the entrances to the parking levels of the stadium, I urinated into the brown water below. The morning sun and the lightest breeze, the quiet City all around; it was very peaceful. I stopped for a moment to take it all in. From below me I could hear the murmur of voices. Looking around, I discovered a set of stairs over the side of the terrace just a few feet down. The stairs led to the giant parking structure below the actual sports arena, one of the few places in the City where you could go underground and below the level of the streets. I climbed over and hopped down onto one of the landings of the stairs for a look. Crisscrossing at steady angles were levels of parking spaces dotted with a few cars, and though I didn't immediately see anyone, the voices I'd heard were a little louder. The ground down there was dry, and there were no people. Knowing that I had nothing but time, I decided I'd come back to this place later on and force out the Army food as best I could in the relative privacy of the parking deck. The thought of escaping the prying eyes greatly excited me. Hopefully the soldiers wouldn't shoot me on sight for being down there.

I returned to my group, but kept my discovery to myself. That was my bathroom. It wouldn't do to have several people going down there and mucking up my virgin, crap-free place. Besides, if the soldiers caught on, they might station a guard on those stairs.

Not long after returning, we heard some shouting and honking horns. A convoy of three Humvees approached our camp from the direction of the tower. Uncle G and I moved into position to catch some of whatever they were handing out. Just as the lead truck got within a few feet of us, a soldier dropped a cardboard box over the side right in front of us, an unopened box containing two or three dozen MREs. Jackpot! With the cases of water we'd gotten yesterday, this would solve the food problem for our group for days to come, but before I could grab the box it was snatched up by a tall young guy with chin-length braids in his hair. He lifted the box, adjusted his falling down baggy pants, and started walking off.

"Hey, those are for everybody," I said to him.

He turned around and said, "No, they's fo' me."

"Damn, man, my mama's sick over here. Think I can get one meal so my mom can eat?"

"Yo mama ain't none a my mutha fuckin' problem. Na you best lee' me da FUCK alone befo' you get hurt." He turned away, calling me a "bitch-ass nigga."

Really, I wasn't shocked over what he said. I totally expected that kind of reaction from just about anyone in this post-apocalyptic scenario we were living out. No time for sympathy, just dog-eat-dog and the fittest will survive. As the remaining trucks passed us, and boxes of food were carried off by these calorie hoarders, Uncle G stood with his hands cupped around his mouth to make sure his voice would carry. To the passing soldiers, he shouted, "Y'all feeding us like this means that white people won't get to eat!" If anyone heard him, they made no sign of recognition. The column of Hummers moved past us and we hadn't scored a single gram of nutrition.

Uncle G was incensed with a fury I'd never seen before. He actually took a couple puffs off a cigarette to help calm his nerves, a rare sight indeed. Not like he was some kind of anti-smoking Nazi, he just didn't do it unless stressed to a precision point.

Morning approached noon, and the sun approached its zenith in the sky. There were few clouds. The air was nice and humid, but the temperature stayed in the upper eighties, so it wasn't the most brutal day of summer, but certainly hot enough. Jimena directed our attention down to where the soldiers guarded the ramp. They were handing out food. Jimena, G, and I dashed down to receive a meal. We each received two bottles of hot water that had apparently been sitting in direct sunlight, and two MREs–enough food for our nuclear family for the time being. And though we possessed a surplus of water, we knew that we'd be out in the sun all day, so no amount of bonus water was going to get turned down, not with the sun and mercury rising higher.

It really started getting hot out there. Mother, Uncle G, and Jimena—even Tom—were pouring water on their heads and necks trying to cool off. I was tempted to do the same, but I thought a hot wet head had to be just as bad as a hot dry head. Probably better to just drink that water. I felt myself getting overheated, too. I took my shirt off and tried to make a turban for my head, with minimal success. Then I remembered Jeanine's bag. The canvas book tote tied nicely into a thick, funky looking piece of head gear, but it worked wonderfully. The lumpy double-layer of canvas created a tiny space in between the layer on my head and the layer getting hit by the sun. That bag really did make for a useful hat. Then I tied the white handkerchief around my neck, and Bam! Successful sun coverage. However, that didn't help the rest of my group. Other people around were making use of the tons of cardboard and other refuse lying around. I ran off and grabbed the cleanest looking box from the nearest trash pile, broke it apart for Mother, and laid it over her shoulders. The flattened box was just large enough to cover her back, neck, and shoulders. Turning the box sideways, it was large enough for all three of them to duck their heads under and into some shade.

"Hang on, guys, I'll go find some more boxes."

Finding pristine boxes in a stadium full of trash is much harder than it sounds. More than once, I'd spot one and pick it up, only to discover someone had used it for a toilet. I walked a ways around the building, past the soldiers, and only scored one good box. I delivered it back to the group and went around the other direction, toward the tower and the big line, in search of that elusive third box. Thousands and thousands of people had crossed the wide walk path in the twenty-four hours since its formation. Thousands of people and not a single toilet had been set up on the walk path. When the breeze caught that odor and blew it my way, I gagged so loudly that a couple ladies nearby pointed and laughed at me. With watery eyes, I waved at them and kept on in search of another box. The line looked as bad as it smelled. In some places, the trash was piled to shoulder height or taller, and just like on the field, narrow pathways formed around the trash mountains. Unlike the field, the wide brick walk path might have been only thirty yards across instead of a hundred yards like the field was with the sidelines. If shots were to ring out and another stampede occurred like on Wednesday night, there would be much less room to maneuver. I pictured people going over the sides of the walk path trying to escape the bullets and falling forty feet to their deaths. As bad as everything had been in the Superdome, it could easily have gotten much worse. A death toll in the tens of thousands hung like a carrot on a string. After moving past the line, I found myself on a section of the terrace that I hadn't been to yet.

Excepting the different view of the cityscape, this section of terrace was visually identical to the end where we'd set up our camp. I worked my way down to the next ramp leading down to street level. The Army guarded the ramp with trucks and barricades. This side of the terrace wasn't getting pounded by the sun like where we were. Off to one side of the barricade was a stack of flattened MRE boxes. Score.

The sounds of breaking glass, hoots, and laughter distracted me from my hunting and gathering task. Instead of grabbing the boxes straight away, I decided to investigate. My curiosity led me to one of the most disturbing things I saw during the whole experience. Worse than the worm tubes, red light district, or the night of a thousand fights.

At some point during this mess, people were given glass beer bottles filled with drinking water. Brown Miller beer bottles full of water, a public service from our local bottling facility during times of disaster. I'd seen this kind of thing before. Once when my grandparents had gone to Panama City for an RVing beach week, they'd gotten caught up in a tropical storm, and, long story short, Papi brought me home a six pack of Budweiser cans full of water. The six pack even had the plastic ring thing on it. The cans were all squishy without carbonation. It was weird.

Some guys had gathered up a bunch of these bottles and were dropping them over the side of the terrace one at a time. I'd heard a bottle break, the next pitcher looked over the side, took careful aim, and tossed his bottle over the side. Instead of breaking glass, I heard a hollow glass bottle *thunk* followed by a splash. Apparently, that was a good sound. The guys in on the game, probably about six or eight of them, cheered, clapped, and hooted to one another. Then there was a high-five. I remember it so clearly.

The man who'd tossed the winning shot raised his arms in the touchdown position exclaiming, "I got hu' ass! I got hu' right tween da shoulders!"

Maintaining proper distance from the group of men, I looked over the rail and saw a young black woman's corpse floating face-down in the brown water. Where her story began and ended, I'll never know, but her remains were beached at the foot of the stadium, resting on the sloped ramp of a parking deck entrance. These guys had made a game out of trying to bounce bottles off of her remains, forty feet below.

She wore jean shorts, a t-shirt, and a pair of black Chuck Taylor Converse shoes. Her arms and legs were swelled out from the sleeves and legs of her pants. Her skin had turned a grayish-yellow, and then I caught a whiff of that repugnantly sweet smell of death. Another bottle splashed in the water—*ploomb*—wide to the right. There was nothing to do but leave.

I returned to the group with five boxes worth of cardboard under my arm. Try to picture it if you can. Merely four days after landfall, a shirtless man wearing a canvas bag for a hat out hunting cardboard for his family, while others are busy desecrating a corpse. It's amazing how quickly society can just dissolve like an Alka Seltzer tablet in shitty brown water and we become *Lord of the Flies*.

As we broke down the boxes, Mother told me she had to pee. I said I'd walk with her to the bathroom or anywhere else she wanted to go.

"Fuck that! I ain't going back into that week-old pile of shit! Naw, help Mama put a box together." We walked away from the camp about thirty yards. After taking her shoes off, she squatted in the box and peed through her pants while pouring two bottles of water over her overheated body. After her bath, she looked better than she had in days, even if she was dripping wet. When I said, "Hey, Mother; did you just piss on yourself?" she said "I ain't pulling my pants down in front of these pervert mutha fuckas." She's the best.

Uncle G sat on a piece of cardboard with a sheet of cardboard balanced on his neck and stooped shoulders. The guy was a cardboard sandwich. He was sorting through our MRE meal choices. I had only gotten one pork rib during the past four days, even though, collectively, thirty MREs must have passed under my nose.

Joking with Tom and Mother, I shouted in my best Joan Crawford, "No more Turkey Dinners, Ever!" Come on, everyone knows the "No more wire hangers" bit from *Mommy Dearest*. Apparently, more people heard me say this than just my immediate audience. I heard someone say, "Whoa, what you lookin' fo', man?"

I turned around and saw that the question had come from a group of guys sitting under the shade of the overhanging Superdome structure. They were pretty tough-looking guys, five of them, three hispanic and two black. I thought it best to tread lightly.

"Do what, now?"

It was one of the black guys who'd spoken. "I said, what you lookin' fo'? What meal? If I got it, I trade you if you got summa dat Beef Stew."

"I got some Beef Stew, bra. You got one of those Pork Ribs?"

"Man, we got it all ova hea'. Come on ova, bra, so we don't gotta shout." The guys weren't but twenty feet away.

I grabbed the Beef Stew MRE and told Mother I'd be right back. And so the

Beef Stew was exchanged for the Pork Rib, and both parties were happier for the trade. Dolja and I were going to enjoy dinner tonight.

"Thanks, y'all," I said to all of the guys there, though I'd only been talking to the one. They all nodded and said, "You're welcome," more or less. I figured these were probably okay dudes.

As I turned to head back to my gang, one of the Spanish guys, the one seated closest to the fella I'd been talking to, said, "Hey, man. We're trying to kill off this bottle before we go get into line. You got time to talk and have a drink with us?"

The thus-far silent older black guy raised up a bottle of clear Bacardi Rum. Ol' Beef Stew slid a 10-ounce Solo plastic cup from a sleeve of cups and handed it to me. The man with the bottle poured me a thick shot and said, "Po' a lil wota on it."

The hispanic guy who'd offered me the drink in the first place lifted up a fresh, unopened bottle of water and said, "Have a seat, man. Sit in the shade with us, have a drink. My man here wants to talk to you."

Damn. Why'd he have to say that at the end of this spectacular moment? *My man wants to talk to you.* What the hell does that mean? What did I do? I had a drink in my hand from out of nowhere, from out of thin fucking air. Five minutes ago, I was another nobody in a sea of nobodies . . . and trash and turds. But, no doubt, I was still me. Now I had a cup full of rum. All it cost me was a pouch of nasty-ass beef stew, and I'd come out ahead a nasty pork rib in BBQ sauce. Somehow in this transaction, I was standing entirely in the shade of the stadium as I sat down on a cardboard box stuffed with other cardboard until it made a halfway decent seat. These guys seemed okay, but I couldn't help but feeling like Ethan Hawke in that scene from *Training Day* where he's playing cards and the guy says he had his "shit pushed in!" and then they almost blow his brains out in a bathtub. What had I done that he needed to talk to me about?

I thought that—my survival mode gut reaction to this gesture—but I didn't "feel" it. I slid my retarded-looking canvas hat off my head and looked around at their faces. Their smiles were genuine.

Beef Stew introduced himself as "T" and the hispanic guy's name was "Oscar." T said, "Man, I respect the fuck outta da way you been takin' caya a yo mama, man. Dat's yo moms ova dea'. I know it is. Fuck, man, fuck. I cooun't neva pictua' my mama up in dis shit, man. My mama fuckin' dead, man, o else she be up in hea' too. Ya know it man. I glad she ain't neva had to see dis, ya unnastan'. Fuck, man, you sittin' dea' kickin' it wit yo mama, fixin hu' kawfee, lightin' hu' cigarette an' shit. Man, dats, ya know, dats some beautiful shit to me, man."

About that time I noticed that all five of them held little plastic cups. T had definitely filled his cup more than once. Maybe it was the heat. "My mama dead, man. I thank ta LORD! that she ain't had to see dis shit, MAN. Fuck, dog, sit cho' ass down and have a drink with me and my boys, man. Yo, man. I tole you I respect that shit, man. Nigga went and got his mama fuckin' cawdbowd, man."

Oscar just nodded and laughed at his buddy. I think T the Beef Stew had filled his cup way more than once. Either way, I hadn't realized until just then how badly I wanted a drink. I cracked open the water bottle, poured some water into my cup of Bacardi rum, and took a sip. For a moment, everything disappeared. The brown water, the worm tubes, the rank piss, and the Army guys, and my tongue went numb. The rum and the water mixed together tasted so sweet and clean and cooling as I sipped it down. I can't describe it.

Back in the days of sailing ships, this mixture of rum and water would be commonly referred to as *grog*. Why would they call it that? Who the hell knows, but I'll tell you this. From that day to this, grog has been my drink. Way better with ice, of course, maybe a lemon or a lime if you're feeling frisky. Grog has ghost-written most of this memoir, that's for damn sure. *The author is enjoying a grog as he writes this passage at one-thirty on a Tuesday night. Grog, dude. I digress.*

Oscar told me that he and the other two hispanic fellas, who spoke no English, shared an apartment and that T and his uncle, the bartender, lived in another apartment in the same building by the fairgrounds, near Paris Avenue. They'd made their way to the Dome on foot. The hispanic guys had taken a city bus to the Dome on Saturday night. Last Saturday night. Remember, this is Friday. I told him our story.

T had kinda started to nod off while Oscar and I talked, but he snapped back to life and looked around, bewildered, for a moment, rose to his feet, looked at Oscar and said to him, "Man, what da fuck is wrong wit cho' Messican ass?"

"Sit down, nigga."

"Nigga? Fuck you too nigga, wit cho' nigga Messican ass. You da worse niggas dey got."

Oscar chuckled at him the whole time. These two had to know each other to clown like that. It was obvious that they did.

Now T turned on me with a twisted grimace, "Man, and what the fuck is wrong with chu, man, tell yo family to get out da sun and get dey ass ova hea'."

Graciously, they accepted and all found a spot to sit in the blessed shade. Two conversations sprung up, one in Spanish, the other in English, Oscar serving as the go-between translator. I sipped my grog while we passed a couple cigarettes around the gathering, and everything seemed alright with the world. Even stone-faced Jimena felt comfortable enough to manage a smile. I finished my cup, and the bartender poured the rest of the bottle into my cup, maybe half a shot.

"We down to da lass," said the bartender as he pulled out a fifth of Grey Goose vodka, over half had already been drunk.

"When T said he found something to drink upstairs, I didn't know he'd found six bottles of the shit. We been drinkin' for days over here, man. But I'm about ready to get the hell out of here for real. Pour this man some vodka so we can get the fuck outta here," said Oscar.

I sipped down the last of the rum, and the bartender refilled my cup with a fat shot of the vodka. I poured in a little water and took a sip…ugh! It was awful. Compared to the sweet, smooth, and dry Bacardi, the vodka tasted like paint thinner, and smelled like rubbing alcohol. I'd be nursing my way through that one.

Mother told me she felt much better after a little time in the shade and excused herself to go sit by Tom. I figured, what the hell, so many people had left through the bus line, I could actually walk around the terrace with ease. I remembered my digital camera and asked Uncle G if he'd mind fishing it out of his bag for me.

"Hey, y'all, I'm going to go for a walk and take some pictures." I walked a lap around the terrace, snapping as many pictures as my tiny 16 megabit memory card would hold, and deleting as many of the pictures as my conscience would permit. In hindsight, maybe I should have erased them all and better chronicled this historic event, but the thought never crossed my mind. Those pictures were the only thing I had with me to remind me that I'd been somebody and been somewhere else before this brown water world.

I snapped photos of a Vietnam War Memorial statue on the terrace, a picture of the smoke still rising from the previous night's fires, but when I looked over the side of the rail down at the drowned woman's corpse with the broken glass all around her, I stopped. I thought that it would be better to live the rest of my life without capturing that image. Taking her picture in that condition, I felt then and still feel now, would have been like shaming her memory and stealing her soul. Instead, I snapped a picture of the cityscape from that spot along the railing, to remind me of the life lost down below. In truth, I didn't need to snap any picture to remind me of her and her pungent, sweet smell on that sunny Friday afternoon. I carry her with me every day.

While making my lap around, snapping photos and scavenging discarded coffee packs, more than once I felt a rumble in my stomach that didn't exactly feel like hunger. Maybe it was the combination of the alcohol and a little bit of walking, but I thought that it might be time to go, in the way I'd been waiting to go for almost four days.

I walked back to the gang and had a swig of watery vodka; I'd left Uncle G in charge of my cup and he'd done a fine job. After gathering about five squares of MRE toilet paper, I started off toward my parking garage sanctuary. Over the side and down the stairs, I crept into the gloom of the sunless parking deck. The ground sloped to my left and, with tons of concrete and stadium overhead, I could clearly hear the brown water lapping down that way. I didn't want to get ambushed with my pants around my ankles, so I walked up around the next corner and came to a completely empty level, only two spaces occupied out of a hundred. Halfway up the level was a busted-up hoopty. Much closer to me was parked a little white pickup truck. The owner obviously made it a point to keep their vehicle clean.

I pressed my sweaty back against the driver's side door and slid down into a squat, fully expecting to create something spectacular. But the Army food again proved too powerful for my weak civilian guts. Thoroughly frustrated, I prepared myself to leave the parking deck and head back to the surface. Just as I was about to climb back up the stairs, I heard the muffled voices again from another level of the massive garage. If there was one thing we residents of the Superdome possessed, it was time, so I decided to investigate as far as I could without being seen or getting wet.

I walked right up to the shoreline of the brown water. Once again, everything got eerily quiet. Down in this subterranean sea with many levels of hollow concrete overhead, the lapping water played its unnerving tune. I could no longer hear the voices, just the pounding of my heart.

I crawled up one of the supporting beams, just above the waterline, until I reached a place where two slanted parking levels crisscrossed, and then slid through the tiny space afforded by the beams and metal railings. I'd crawled into an entirely new, unreachable section of the garage. This area was nearly pitch black and the death smell was powerful. For all I could see, there may have been a corpse just a foot in front of me. I tried my best to hold it in, but couldn't contain the urge to retch, and more than once I coughed quite audibly. Then the voices. From out of the darkness.

"Did you hear that?"

"Who's there?"

I held my breath. My God, I've never been so scared. I saw the beam of a distant flashlight. I'd definitely stumbled onto something I wasn't supposed to find. The overpowering dead smell led me to believe I'd found some kind of mortuary underneath the stadium. Surely, I'll never really know. I didn't want to wait down there in the dark until these guys found me and did whatever they were doing to nosy intruders, so I did the only thing I could. I crawled back through my hole and ran up the beam toward the stairs leading back to the terrace. It didn't bother me at all that I'd gotten my shoes wet on the way out, I just wanted to get back to my family in one piece.

Back on the terrace, as I approached the gang sitting under the shade of the building, a burst of laughter greeted my ears. Oscar, T, and the other guys were gone. Uncle G, Jimena, and Mother returned to the shady spot in my absence and sat with another person. Holy crap, it was Glenn! We hadn't seen him since the previous morning. Mother told me later they'd spotted him wandering down the terrace, kind of shell-shocked, and Mother shouted, "Whoa, Glenn! Get yo' fine ass ova hea' boy."

Glenn had lost his bag and his blanket, yet somehow he'd gained a black eye. When I asked him about it, shrugging his shoulders and shaking his head, he said, "What? No, no, it's okay."

We sat down with Glenn in the shade for a bit. Dolja even had the good form to make love to his arm just one more time. Glenn talked casually with Mother and Uncle G, but to me he seemed a little distant, different even. I just assumed he'd been robbed or otherwise confronted. I didn't want to press the guy. Glenn's shit, at some point, had gotten *real*. Whatever had occurred, I didn't see the need to force him to relive it for the sake of my interest. Very recently, my inquisitiveness had me crawling through holes like a rat. The line had to be drawn somewhere. Whether I got his story or not, it was good to see him.

Crawling around on all fours in the parking garage made my hands very dirty, and that's coming from a guy who hadn't washed his hands in several days. I sipped my cup of vodka. It didn't taste nearly as good as the rum had, so I spit some on my hands to loosen the dirt. It helped, but what a terrible form of alcohol abuse. I grabbed a bottle of water to rinse with instead, and about then I had a really fantastic idea—well, more like a series of thoughts coming together to form a plan.

I wanted to wash up. We had plenty of water, but no soap. There was no soap in the MREs, but I had a hunch there was still plenty of soap in those filthy bathrooms. The water had stopped running early on in this mess, hence the deplorable state of the facilities. No one in this place had washed their hands in days. The soap was in there, but people had totally given up on the bathrooms. They were just SO SO gross by that point, a ton of excrement slowly braising in a subtropical oven. Just walking near the filthy fucking things made me gag. How could I ever stand walking right into the unholiest place on Earth to get to the soap and make it out alive?

Vodka, that's how. I still had Jeanine's handkerchief around my neck. I thought that moistening the handkerchief with alcohol and placing it over my face would protect me from the smell long enough to get in and get out. And with this plan, I entered the actual stadium for what would be the last time. People still filled the outer corridor, but it was considerably less full. I didn't have to dry hump fourteen people just to get through. Down the little escalator and into the old concession corridor, the rotting shit smell hit me. As soon as it did, I pulled the handkerchief up over my nose and filled my mouth with my last swig of vodka water and liberally soaked the rag covering my face. Getting closer, the smell hit me so powerfully, even with the vodka rag, I thought I would die right then. I clicked on the flashlight and stepped into the Chamber of Sorrow. I won't describe the visual in detail, I'll leave that up to the reader. I will say this, whatever you're imagining a Superdome bathroom might look like after 20,000 people used the facility without a single flush for a week, whatever you're imagining, it doesn't come close. Take your mental image and multiply by a gross factor of fifty. Now you're getting close.

I furiously pumped pink soap from the dispenser into my hand, trying not to breathe. The alcohol began to evaporate and, without its protection, I instantly started dry heaving. I needed to get out of there immediately. I held a palm full of soap. That would have to be enough.

Once I cleared the door, I gasped for a breath to ease the aching in my lungs, but I hadn't gone far enough. I got a breath of rotting urine and poo and retched watery vodka on my bare chest as I ran back to the escalator and the outdoors.

I'd gotten in and out of the stadium as quickly as possible. However, I did notice just how empty the field and stands were. Not completely empty, but maybe one in four people remained indoors, compared to when we abandoned the field only yesterday. A couple of diehards still wandered the trash-covered field.

Everyone in the gang took a little soap to wash their hands with, and I still had enough to wash my face and armpits, as well as thoroughly washing my hands. I offered to go back for more, but Mother dissuaded me and said a little soap wasn't worth sending me back into the filth. Uncle G and Jimena agreed with her and thanked me for the clean hands.

Several hours before, while I was hunting cardboard, a nearby family of Mexicans had started working diligently on a construction project that didn't make a whole lot of sense to me at first, but was now taking the shape of a marvel of modern engineering. There were fifteen people in this group, half of them children. We'd talked briefly to the group earlier in the day. They'd found a broom and were sweeping the section of terrace that served as their Superdome residence. Jimena asked to borrow the broom and tidied up our space. The broom was offered to others, and they all declined, black and white. I found it interesting that only the hispanic residents of the Superdome cared enough to tidy an area. Everyone else seemed too jaded to want to do anything about their surroundings.

The men of the Mexican family climbed up into the bed of the stalled-out, abandoned Army truck and removed one of the four arch-shaped supports that stretched the optional canvas covering for the truck bed. They moved the oversized upside-down letter U over to their campsite and then went in search of materials. Each cardboard box of MREs contained a single strip of cardboard kind of wound in among the meal pouches to prevent them from being crushed. Stretched to length, these strips measured about one foot by five feet. The Mexican family gathered about two dozen of these strips. They also gathered several wads of the plastic wrap that at one time covered the stacks of MRE boxes while they were still arranged on palettes. Hundreds of these wads of balled-up plastic wrap littered the ground. As the children kicked around one of these wads like a soccer ball, the adults got busy. The wads were unraveled and rolled into long strands of plastic rope. The first wads were used to tie the canopy beam to the terrace railing, standing it up. I was intrigued, but still didn't have a clue what they were up to. A trio of patrolling soldiers stopped for a moment to watch their work, unsure whether or not they should stop them and reclaim the piece of government property the builders had commandeered. In the end, the soldiers moved off and the family carried on with their work.

Next, small holes were made at one end of the cardboard strips and, using more plastic wrap rope, the strips were tied to the canopy support to hang down vertically. The process took hours, but two dozen vertical cardboard strips later, they'd made a fully functional, extraordinarily practical, outdoor vertical Venetian blind. The entire family sat comfortably in the shade while the long cardboard strips swayed in the gentle downtown breeze. The true genius of the design became apparent about an hour later when part of their shade was again being hit by direct sunlight. The guys levered the end they'd tied to the railing and turned the free-standing leg to whichever place it needed to be to maintain optimal shade. I must say, I was thoroughly impressed with their post-destruction ingenuity. They'd turned so much trash into a functional sun-blocking device, increasing their comfort level exponentially. I felt like some kind of lowland gorilla sitting there with a sheet of cardboard over my head while these *Homo sapiens* had actually built something so very useful.

Slowly, dusk turned another day into night. The giant floodlights on the towers illuminated the omnipresent bus line. Fewer and fewer people wandered the terrace, and in direct proportion, they were replaced by a greater number of soldiers patrolling the terrace in teams of four to seven individuals. When I asked where they were from, these soldiers would say things like New York, Ohio, Teyuck-suss. Most carried shotguns, but others carried these awesome little sub-machine guns—a D5K Deutsche, if you're playing *Goldeneye* on Nintendo 64. It amazed me how clean, crisp, and perfectly starched their uniforms appeared. All of the Louisiana Guard soldiers' uniforms I'd seen in the previous days looked as though they'd been dipped in Lake Ponchartrain, then beaten against a brick wall. The Louisiana Guard, those men and women worked their asses to the bone that week. They worked until their fatigues were soaked through with sweat, and then worked some more. They were working for us. I don't know if anyone has ever said this, but to the men and women of the Louisiana National Guard present during that shit storm of human suffering: for what it's worth, I want to say "Thank you." Ladies, gentleman, soldiers, don't get me wrong, you didn't exactly make the experience pleasant, by any stretch of the imagination, but you gave me water and food. No one else was giving me water and food.

Also, there was not an all-out riot in the stadium. There were times when I really thought there would be, like the Night of a Thousand Fights and the Charge of the Gazelles. I'm going to go ahead and give you soldiers credit for preventing that riot, too. Again, for what it's worth, my family and I thank you for being there. I cringe when I think of life in the Dome with no Army presence whatsoever. No water, no food, tens of thousands of people . . .

At the time, I had no way of knowing that more than ten thousand people were also stuck at the Ernest N. Morial Convention Center, New Orleans' principal convention venue, living under those exact conditions—no food, no water, no Army. My heart goes out to each and every last one of them.

The sun had departed on that Friday, September 2nd, probably around 8:30 p.m. The sun, the rum, and the sleepless nights hit me hard. Earlier in the day, we added a pristine Army cot to our collection of camp furniture, which until then consisted of cardboard, random cushions taken from abandoned camp sites, and two black, metal folding chairs that had been Oscar's and T's. Mother noticed me drooping and insisted I lie down and sleep, saying that I'd been awake for too long. When I tried to protest, telling her that someone needed to keep watch, she took my hand into hers and, with a quivering chin and tears swelling in her eyes, said, "Let me and Tom get this one, baby. You've done so much in the past few days to look out for me, let me get this one." She handed me the plastic bag with the hippo inside and said, "Here's Klausie. He's tired, too."

I used the hippo to prop up my right knee like I would do if I were in my own bed and laid back to look at the stars. I laid there imagining myself soaking in an oversized Jacuzzi tub, the water warm and sudsy as I fell asleep.

The Phone Call

It's one o'clock p.m. on Friday September 2nd, 2005. My grandparents are sitting in the living room of their daughter Helen's house with her husband, Uncle Nick; all four of them are glued to the television. They'd been glued for days. Their children, their daughter-in-law, and their only grandson were somewhere on that television screen. They just hadn't found them yet. Maybe, if they just watched a little longer, they'd find us and know we were safe. Countless other Americans watched the coverage from their living rooms as well. They could only see what the camera lens and the editors showed them. Each news segment provided only a glimpse, a meager sliver, of the large-scale panorama of flooded New Orleans.

I saw a handful of news teams with their lights and their cameras filming in the Superdome. None of them, not a single one out of the at least seven film crews I saw, stayed for more than twenty minutes among the crowd. They would take a snapshot, beam it via satellite to America and beyond, and then disappear. I think they preferred the distance the helicopters afforded. Once we left the field and sat out on the terrace, it seemed the helicopters were working in shifts. During the daytime, especially, there was always at least one chopper right above my head.

But now I'm talking about an elderly couple sitting in southwest Florida watching this madness on television on a Friday afternoon. Right about then, I was probably hunting after cardboard boxes, wearing my camouflage slippers and a canvas bag for a hat.

At dinner the previous night, my grandfather had refused to eat, saying, "How can I eat when I don't know if they have food, or if they're alive, even." After he got this sentence out, he broke down in tears. All my life, Papi has been the rock, Abuelita did the crying for both of them. He was her rock, our rock, the Rock of Gibraltar's rock. Papi is the warmest, most beautiful, and kind man. His blood pumps hard with emotion, with love, but I don't remember ever really seeing him gnash his teeth, heave, and cry like a fountain. Abuelita, my beautiful grandmother: I knew she was somewhere worried to death, with big alligator tears rolling down her brown cheeks, a single tissue cried and snotted into near oblivion. That I could see with my mind's eye as I crawled among the trash piles, but I could never imagine my grandfather breaking down and sobbing over his home-cooked meal that Thursday night.

Suddenly, their phone rings.

Aunt Helen answers, "Hello?"

"Helen Sanford?" asked a woman's voice.

"Yes, who is this?"

"That doesn't matter. I have a message from your family."

"My family? What do you mean my family? Are they okay?"

"Yes, I spoke to them. They want you to know that they're together and they're safe."

"Oh, my God. Who did you speak to? Where are they?"

"I don't remember the woman's name."

"Was it Cecilia?"

"Maybe, I don't remember."

"What did she look like?"

By this point the TV was off and all attention in the room focused on this oddly emotional phone call.

"She was Spanish. She was speaking Spanish to two other people she was with."

"Did she have black hair and a pretty face?"

"A beautiful face."

"That's my sister, Cecilia! Oh, my God! Is everyone okay?"

"They were when I last saw them. They're at the Superdome. They want you to know they're together and they're safe. That's the message. I have to go now."

"Wait. Who is this? Where are you calling from?" asked Aunt Helen in hysterics.

"Ma'am. They asked me if I would call you. I have. I have to go now." And with that she hung up.

An earthquake of emotions shook that living room in Florida. A strange mixture of despair multiplied, divided by, and added to hope. Aunt Helen tried to *69 the number to call it back, but she got the whe wah whew ah nuh nuh nuh nuh sound like a fax machine or an old modem. The phone call had created more questions than it had answered. We wouldn't know this until later on, but when we heard about this odd phone call, Mother and I could only smile, knowing that Becky and Isaac had made it out of the stadium and that Becky had been true to the pledge she'd made my Mother on Wednesday evening before the gunfire and the charge of the thousands of panicked spectators on the field. She'd made the call to our family. At least they knew that someone had seen us alive in the flesh.

SATURDAY
SEPTEMBER 3RD, 2005

Together We Burn

Splish, Splash

I could feel the warmth of the water, smell the fragrances of my bubble mixture. Everything just felt so perfect, like nothing could go wrong. But if everything was so perfect, then why was there so much shouting? Why is someone shaking my foot and calling my name?

I opened my eyes and saw a black sky deep in the overnight hours. I saw my mother. She'd been the one shaking my foot, frantically trying to wake me. I heard the shouts, and the beams of dozens of flashlights were crisscrossing through the darkness like the glowing eyes of a many-headed hydra.

"Wake up, baby, something's happening," Mother said, with a tinge of disgust in her voice.

After days of madness, we'd finally found a comfortable spot where we felt safe. She just wanted to be left alone, but that wasn't going to happen, not tonight. The shouting and the flashlights pressed closer, deep growling voices. Tom told me that it was about five minutes after twelve. He'd been watching the soldiers forming up, and this new calamity began right at the stroke of midnight.

"Move it! Everyone into the line. Leave all of your belongings! Into the line, NOW!"

About three dozen soldiers wielding flashlights and shotguns pushed the crowd on the terrace before them like a human broom sweeping so much dust. As people began to gather their things and shoulder their bags, they'd shout, "Drop it. Leave your belongings. Into the line, NOW! Everyone move!" A rude awakening, to say the least. We couldn't help but be moved ahead of them as they pressed forward.

We had the dog, the hippo, Uncle G's and Jimena's backpacks, Tom's bag, and our food and water supply. The soldiers, out-of-state National Guard, told us to drop everything and move it.

"What is this? You can't make us leave the only things we have left in the world," Mother protested.

The soldiers told us that we would be able to come back for our things in about an hour. They just wanted to get a count of everyone who's left.

Uncle G said, "Man, people are stealing anything from anyone. I can't leave my wallet and ID here in my bag."

"Leave the bag, sir. Your possessions will be looked after. You'll be back here in an hour."

We stuffed our bags and the hippo underneath the cot and tossed some cardboard over it to, I guess, make it look more like trash. Not likely, in what was obviously a neat little campsite.

"Ma'am, you can tie up the dog, too. We just need to count the people."

Mother looked at him through narrow eyes. She set her feet into a kind of boxing stance and rolled her neck around her shoulders, making an audible *crack* as she did so. "Watch me." She took a couple steps back, turned on her heel, and the five and a half of us marched ahead of the battle line of soldiers.

"Move. People, we need everyone in the bus line. Drop everything you have. You'll be back in an hour."

The number of soldiers in the stadium had increased dramatically over the previous twenty-four hours, in direct proportion to the decreasing number of New Orleans residents in the Superdome, but people had been getting onto buses for thirty to thirty-six hours. Instead of mob rule, it had become a police state. From then on, I would feel much more like we were being treated as if we were prisoners of war or foreign refugees, not citizens of the United States of America. The Pennsylvania Guardsmen who woke me up from my first good sleep in six days with their shotguns and flashlights were a far cry from the sweaty young Louisiana National Guardsman who told me he lived in Arabi, St. Bernard Parish, and was worried about his wife and baby girls.

The Army had really taken over, and we were simply a military objective now—people who needed to be moved—no different from taking a hill or digging a latrine.

I know Uncle G was sore at having to walk away from his and Jimena's bags. She hadn't yet been fully naturalized as a citizen. Her papers were in those bags. If the Army just whisked us away, who knows what could happen to her. Me, I'd shoved my hippo under the cot and, leading Mother through the dark holding hands, walked away. I asked Mother if she thought Klaus would be okay. She told me that they'd have to shoot her ass dead before she would get on a bus without her grandson. She glanced over her shoulder at the soldiers, curled her upper lip, and snarled like a Doberman.

As we neared, I could see that there were several teams of soldiers driving people like sheep. From around the other end of the terrace came a horde of people, closely followed by another phalanx of flashlights. From out of the stadium doors emerged a shuffling procession. They had the appearance of fans exiting the stadium after a very long, sweaty, and sad game, which the home team had desperately lost.

"Move into the line, everyone. Push your way as close to the front as you can. Keep pushing, people."

Foot trails meandered through the stacks of cardboard and cots and other more personal effects like chairs, pillows, clothing, and blankets. Without the walking paths through the garbage, navigating our way through this trash heap in near complete darkness would have been impossible, especially for Mother, who couldn't see anything to begin with.

Worse than wandering in the dark through a landfill in midnight blackness, we were also walking through a giant toilet bowl. An unknown number of thousands of people had traversed this brick concourse. How much time the average journey from one end to the other took, I didn't know. Undoubtedly, several hours. Let's estimate that every person needed to use the restroom at least once while crossing the terrace. That's, I don't know, fifteen-thousand bowels and bladders emptied. Granted, we were outside. The human waste hadn't been composting in a dark steamy bathroom like inside the stadium. Still, it goes without saying that the odor was as powerful as it was inescapable. We were just standing right in it, walking right through it. Some trash piles were definitely more pungent than others as we moved toward the barricade.

"Push to the front, everybody. We need everyone to pack in as tight as we can."

We were caught about halfway across the expanse, stacked up like toothpicks in a box. I and everyone around me were forced to climb up on piles of garbage as the soldiers pushed us forward, tighter and tighter into the space. I tried to climb one of the taller piles, hoping to gain a vantage point from which I could see our campsite and keep an eye on our stuff, for all the good that would do. Hundreds of bodies, tons of trash and a line of armed soldiers separated us from those items. Cramped in that line in the middle of the night, I had no faith in what the soldiers told us, that we'd be allowed to return to our things. Looking behind me, I saw the line of soldiers, crisp uniforms, holding their weapons. Some appeared to be mocking us and our wretchedness, others were simply disgusted with their surroundings and the entire situation, while other faces were more sorrowful and appropriate to the suffering all around. The scores of faces I could see of my fellow residents all carried some deviation of the same taciturn expression. The Moai statues of Easter Island come to mind. Hundreds more faces were hidden by the darkness. All I could see were the ghoulish reflections of their teeth and eyeballs.

Then, no more shouting, no more pushing. Something resembling quiet had descended over the crowd. The stillness and inactivity served to exacerbate the nervous tension among us, not to mention the claustrophobia factor of being smashed into these tight quarters with piles of garbage, breathing shit and piss with every inhale. It wasn't long before the murmuring of the people became vocal shouts of protest directed at the soldiers, the smell, the situation *en masse*. Translated, they were all saying the same thing "Let me out of here! In one direction or the other, let me out of this line!"

I felt so tired, all I wanted was for them to let us go. I wanted to go back to my cot, stretch out, and go back to sleep. But there was nothing to be done. Jammed in line like we were, lying down would be totally impossible. All one could do was stand on, sit on, or cling to their respective island of trash and wait, wait, wait. Instructed to leave even our water behind, thirst became an added temporary discomfort as we moved well into our second hour with no word from anyone as to exactly what was going on. If boredom could kill.

Mother had woken me at five past midnight, when we were shuffled into the line. Finally, at three-fifteen, they announced that we could go back to our places. They thanked us for our cooperation, to which many sneered, and assured us that each one of us would be on a bus by the end of the day.

As we made our way out of the line and back to our camp, the line of soldiers marched ahead of us, keeping track of us and making sure that no one made it through their line of battle. The people reentering the stadium itself first walked through a regiment of camo-clad soldiers who dispersed before them, keeping track of each individual. We made it back to our blessedly intact campsite.

Once again, I was urged to take the cot and sleep. I didn't protest. I'd gathered up plenty of coffee early that afternoon and, true to form, Mother and the rest of the gang were mixing up a late-night bottle of coffee water.

Lying down, closing my eyes, I soon fell asleep again. I don't remember dreaming this time, but I do remember thinking about what the soldiers said as they let us out of the line, "Everyone will be on a bus by the end of the day."

I would estimate there had to be at least two thousand people in the line that night. Maybe more, maybe less. It was dark and, believe me, I'm no mathematician, but I'd say there were two thousand people remaining in the Superdome. Two thousand people, fifty people to a bus; that means that it would require about forty buses to remove us all from the stadium, the City, and everything we thought we knew. Forty buses and a new tomorrow awaited.

Regardless of the multitude of challenges our current lodgings presented, I'd learned to cope with life in the stadium. A new fear of the unknown gripped me like the fear of leaving our attic and climbing into that boat four days before. Forty buses, to me, seemed a perfectly manageable number of vehicles to appropriate. I believed that we would be leaving tomorrow, but then what? Leave and go where? And what do we do when we get there? Get jobs and apartments? For the first time since we'd abandoned it, I thought about when I'd be able to see our house again. When would that be? The brown water hadn't gone anywhere since we got out. I fell asleep wondering if I would ever see my home again, if the water would ever go away, or if New Orleans was just plain dead. I didn't want to think that, but very little of what I'd seen recently could convince me otherwise.

Sweet sleep. After so many days of trying to sleep in stadium chairs or on astro-turf, the simple Army cot felt like a fine feather bed. Compound this with the exhaustion of an unbroken string of sleepless nights and you can imagine just how lovely it felt to be lying down again after a few hours in that miserable line. If only the Army would allow me nine hours of sweet, sweet sleep.

Unfortunately, the Army had other plans for us. Shouting and a hand shaking my foot, and boom, just like that, I'm awake once again.

The sky was still dark, but rays of pink and orange announced the approach of the unstoppable dawn. The air was close and dead still. Today would be a hot one.

As we roused ourselves from our varying degrees of slumber, Uncle G's watch read six thirty-five a.m. Approximately three hours since we'd been released from the line, the battle ranks of soldiers had reformed to sweep us from our camps and back into the landfill line.

It became apparent very quickly that the overnight sweep had been a dress rehearsal for this morning, with one subtle, yet important, difference in the verbiage of their commands. Instead of "Leave all your possessions, drop everything, you will be returning to your campsites," the soldiers were shouting "Bring anything and everything you want to take with you, you will *not* be returning to this area. Everyone is to enter the line right now. Repeat: You will NOT be returning to this area."

So this was it. This would be the final push to clear us out of the stadium and evacuate the City once and for all: Martial Law. We gathered our bags, Klaus the hippo, and all of the water we could carry (which wasn't much). We hadn't received any new food or water in close to twenty-four hours. We thought that we were well-stocked, but in reality we were down to two bottles a piece, one liter of water per person. We also grabbed a couple of the cushions we'd been sitting on just in case it took a while. With the urine and feces staining most of the surface of the pathway, we thought it best to have somewhere clean to sit down. The five and a half of us, including Tom, were walking into the great unknown future as the sun climbed, now filling half the sky with glorious light.

In response to the increasing police state, after we made it back to our camp from the line, Tom said that he thought the Army might confiscate our cameras when we left the stadium. Mother volunteered to stash the memory cards from our cameras on her person as a precaution. This may sound extreme, but I agreed with him wholeheartedly. The disconnect between us residents and the newly arrived Guardsmen from other states had grown into a yawning chasm. Their treatment of us made me feel more like an internee at Guantanamo Bay than a citizen of the United States of America. The notion that they might strip search and gang probe any or all of us seemed very, very plausible.

The soldiers packed us onto the walk path, though not as tightly as they had the night before. There was nothing left to do but wait for liberation and stumble forward among the trash piles every so often as more people passed the barricade.

By nine in the morning, we were starting to feel the heat. By ten we were definitely uncomfortable. By noon it was sweltering. Unfiltered sunlight blasted down upon our huddled mass there on the walk path. There wasn't a cloud in the sky. The Army had us sandwiched in on either side, there was nowhere to hide from the brutal pounding the sun was giving us. The heat index had to have been well over a hundred degrees.

Many of the Superdome's remaining residents were elderly, or people with small children, who, like us, opted to wait while everyone else fought their way through the two-day lines. Now we were all piled in together on what I'd wager to be the hottest day since before Katrina made landfall on Monday morning. Even hotter than Tuesday, when we roasted on the roof waiting for the boat to come back.

Mother and the rest of the gang were again pouring their precious water over their heads in an attempt to cool themselves, but this only provided momentary relief. Then the sun would hit and start cooking their wet hair, creating a sauna effect. Other than wetting Jeanine's handkerchief tied around my neck, I thought it would be better to drink that water than just pour it out for a moment's relief from the broiling sun.

Each minute that passed was pure agony in that heat, every hour a nightmare. But we couldn't do anything about it. Just sit and cook.

One by one, people were overtaken by the heat, and cries for help would fall on the seemingly deaf ears of the soldiers, police, and EMTs who stood all around us. These were the first police officers—genuine NOPD—I'd seen since our "Longest Day," when the police had given us rides in a boat, and later in a truck.

To help us battle the heat, they began passing water bottles to the crowd from crates that were exposed to the same broiling sun. This water can only be described as fucking hot. It was hard to drink it down, and it did little to cool our overheated bodies. The people shouted volleys of complaints at the soldiers and police, and the line hardly seemed to be moving. The most severe cases of heat stroke, mostly elderly people, were fished out of the crowd and taken down into the shade of the parking deck. A few were passed by hand over the heads of the people up to the barricade, like they were crowd surfing at a rock concert.

After so many days of stress and uncertainty in the stadium, I really did feel that all the worst was behind us and we'd simply step onto a bus with no trouble and go to Houston or wherever the Army dropped us. But this day spent in the line has to be the most terrible part of the experience, and the closest we came to actually dying or suffering lasting bodily harm. Flying bullets and a stampeding crowd were one thing, but they pale in comparison to the inescapable torment of the subtropical heat, standing in an open toilet. I suppose it's only fitting that the worst be saved for the last. I thought longingly of the vertical cardboard blinds that the Mexican family had constructed, or all of the sheets of cardboard we'd left behind at our camp; that little bit of shade could be the difference between living and dying. Random pieces of cardboard lay everywhere around us, but you couldn't trust the stuff in a cesspool. Every piece we lifted hid a surprise underneath, and eventually we gave up this pursuit. There was nothing we could do but sit and roast.

A young woman carrying her two-year-old child approached the officers, telling them that her baby was sick. He was too hot. She asked them to do something to help her. They offered her a bottle of hot water and told her to get back in line. She remained obstinate, dropping the bottle of hot water on the ground and telling them they needed to do better than that. After several more attempts to get her to return to the line, a gruff-looking older policeman shouted to an underling and held up one finger. The young officer walked up to the woman and gave her an ice cold bottle from their private stash, drops of icy goodness ran down the sides. She held the bottle to the child's cheeks, which revived him enough to take a few sips. I was so jealous of that kid. I'd have done anything for a cold bottle of water like that one, but I knew to ask for one wouldn't do any good.

It's really messed up that these people sworn to "protect and serve" would try to move this woman along and offer her hot water for her child, who was obviously having difficulty, that they just sat and watched as scores of people collapsed from heat-related exhaustion, while they had hidden generators powering hidden ice-making machines for their own comfort. Where's the humanity in that? I guess I should be thankful that we were given water of any temperature, and I am, but knowing and seeing that such a separation existed between *us and them* really floored me. I'm not talking about creature comforts. I'm talking about life and death.

I'd given Mother Jeanine's canvas bag to wear on her head. The heat and the hot water weren't affecting her as badly as I feared they would, but I would still look over and check on her every few minutes. I spent most of the day hunched over, staring at the ground. More often than not, my eyes were closed. The sun shone fiercely bright. Several times I felt myself slipping out of consciousness, not falling asleep, but passing out from the heat. The other members of my group must have been feeling the same way, too. I'd covered Dolja with a scrap of cardboard, but the rest of us, including Tom, just sat motionless, not saying a word, fighting to maintain. Every so often someone would kick a foot or jerk an arm, shaking off the gathering darkness as they felt themselves slipping away. The others might open a squinted eye to peek and make sure they were alright, but that was it. For hours we just sat in this breezeless, cloudless, blazing sauna while our brains and organs cooked.

The line moved forward again, and we began situating ourselves on new piles of trash. We'd made it close to the barricade by now, maybe fifteen feet of garbage dotted with people separated us from the line of soldiers, the open glass doors of the New Orleans Centre, the cool darkness inside, and the mysteries beyond. Shielding my eyes with my hand, I checked out the soldiers ahead of me. Most of them were National Guard grunts in camo, but there were also a handful of some really hardcore-looking guys I assumed were Special Forces. One in particular caught my attention. He wore the label *Air Force* on his dark blue combat gear. Something about the way he stood, the way he held his weapon— there was no way this guy's specialty was walking down a tarmac waving glowing orange wands. He was a professional, not a reservist. Of course, in 2005, the Iraq and Afghanistan wars were in full swing. The United States military was fighting all over the world; now they'd sent one of their most lethal killers to babysit a bunch of stinky flood victims. He stood stone-still, like a Beefeater in front of Buckingham Palace, though I know his eyes were moving behind the opaque lenses of his sunglasses. The heat didn't seem to bother him at all. He was standing in a shaded spot, but with a long-sleeved uniform, gloves, body armor, and a full battle kit, he must have been sweating profusely under those layers. He held a snub-nose submachine gun with a long clip extending underneath. He also carried enough extra magazines of ammunition to take out the entire crowd. I'd been watching him for a couple hours. He hadn't taken a sip of water or shuffled his feet, not once. He was very impressive, probably the coolest action figure I saw in that crazy box of G.I. Joes. I liked the guy. I liked his style. I wished that I could hear some of his bad-ass stories.

By three-thirty, we'd made it to within the first four rows of the barricade. With any luck we'd be on the next bus. Only three or four hundred people remained. Soldiers formed a line at the rear of the walkway and started pushing the crowd forward, tightening us up. These people had been cooking in the sun all day. They were ornery. A resident a few rows behind us shouted something back at the soldiers. Some of his neighbors joined in the shouting. Someone threw a water bottle. Now both sides were shouting. The totally trained killer guy in the blue uniform I'd been admiring raised his machine gun to his shoulder and leveled the barrel at the crowd in front of him. I was at his twelve o'clock, and, for a moment, the gun was aimed right at me. Then he shouted, "Get down. Everybody down. Now!" And that's just what we did, no doubt. I wasn't about to fuck with that guy. I got down. Thankfully, no shots were fired and none of us ended up as one of his bad-ass stories.

The line opened again and we moved forward a couple of feet. As the afternoon progressed, sections of the line had become covered by the shadows of the surrounding skyscrapers. We'd moved forward into one of these patches of delightful shade. Before long, our bodies began to cool enough for us to look up and start to talk again. We drank a little hot water while Tom passed around some cigarettes from his pack. Earlier in the day, Tom paid a guy twenty bucks for an unopened, pristine pack of Kool Filter Kings. Twenty whole bucks! My jaw dropped when I saw him slide the crispy bank note from his wallet and hand it to the man. We'd exchanged a single dollar for a single cigarette or two, so Tom rationalized his purchase by saying that he'd bought twenty individual smokes. Hell, I couldn't believe that he'd been sitting on his wallet for a week straight without accepting the total evaporation of commerce as we know it and just stuffed the thing in his bag.

Moving into the shade was amazing. It felt like a reward for the hours of exposure to the vicious sun. I was sitting on a pile of trash and cardboard. I'd finished my cigarette and as I pressed the butt between my shoe and the piece of cardboard underfoot, I felt something odd beneath me—an item of irregular shape and dimension. I stepped down again, and there it was. I started moving cardboard around, digging through the layers of cardboard and trash compressed by heat and hundreds of feet and asses until it had become like metamorphic rock. Mother told me to leave it alone and stop digging in the garbage, but by now I was determined to see just what the hell I was standing on. Remarkable, I'd shoved away a layer of junk about a foot and a half deep and still hadn't found what I was searching for, but I knew I had to be close. I could feel it. I hoisted up the last flap of cardboard, which raised about forty pounds of adjacent trash, and a dark cavern opened. I reached inside. It was heavy. I raised it up in the light where I could see.

"Wha-ha. Yes, yes! Ha-ho-ho shit!"

Mother looked over and said, "Baby, what's wrong?"

"LOOK!"

What was there? What did I find? I'll tell you, what I found was better than if I pulled up the Holy Grail, the Easter Bunny, or a sack full of pirate treasure. The weirdly shaped thing under my feet turned out to be a half-size three gallon plastic jug of water, the kind that would fit onto the proverbial office water cooler, where so many of society's taboos are discussed. The solid plastic with the blue tint had prevented it from being crushed beneath, I don't know, a quarter to a half ton of trash and people. Buried under layers of garbage for what must have been days, given its depth, had insulated the water from the heat. In fact, this water probably hadn't seen sunlight for several days. The outside of the bottle was cool to the touch. The plastic ring around the top looked perfectly intact. This was real Kentwood brand artesian spring water, the best in the world, and it was virgin and pure, untainted by the brown water, or the twenty thousand turds, or the scorching sun. I gripped the tab and unwound the waxy plastic sealing the top. I raised the lead-weight three gallon bottle to my mouth.

The water was as cold as if it had been left in a refrigerator overnight. It hurt my teeth. It raised goose-bumps on my skin as it cascaded down my chin onto my chest. I pulled away my lips and just let the jug glug-glug-glug me in the face, on my eyeglasses, and nappy, knotted hair. To my still-overheated body, the water shower felt like jumping into a cold swimming pool. The initial shock hit me. I thought my heart would stop. The water just tasted so clean and unbelievably cool. I'd estimate a temperature of forty to fifty degrees. This was the coolest thing I'd come in contact with since the electricity had gone out days before.

Without warning I started dumping water on Mother. She froze up for a moment and then drank big swigs as the heavenly, cool fountain poured over her. I handed the jug to Uncle G, and the five of us passed the jug around several times.

Maybe my water discovery didn't exactly save our lives; the revolving of planet Earth and the spread of afternoon downtown shadows had assured our continued survival, but the hidden jug of beautiful, cool Kentwood water nourished us, revived us, refreshed us, and reminded us what it felt like to be a human being living in the 21st Century.

The week of brown water and artificial turf just evaporated. The cool water refreshed me into believing that I'd reached the finish line. The end. I'd been baptized, washed and cleansed inside and out. I was ready to start the rest of my life. Cradling the jug as if it were a newborn baby, I vowed to my mother that I would drink the whole thing if it killed me.

The Road to Freedom

Not ten minutes later, the Army guys started shouting at us, and the barricade was opened. They were waving through the next busload's worth of people. The soldiers behind us shouted at us to move forward. I grabbed my jug of water and advanced. As we cleared a couple of trash mounds, it became evident that we were going to make it through. Mother noticed I was struggling with the heavy water jug and urged me to drop it and leave it for somebody else. She was right. That's what I should have done, allow the blessed water to maybe help out other people, but instead, I waved her off and sauntered away with my prize, sloshing around with each step, more than twenty pounds of dead weight. A little farther and we were through the barricade.

Goodbye, Superdome!

We stepped through the glass doors of the New Orleans Centre, a three-story shopping mall that would not reopen after Hurricane Katrina. The interior loomed cavernous and dim, and achingly quiet. The last time I'd been in this place must have been two years before, partying before a Saints game, partying with thousands of other pumped-up fans. The only light inside filtered through the art-deco skylight cresting the building—shadow light. The building stands completely surrounded by taller high-rises. Our footsteps echoed around the empty space. Tom led Mother by the hand through the darkness. Jimena carried the dog. I had Klaus and the water. We walked the length of the building, were directed down a busted escalator by soldiers, and again walked the length in deeper gloom than above. The skylight shined less effectively down here. Weakened by a long day in the sun, the water jug really slowed me down. I began to lag behind. Again, Mother recommended I just let it go. She said we were alright now, that we'd made it. She told me that I should let it go. This time, I did what she said and set the jug down, hoping that someone else might see it and take a drink, but odds are people walked right past it, paying it no attention whatsoever. I know that's what I would do if I happened upon a random jug of open water, especially one found anywhere near this place.

I saw sunlight ahead, and broken glass. The doors leading out to the street had been shattered into a million pieces, smashed by the soldiers, I assumed. The glass crunched underneath my camo slippers, and the five and a half of us stepped out onto LaSalle Street, greeted by a row of idling buses. Not school buses, but big, towering coaches, three of them, parked bumper to bumper. Soldiers directed us onto the bus at the rear of the convoy. A smiling, middle-aged black man in a crisp white shirt with a blue tie and red chauffer's cap welcomed us as we stepped on board. He told us to make ourselves comfortable, but no smoking please. Artificially cooled air and a strong smell of Pine-Sol, Lysol, and other disinfectants nearly knocked me down. I hadn't felt air conditioning in days, and my clothes were still damp from my Kentwood water bath. I never thought I'd actually feel cold ever again. Within minutes of climbing aboard, I started shivering.

I took the window seat, with Mother and Dolja next to me. Uncle G and Jimena were in the row ahead, and across the aisle sat Tom. I sank into the softly padded, clean, cool seat. Mother turned to me, she looked tired and happy. She had tears in her eyes. Giving my hand a squeeze, she said, "We made it, B."

Twenty minutes later, the bus driver stepped on board and declared that his heart really went out to each of us, that he was proud to be here driving us in his bus, and, most boisterously of all, he hoped that we knew somebody in the great city of Houston, Texas, because that's where he's from and that's where he was taking us. The fifty people on the bus gave a cheer. Although downtrodden and dejected, these were New Orleanians on this bus. Being loud is part of what we do.

Someone reminded the driver that Houston is at least five hours away. Would there perhaps be somewhere we could stop and eat along the way? The driver assured us that we had no need to worry. We were going to be taken care of from here on out. Man, that sounded good, better than my comfy seat felt. To say our spirits were high would be an understatement. We raised another cheer as the bus started rolling.

Contrary to my expectations, we didn't make a direct line for Interstate-10 westbound, the most direct route out of New Orleans if one were Houston-bound. The Interstate is literally right there above Claiborne Avenue, visible from the line we were just in. Instead, we turned toward the river. After I thought about it, this path made sense. Driving through a City inundated by water, the higher ground lay closest to the river levees. The bus turned right onto Convention Center Boulevard, and for the next mile we drove past the Ernest N. Morial Convention Center. Unless you've driven past it, it's difficult to imagine a single continuous building over a mile in length.

We'd been isolated from the rest of the world for a week. Our only news source had been the rumor mill circulating through the Superdome. We had no idea that several thousand people had been living in the Convention Center for days without proper distribution of the most basic essentials, water, or food.

It shocked me to see so many people standing there in the sunshine. To me, it looked like the Superdome four days before. Only a smattering of police and the handful of Army guys present were busy unloading pallets of MREs and distributing bottles of water.

As the bus slowly drove past that mile-long line of solemn faces, I learned what it meant to be truly hated and despised. It really broke my heart, and I don't blame them in the least. All this time I'd thought the Superdome was the worst place anyone could ever be, and it really was, but the people I rode past outside the Convention Center humbled me. I could see it written on each one of their faces as the bus rolled past. They'd been watching buses roll past for three days, and only now were soldiers unloading water and food for them. After we'd driven a quarter-mile up Convention Center Boulevard, I wanted to crawl and hide. Every miserable soul who stood there seemed to be staring straight at me. Behind the tinted glass of the snazzy tour bus, our faces were hidden; we were just another busload of anonymous assholes being driven from the City to anywhere else. Where didn't matter. And they were still standing in the same place they'd stood for days. In each set of eyes I saw a hurt, expressions of both jealousy and shame. The jealousy, I could understand. They wanted to be on this bus. I totally get that. The shame, that was more subtle. It has to do with the underlying pride in one's self, the very chemistry of individualism and what it means to be human. They knew that other citizens were loaded onto those buses, other *residents*. To hell with the police, the Army, the news reporters, and the rest of America watching from the comfort of their living rooms; they knew that the people inside those buses were their peers, their neighbors, and we were sitting behind tinted glass on an air-conditioned bus, while they continued to stand in the same hot sun we'd just been rescued from. They hated us because they knew that we were looking at them like they were some wretched mass, like we were better than them all of a sudden. We were merely tourists now, hidden behind one-way glass. I wished that we had been boarded on a big yellow school bus with open windows so they could see the pain on our faces. We weren't pompous voyeurs. We'd been exposed to our own slice of Hell. I mumbled a prayer and wished them luck, but after three quarters of a mile rolling at six miles an hour, I had to look away. I couldn't stand their scornful eyes any longer. I couldn't face the guilt I felt for sitting on that air-conditioned bus.

After a couple of tight turns on city streets, the bus merged onto the Crescent City Connection, the G.N.O. Bridge; we were crossing the river and headed to the westbank. This is the same bridge I would later find out Simone walked across on Thursday, the "Day of Days" in her Katrina story. I thought to myself, *This is some crazy route to take to get to Houston.* However, in the greater scale of Katrina devastation, there was no way the bus could travel across the City in its present condition. I had no concept of how widespread the flooding truly was.

The bus turned off the Westbank Expressway, and, for a long stretch, we drove up River Road, closely shouldering the river levees. Houston was a long way away, plenty of time for a nap. But falling asleep sitting upright has always been difficult for me—even if the seats on the bus were a thousand times more comfortable than the seats in the Superdome. Mother zonked out in no time, but

I just sat staring out the window at downed power lines, signs, and billboards. I tapped Uncle G on the shoulder, and, after digging around in his bag for a moment, Dolja and I were eating the Pork Rib in BBQ Sauce I'd bartered T for the previous day, along with some Army crackers. That mashed-up rib thing tasted way better on an air-conditioned bus than a murky field of moist turf. We washed it down with a bottle of warm water. I wished I'd kept that jug of cold Kentwood water. It was tough going back to the hot stuff after that cool deliciousness. I wish I still had that jug, the last angel.

The bus passed through Bridge City, underneath the looming Huey P. Long Bridge, and continued heading west. Just getting that far had taken over an hour. At that rate, we might get to Houston by Halloween.

A little farther, and the bus turned off of River Road, merging onto the Interstate 3-10 Luling Bridge, back across to the east bank of the river. By this time, most of the passengers on the bus had fallen asleep. Of course, I could not. I sat in my chair petting the dog, listening to the rest of them snore, listening to the sound of the engine, and trying to eavesdrop on the bus driver's radio conversation. Our row was well to the rear of the long coach. I couldn't make out much of what he said. It didn't really matter, as long as he kept driving.

Once we made it over the river, instead of turning onto I-10 westbound— the most direct route to Houston—our driver merged the bus eastbound, back toward the City. Right then, I knew something was up. The New Orleans International Airport, now known as Louis Armstrong International, is situated on the very western edge of the habitable strip of land comprising Orleans and Jefferson parishes. Past the airport lies massive Lake Ponchartrain and the edge of the world. The driver exited the highway and made for the airport. I woke my companions from their brief naps and told them the news. All agreed that flying to Houston would be way quicker than driving, so this sudden change in plan appeared to be a blessing, but still I felt apprehensive.

Flying Machines

The New Orleans Airport is separated into two massive levels. The lower is for Arrivals and the upper is for Departures. Both are covered to protect travelers from the elements. The bus climbed the ramp to the Departure level and we joined the end of a long line of buses all pointing in one direction. On the broad sidewalk to our right, a massive line of thousands of people was formed, facing the opposite direction. As the bus inched its way forward, past rows of ambulances and police cars, I knew my prior misgivings were sound. We weren't riding this bus to Houston. Oh, no. We were going to be dropped at the end of this line, ten people wide and a half a mile long. We stepped off the bus at six-fifteen p.m. and took our place at the tail-end of this enormous human snake. Our spirits sank to an all-time low.

Nearby, a camera crew filmed a reporter doing a news piece on the refugees. It turns out that they worked for a Spanish language station based in Los Angeles. Uncle G has always been kind of shy, and Jimena didn't want any part of it, so Mother stepped up and volunteered to be interviewed. In total, Mother talked to the female reporter for close to twenty minutes, the cameras rolling the entire time. Halfway through, the reporter was in tears. I'm not fluent in Spanish, far from it, but I know enough to tell you that she didn't hold anything back. She eloquently described the Superdome experience in full detail, no sugar-coating and no exaggeration. Just the facts.

Later, we heard from aunts, uncles, and cousins in southern California that they'd seen Mother on television. Fuzzy teeth, filthy clothes, all that. Like the rest of us, she hadn't showered or brushed her teeth in a week. I'd like to find a copy of that interview to hear what she had to say about our Superdome time only hours after it had ended.

As they were parting ways, Mother gave the reporter a packet of coffee from her MRE. New tears welled up in her eyes. She tried to refuse the gift, saying she couldn't take something from someone who'd lost everything. Mother said she wanted her to have it to remind her of what she'd seen here in New Orleans, and to remind her of the kind of people we were. Finally, she accepted the gift, after Mother told her, "Besides, girl, I don't want to see another one of these mothafuckas as long as I live." The reporter embraced my filthy, stinky mother outside the New Orleans Airport, vowing that she'd remember her always, and that she would tell the world what she really saw that September day in 2005.

It was Saturday, after all. Across the country, people were attending or watching college football games on television. After living in a football stadium for six days, I couldn't fathom the idea of people buying tickets and cheering on their teams. That kind of image was simply too far removed from the broiling hot, turd-dodging, cardboard-hunting, survival mode I'd been living. Nachos and beer? Try Army cheese and coffee water. I didn't think I'd see a hot dog ever again, let alone a cold beer in a souvenir cup.

The line would advance thirty paces every half hour or so. We'd totally stopped caring about dirtying our clothes, and just sat on the ground until it was time to move forward again. A row of ambulances, police cars, and fire trucks stretched as long as the line of people did. All were running on idle. As mentioned, this drop-off zone for departures was covered by an awning running the length of the multiple gates for different airlines. The exhaust fumes of all these running vehicles were trapped under the awning on this breezeless afternoon. The smell of burning diesel fuel hung heavy in the air and did nothing to decrease the anger brewing inside each one of us. After an hour, we all had splitting headaches from breathing the noxious fumes.

Walk two dozen steps, then sit down again, walk a dozen steps, then sit. This process of walking and sitting seemed like it would never end. We were all recovering from near sunstroke after a day in line in front of the New Orleans Centre. Now, we were drowsy from inhaling carbon monoxide, but we weren't allowed to rest on the dirty concrete beneath our feet. As soon as I would sit down and readjust, it was time to walk again. How I longed for that comfy Army cot I'd napped on the night before!

Hours later, the line turned into the building and we thought we were almost there, but alas, once we finally got our bodies inside the door, I could see the line extending past the ticket counters, concourses, and beyond. We hadn't made it anywhere, but at least we'd cleared the carbon monoxide gas chamber outside. Tom and I had a good laugh when standing behind the ticket counters we saw disgruntled soldiers in the place of disgruntled airline employees.

U.S. Airways, Delta, Southwest—they didn't exist anymore. The only airline flying today was the United States Air Force.

Slowly, ever so slowly, we moved past the ticket counters and baggage checks of the domestic and international airlines that fly out of New Orleans, past the now-dormant security checkpoint, and into an actual concourse with flight gates and newsstands, a Burger King, and similar stuff. The signs above the shops, the rows of familiar products, they resembled my memories of a time long ago, a time before I'd turned savage while living in a world of shit and combat boots. I even found myself wondering what hot French fries would taste like with a little warm Army cheese on them. That's how demented I'd become.

High overhead in the airport atrium is an artistic model of Leonardo da Vinci's flying machine. It replicates the figure of an anonymous man surrounded by wires and pulleys attached to wide-sweeping batwings. The sculpture is quite beautiful and very gothic, it looks as much like one of Lucifer's fallen angels as it does an innovative design for a Renaissance flying machine. Da Vinci's machine never did take flight, and I was feeling the same way, like I'd never get off the ground.

The line paused again. Our gang stopped right near a group of three soldiers standing off to the side, talking among themselves and just keeping an eye on the people shuffling by. Just like everywhere else these masses of people passed through, the ground was strewn with trash, mostly empty water bottles and MRE envelopes. A crunched-up cardboard box lay on the ground, between our spot in line and the trio of soldiers. Dolja's phone cord leash had been discarded in favor of a length of orange mystery wire we found outside the airport. He took a look at the soldiers, growled, and sent a few barks their way. One of them laughed at the little mutt. The other told me that I'd better control my animal. I thought to myself, *Or what? Was this guy going to shoot my dog for barking while we were standing in line to be evacuated?* What a jerk. Apparently, Dolja felt the same way. He walked over, lifted his leg, and pissed all over the crumpled box, and scratched his claws across the smooth floor. The soldier turned red, the other laughed even harder. Dolja said what he needed to, and then rejoined us in line.

After another twist in the concourse, we finally saw the line going through a door down some stairs and onto the tarmac. Through the floor-to-ceiling windows that looked out to the runways, I saw a large gray military cargo plane sitting with its tail raised high in the air and the people filing into the open loading bay. I thought it was a C-130, but Tom assured me from the shape of the wings that we were looking at a C-117.

I couldn't believe how spacious the inside of the plane looked, but I suppose it needed to be large to fly around tanks and pieces of artillery. All of that large cargo was secured to pallets on tracks that rolled onto the plane and locked into place. They'd replaced these with cargo pallets full of tiny passenger seats and locked them into place in rows. The sides of the plane were lined with permanent seats for soldiers and crew. Dolja and I were directed to one of these seats along the side of the plane, while the rest of the group was seated on the cargo-pallet chairs.

A young airman sat next to me, and he, too, commented on the value of a dog like Dolja for killing rats and other varmints. All this time, I thought of him as a harmless pup. I had no idea he possessed such killer instinct, so readily identifiable to others.

The pilot came out to address us with a very kind speech, though his tone came across as robotic and flat, very military. Other crewmen instructed us to fasten our seatbelts. The loading door raised and closed. The young airman next to me had Dolja on his lap while we taxied for takeoff. He and Dolja became immediate friends.

I'd never flown in a plane without windows before. I found this both disappointing and disorienting. The pilot opened the throttle and the plane hurtled down the runway. A moment later, we were off the ground.

I didn't know if I'd ever see my home or my City again.

I asked the young airman where this bird was headed. He told me that the pilot would tell us any minute, after receiving his orders. Wow. A hundred people were on this plane heading toward an unknown destination. How poetic. I mentioned something about Houston, and he was certain that wasn't where we were going. "Houston's full up," he said.

Still dazed with disbelief over the fact that not even the pilot knew where we were going, I asked one final question of the man as he passed the dog back to me. I asked if he knew what time it was. He looked at his wristwatch and squinted up an eye, asking me if we were in the central time zone. I assured that we were. "One-forty a.m., central time."

One-forty in the morning, Sunday morning, and Tom and my family and I were on an airplane flying out of the City, after spending more than seven hours in line at the airport. Add that to the nine-plus hours we baked in the sun earlier today and that equals an absurd amount of time to force someone to inch their way through literally miles of lines. Just think, it was one-forty in the morning. We'd been standing in line since dawn. And now we were flying thousands of feet in the air without a clue where we'd find ourselves by the time the sun came up.

SUNDAY
SEPTEMBER 4TH, 2005

COFFEE AND DONUTS

Thirty minutes or so after takeoff, the pilot again stepped out from the cockpit to address his *cargo*. The looks on everyone's faces must have caught him off guard. Normally, the person driving a vehicle, any vehicle, bus, plane or train, doesn't walk away from the driver's seat for a chat. He recovered himself quickly, assuring us that his co-pilot had the plane well under control. The pilot said that he couldn't begin to imagine what we'd gone through for the last few days and that, on behalf of himself and the U.S. Air Force National Guard, we could start to relax. The worst was behind us. He informed us that we were heading to an Air Force base at Fort Chaffee, Arkansas, in the northwestern part of that state. He told us we should get comfortable upon arriving, as we'd be there for a couple days while the evacuation of the City was completed. But, not to worry, we'd pass the time taking hot showers, putting hot food in our stomachs, and making contact with our families. He concluded with, "So, come on folks, how does a hot shower sound, right about now?" The human cargo gave a lusty cheer over the thought of getting clean.

Personally, I had some misgivings about the whole scene. First, what's Fort Chaffee? Second, what the hell is in Arkansas? I know Houston. I'd been to that city time and again on both business and pleasure, but I'd never been to Arkansas. I searched my brain to come up with things I did know about the place, but not much came to mind. Facts: Arkansas is Louisiana's neighbor to the north. The capital city is Little Rock. Geographically, the state is kind of square in shape and not very large, maybe the size of Louisiana if folded into a square.

Then I thought about the myths and stereotypes associated with Arkansas. An image of a man with missing teeth, wearing a straw hat, and chewing a piece of straw after rolling in the straw with his sister came to mind. I shuddered in horror. Surely, it can't be like that. This is the 21st Century, for God's sake. Apparently, they've got an Air Force base and hot running water. For me, right then, that was enough. Just the thought of soap and water made me want to start crying.

About an hour later, we began our descent into Fort Chaffee. You could feel the excitement on board the aircraft. Everyone wanted to be off of the plane so they could check out their new surroundings. A common sentiment, also, was the prospect of eating food—real food, not MREs. I heard one passenger talking about how badly he wanted to drink an ice cold Coca-Cola. We were all just hoping to find something familiar, I think.

As the plane landed, I thought about how, unless they were going to issue us camouflage uniforms, the idea of showering sounded like a mixed blessing. I couldn't wait to get clean, but there's no way that I was going to put these clothes on my body ever again once they came off. They needed to be burned, not re-worn. But, the United States Military was in charge of things now. They'd have all of these mundane details figured out; at least I hoped they did.

We were told to remain seated. The crew stood in the aisles. Hydraulic machinery at the rear of the plane started to whine.

Verrrrrrrrrrrrrrrrrr

Slowly, the bay door opened. In my mind, I pictured a row of fat Sergeants armed with ladles stirring huge cauldrons of steaming soup. Instead, we saw the silhouettes of a dozen armed soldiers standing in the headlights of a half-dozen Hummers. Before them, they'd set up a long folding table, upon which sat a coffee machine and a couple of boxes of donuts. The airmen told us we had twenty minutes for coffee and donuts, then we'd be taking off again.

Twenty minutes? I thought we were staying. Coffee and donuts? They said hot food and showers. What the hell was going on here? What an incredible letdown. Of course, the rest of my family poured themselves some coffee and were ecstatic over a cup of for-real, fresh, brewed coffee, not the Folger's Crystals in the MREs; but I just wasn't feeling it. I decided to hang back with Tom and smoke a cigarette. This caused some alarm among the soldiers and airmen. After all, we were standing on government property, twenty yards from a large, open airplane. Our request to smoke went all the way up to a Captain standing around the trucks with the blinding headlights. Once assured that the plane wouldn't be refueling while on the ground, he gave us permission, "Light up."

Standing there in the middle of the night, hundreds of miles from home and still not knowing where we were going, I dragged angrily on my Kool Filter King. This was some real bullshit. We were getting jacked around. Was there no place for us in the entire country? Or was every town and city "full up" like the airman had said Houston was. Maybe it had more to do with lack of sleep than anything else, but I was super angry and unhappy and really did wish, for a moment, we were back in the Superdome, back in our City, where things were familiar and made more sense. I mean, where would we go next? Topeka, Kansas, for bagels and cream cheese?

We were ordered back onto the plane. I felt more like a parcel than a person, a parcel addressed to nowhere that nobody wanted. I've never felt so unimportant, useless, and like such a burden weighing upon the strangers surrounding me.

Shortly after taking off again, the pilot stepped out from the cockpit to address us. He apologized for the mix-up and told us that we were now headed to Little Rock Air Force Base, and that's where we were going to stay. Facilities and food were waiting for us there, all the confusion would be put to rest, and we would receive that hot meal we'd been promised. I took in his words with several grains of salt. The bus driver had promised us the same thing twelve hours earlier. I was done with promises. I wouldn't believe anything they said until I saw it, smelled it, and tasted it.

On the plus side, Arkansas isn't very large. Tom and I figured that if we'd just taken off from the northwest corner of the state bound for Little Rock, We'd probably be there in thirty minutes or so. Little Rock, like many state capitals, is situated at the very center of the state.

An hour and a half later, we still hadn't landed. We'd heard nothing from the pilot or crew. Once again, I felt myself getting really antsy. What was the hold up? How long were they going to keep us hanging in suspense?

Tom thought that the plane was circling. After surveying the slant of the cabin and the manner in which the crew walked, slightly stooped over, I wholeheartedly agreed with this assumption. But again, I asked, why? Unless there were really that many Katrina people flying into Little Rock, I could see no reason for the delay. For the millionth time in the past twenty-four hours, something must be up.

An hour after that, I was ready to kill someone if they didn't let me off that plane. Through the one tiny window embedded in the door across the plane, I could see the first rays of dawn beginning to lighten the sky. Officially, an entire day had passed since the Army guys woke us up and forced us into the bus line. An entire day spent either standing in line or flying in line, as it appeared we were now doing.

Delirious with impatience and loss of sleep, Dolja, Klaus, and I started concocting a plot to storm the cockpit and *force* a landing. Just in the nick of time, the pilot's voice came over the public address system: "Buckle up, folks. We're beginning our descent into Little Rock." This time no one cheered.

Urp Urp Urrrrrp

Flight 4899 Mandeville Street touched down at Little Rock Air Force Base a few minutes before seven a.m. Sunday, September 4th, 2005. Six days and sixteen hours after Katrina made landfall.

Though forlorn, filthy, and exhausted, a wave of electricity flowed through the passengers on board the plane. The hope—the prayer—that this was the end of the line. That this was it. This would be where we reconnect. Where we finally get to place that phone call to that special someone, friends and family, or our worst enemies, anyone. Just to let them know that we're alive. Let them know that we'd made it out of the City, just to let them know, so they could stop worrying. Certainly, everyone on board had their calls to make to worried loved ones and friends.

The plane stopped rolling, and once again we were instructed to remain seated. We were going to be greeted here at Arkansas' state capital by a very important visitor. I thought to myself, "Holy shit. Bill Clinton is about to step on this plane!" I prepared myself to meet the former president and ask him if he could spare me one of his cigars.

The cargo bay opened. A trio of soldiers in camo escorted three men in black suits onto the aircraft. I didn't recognize these men in black, but could tell that none of them were *Big Bill*. Two of the suits stood on either side of a taller man with dark hair and folded their arms while the man in the center began to speak. He informed us that his name was Mike Huckabee, the governor of Arkansas. He'd been boarding each plane of New Orleanians as it landed to welcome us to "The Natural State." He also made us a promise. He told us that if anyone in the entire state during our stay in Arkansas didn't greet us with a smile, didn't accommodate us to the utmost of their ability, or even so much as sighed when speaking to us, we were to report this directly to him and he'd deal with the offender himself. That was the first promise made to us that was kept. Or at least, we never had to enforce it. Every person I met in Arkansas, old or young, black or white, they treated me and my family with the epitome of kindness, dignity, and respect.

I must also add that this speech, though gracious, was poorly timed. I know I wasn't the only one on board who just wanted to be done with all of this traveling and standing in lines. We wanted to be wherever it was we were going. We'd been flying for six hours. We could have flown to Los Angeles in that amount of time, and the fact that our plane was made to circle the Little Rock Air Force Base for two hours so the governor could board each plane and make his speech seemed perverse. Why torture people who'd been through hell any longer than necessary? A few days later, I shared this sentiment with a Red Cross volunteer and she told me that Mike Huckabee had big plans for his future, possibly a run for president in the next few years. You know, you can say anything you want about democracy and the political machine that runs this country, but come on! Let a guy get a shower before you try to add him to your constituency. Let a guy regain some sense of normalcy in his life before you try adding him to your mailing list. Do your campaigning on your own time, not on evacuees' time. There is a time and a place for everything, especially politics. Seven a.m. on board a plane full of refugees is neither the time nor the place. Regardless of his party affiliation, any time I hear the name Mike Huckabee, I can taste the bile rising in the back of my throat.

We were led off of the plane and directed toward two big touring coaches like the ones that carried us from the Superdome to the New Orleans Airport. The morning was cloudy and relatively cool, I thought, for early September. In New Orleans, we'd been sweltering, but here in Little Rock, an hour after sunrise, the air remained crisp.

I asked one of the soldiers we passed if we were going somewhere else. We'd been told that we would be staying in Little Rock. He informed me that we would be taken to an emergency Red Cross shelter set up at the Pine Bluff Convention Center. After I asked him what and where Pine Bluff is, my voice wavering with anger and exhaustion, he told me that we'd be at the shelter after a forty-five-minute bus ride.

"And then where are they going to take us?"

"Nowhere," he replied. This was our designated emergency shelter. He'd just left from there. They had food, water and other drinks, beds, clothes, showers.

The only thing missing was us.

I boarded the bus, still quite skeptical as to what would happen next. I'd lost all faith in the military monolith, politicians, and the words they say. We stepped onto this new bus, I took the window seat, and Mother was next to me on the aisle. Both she and Dolja were asleep before the bus started rolling. Departing the Air Force base, the bus hopped on a U.S. highway laid out just like an Interstate. We passed the largest church I think I'd ever seen, white and brick, a Pentecostal church. I couldn't remember ever seeing a Pentecostal church in New Orleans, but if the size of this church was any indication, there must be a hell of a lot of Pentecostals in Little Rock.

Verdant hills and neat homes set on tree-lined streets are what I saw from my window on this overcast morning as the bus drove us to the refugee center. We crossed a bridge with a broad river below, not Mississippi River-broad, but no stream either. A building right on the river had the words LITTLE ROCK spelled out in large letters. I had no way of knowing it at the time, but life and love would bring me to this city again almost exactly three years from that day, and it would become my home for most of the coming decade. Crossing that bridge, seated on that bus, I could imagine nothing so far into the future. Difficult years still separated me from the wife I'd yet to find, fall for, and marry. In mere minutes, we'd driven past the towers of a few tightly grouped skyscrapers, past a neighborhood or two, and, just like that, we were driving through forests and farmland. In five minutes' time, we'd driven through the City and into an episode of *Green Acres*.

We continued on through these patches of farm fields bordered by trees. A gentle, drizzling rain began to fall, dotting the windows with tiny droplets of water. This was the first rain I'd seen since Uncle G and I went on our short walk to assess the damages the storm had wrought on our neighborhood. The walk on which we'd discovered the brown water churning up from the manholes and collecting in the streets of Gentilly. That walk seemed to have happened a lifetime ago, as if it had been someone else walking on that dry sidewalk hundreds of miles away from this cruising coach. The bus rolled on, and the light rain continued to fall, as if it were washing all of that away one tiny drop at a time.

SUNDAY
SEPTEMBER 4TH, 2005
AND BEYOND

BACK TO SQUARE ONE: THE FUTURE BEGINS

I had continued misgivings as the bus neared the city of Pine Bluff. The U.S. military's largest chemical weapons storage facility is just outside of town. I told Tom that they'd brought us here to gas us all. The entire convention center, a building encompassing square acres in size, had been taken over by the local chapter of the American Red Cross.

We were led to an open arena with a smooth concrete floor, surrounded by stadium seats, and raised basketball goals hanging from the ceiling. The gymnasium served as the cafeteria, and, unfortunately, we'd arrived too late for breakfast. All the hot food they had left were some dried-out biscuits. That's not to say there wasn't any food to be had. A great assortment of snack foods, sweet, salty, and savory, were lined before us. After grabbing some juice and a donut, I headed over to a table to eat my food.

A large television set was plugged in, and, for the first time, I saw what the nation had been watching for a solid week. This entire time, I'd only seen what I'd lived, a very narrow, first-person view of the events. Those first on-screen images I saw of the magnitude of the devastation practically knocked the wind out of me. Humbled, I could only sit and stare. Everything was ruined, and the flooding seemed endless. I'd just made it out of that mess. That was a sobering moment.

They'd moved the entire contents of the Salvation Army retail location in town to the Convention Center so that we'd have more than just clothes to put on, but a choice of clothing. They'd even set up a small kennel. Dolja received a bath, and was taken for regular walks.

As promised, one of the first things I did after arriving was find a pair of scissors. A lovely woman, married and a mother of three children, held my knotted ball of hair and snipped it away from the back of my head, taking me from chest-length hair to strands that barely reached my chin. After my turn to shower and wash myself, I stood in the mirror combing my newly shortened hair. And, as I dressed myself in Salvation Army clothing, my Superdome rags had been added to a giant bin of other people's discarded disaster clothes. I had the first of many epiphanies that would have to come in order for me to mentally continue with the readjustment to post-disaster life. I was alone in this large bathroom with toilets, sinks, and showers for an entire basketball team. I'd gotten dressed, and, as I ran the comb through my hair and looked at myself in the mirror, I realized that the storm had taken so much from me that I no longer owned the clothes on my own back. I owned nothing anymore. A new life began that very moment, gazing at that peculiarly familiar reflection on a steamy mirror. I'd found my rock bottom, and would use that as the foundation to start over.

That first day, everyone was encouraged to visit the volunteer medical staff, just to get looked over. They'd seen the conditions of the stadium on television and were worried about infections and diseases resulting from direct exposure to human waste. My left side and back were covered with scrapes and scratches from sliding off of the roof. I'd forgotten all about them. The nurse said my scratches were all healing and showed no sign of infection.

Later that day, a sweet, older woman named Mary drove me to the local Wal-Mart and bought me a pack of boxer shorts (only briefs were provided at the shelter), a McDonald's combo meal, and a new cap with Sergeant stripes on it.

Not only had they brought the clothes when they cleared out the Salvation Army, they'd brought toys, books, and games. A maintenance man permitted me to find something to read, and I selected a hardcover copy of Henri Charriére's immortal tale, *Papillon*. A first edition, nonetheless. I'd heard of his story while watching a documentary about Devil's Island. *Papillon* is a tale of perseverance and hope, and eventual escape from a place that only exists to destroy individuality and devour the human spirit. Needless to say, I found many corollaries between the French prison in South America and the Superdome in south Louisiana. I found other similarities between his story and my own recent experience, like walking. He would walk from one end of his cell to the other for several hours a day, which reminded me of the dozens of laps I'd walked around the field on Wednesday. Papillon's story of self-reliance and ingenuity really spoke to me at that time in my life and filled me with the hope to continue, to carry on, and to eventually rebuild.

A huge banquet room lined with rows of cots and divided by a partition separated men's and women's sleeping quarters. This did not sit well with many couples and families who had just been separated from everything they thought they knew. Welcome to the Bible Belt. Mother, Tom, and I pulled out some Greco-Roman wrestling mats and made beds with blankets and pillows to sleep on in front of the big screen TV in the gymnasium-turned-cafeteria.

Mother and I didn't want to leave Tom, but Uncle G and Jimena were ready to go. They flew out on Tuesday, September 5th, to join my grandparents and Aunt Helen. We thought it best to send Dolja with them, since we were about to attempt to board a plane with no identification—no small feat in post-9/11 United States. We successfully flew out to Florida the next day. The night before our flight, I became very sick, complete with chills and a high fever. I spent that night and most of the next day before our departure wrapped in blankets, shivering. It was really hard to leave Tom by himself in Pine Bluff. He'd been so helpful and wonderful to us. It felt like saying goodbye to a comrade I'd fought beside through combat. Tom would catch a plane Thursday morning to Orlando, where the company he worked for had another office. We got to

Florida late Wednesday night. There was nothing to do but hug and kiss my grandparents—with us all reunited, they could finally rest—eat a little bit, and go to bed. Cleaning Klaus the hippo presented a different kind of problem. He's a big guy. Way too big for a washing machine. I attempted to surface clean him with some detergent and a toothbrush, but he still smelled like a musty mess. Two days later, I would totally gut him, remove all of his stuffing, and hand wash his hide. Cutting open my hippo in Aunt Helen's backyard was the first time I truly let the emotions pour out of me, and I sobbed for a long, long time that afternoon in the south Florida sunshine.

The day after we arrived in Florida, I went for a walk around Aunt Helen's neighborhood. There are canals running through these neighborhoods so people can launch their boats from their backyards to go fishing, not unlike Venetian Isles in New Orleans East.

As I walked along one of these canals, I saw two great gray manatees swimming in the water, graceful and carefree. I ran back to the house to fetch my camera, and when I returned, I found myself looking at four manatees where there'd only been two just minutes before. Two little manatee pups swam alongside their much larger mothers. They'd just given birth right there in the protection of the dead-end fishing canal, and now they were headed back to more open waters to raise their offspring and prepare them for this new phase of life.

The manatees were as good an omen for the future as I could have hoped for, I thought as I sat down on the flattened futon sofa, which served as my bed in Aunt Helen's house. Everyone else had gone to sleep, and, except for Mother's snoring on the twin bed set against the opposite wall in the room, I was alone with my thoughts. So much had happened in those ten days that sitting in my aunt's spare bedroom in southwest Florida, clean, and loved, and well-fed, seemed an anticlimactic end to such a momentous experience.

I knew that the only thing to do for myself and for my City was to pick up the pieces and start over. Actually doing so would come in time; but that night, alone in the dark, I wasn't ready to let go yet, and, ten years later, I still haven't figured out the correct way to heal, only ways to cope.

I clicked on a lamp and lifted the receiver of the telephone on the end table and dialed my phone number. The number to 4899 Mandeville Street in the Gentilly Neighborhood of the City of New Orleans. The number I'd memorized as a child and will never forget until the day I die. The first thing I heard was a recorded message stating that, due to the effects of the recent hurricane, my call could not be completed at this time, and soon after the message ended, the phone began to ring. It rang and rang. In my mind, I pictured the ring bouncing through the flooded rooms full of floating furniture—empty chairs and empty tables that I imagined were feeling as lonely as I was. After a while, I clicked the lamp off and laid down, pressing the phone a little harder to my ear, trying to contact the person I'd been before Katrina entered my life. No one answered. The phone just rang and rang, and eventually I fell asleep.

ACKNOWLEDGMENTS

Very special thanks to the people of Pine Bluff and White Hall, Arkansas, who graciously volunteered their Labor Day weekend to serve at the Pine Bluff Convention Center. Upon our arrival, there seemed to be more volunteers of all ages—from middle-schoolers to the middle-aged and elderly—than there were refugees. Each person's commitment to help was pure and genuine, though they'd never met a single one of us until we were dropped at their doorstep a busload at a time. It was a momentous outpouring from these communities, and, on behalf of myself, Mother, Tom, Jimena, and Uncle G, I'd like to thank every person who volunteered their time to assist their distant neighbors to the south. You brightened my life when the world looked so very broken and unpromising. Thank you.

Hurricane Katrina chewed me up and spit me out, destitute and full of post-traumatic stress. The next few years would be the darkest and most difficult of my life, thus far. Between September 2005 and September 2008, I packed up Dolja, Klaus, and my few meager belongings and moved no fewer than eight times. From Florida to the North Carolina Coast, the Texas Hill Country, and eventually back to New Orleans in mid-December 2005. I am forever indebted to my extended web of family and friends who opened their homes to me. You know who you are.

I'd also like to thank R-20, the Cimarron Kid, my sounding board throughout the writing and editing process of this memoir. You've helped this project more than you'll ever know.

Very special thanks to Erin Wood and everyone at Et Alia Press for giving a first-time author a chance to tell his story, when so many others brushed this work aside.

Foremost, I'd like to thank my beautiful wife for opening her heart to a wretch like me. I've spent the majority of my post-Katrina life loved and accepted by her and our lovely daughter, now a young woman in her own right. Honey, you're my inspiration, my guru, my editor, and my biggest supporter. Without you, this book could never have been written.

Last, but certainly not least, I'd like to thank God. He who makes all things possible. Life, laughter, love, even Hurricane Katrina.

ABOUT THE AUTHOR

Bruce S. Snow fills his spare time with writing and various musical endeavors. He is currently working on several fiction projects. Bruce earned a B.A. in History from the University of New Orleans, and has lived in Little Rock, Arkansas, since 2008. He and his family will move back to New Orleans in the fall of 2016.

CPSIA information can be obtained
at www.ICGtesting.com
Printed in the USA
BVOW07s0235080217
475611BV00008B/87/P